EXPLANATORIUM

OF HISTORY

EXPLANATORIUM

OF HISTORY

Senior Editor Jenny Sich
Senior Art Editor Stefan Podhorodecki
Editorial team Kelsie Besaw, Michelle Crane, Sam Kennedy, Anna Streiffert Limerick, Georgina Palffy, Vicky Richards
US Editor Megan Douglass
Design team Sheila Collins, Mik Gates, Rachael Grady, Jim Green, Kit Lane, Gregory McCarthy, Lynne Moulding
Illustrators Ed Byrne, Dan Crisp, Simon Tegg, Jack Williams
Picture Researcher Sarah Hopper
Creative Retouching Steve Crozier
Managing Editor Francesca Baines
Managing Art Editor Philip Letsu
Production Editor George Nimmo
Senior Production Controller Samantha Cross
Senior Jacket Designer Suhita Dharamjit
Jackets Design Development Manager Sophia MTT
Senior DTP Designer Harish Aggarwal
Senior Jackets Editorial Coordinator Priyanka Sharma
Managing Jackets Editor Saloni Singh
Publisher Andrew Macintyre
Art Director Karen Self
Associate Publishing Director Liz Wheeler
Publishing Director Jonathan Metcalf

Contributors Simon Adams, Peter Chrisp, Amani Gordon, Susan Kennedy, Ann Kramer, Seun Matiluko, Lizzie Munsey

Consultant Philip Parker
Specialist consultants Dr. Fozia Bora, Dr. Vivian Delgado, Professor Steven Hooper, Dr. Jagjeet Lally, Dr. Andy Pearce, Dr. Caroline Dodds Pennock, Dr. Leon Rocha, Robin Walker, Dr. Ogechukwu Williams, Professor Jamie Wilson

First American Edition, 2021
Published in the United States by DK Publishing
1450 Broadway, Suite 801, New York, NY 10018

HUMANITY EMERGES

CIVILIZATION BEGINS

MIX
Paper from responsible sources
FSC™ C018179

This book was made with Forest Stewardship Council ™ certified paper – one small step in DK's commitment to a sustainable future.
For more information go to
www.dk.com/our-green-pledge

TRADE TAKES OFF

CONTENTS

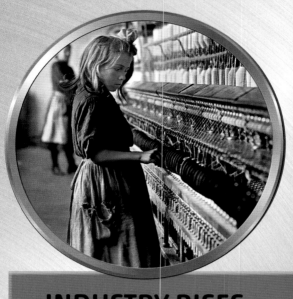

EMPIRES EXPAND

INDUSTRY RISES

TECHNOLOGY ADVANCES

REFERENCE

Our earliest **ancestors** were apelike creatures that lived in **Africa** 6 million years ago. From these distant beginnings, many species of **early humans** evolved, but our species—*Homo sapiens*—is the only one that remains. Early humans learned to **use tools** and **harness fire**, and created the world's first **art** and **music**. As we began to farm the land and settle in one place, the **first towns** were built and **human society** began to take shape.

HUMANITY ·

EMERGES

TIMELINE OF
PREHISTORY

The time before written records began is known as prehistory. Our knowledge of this period comes from things people left behind—the tools they used, the art they created, and the structures that still stand. By the end of this period, people had begun farming, building towns, and domesticating animals.

4 MYA
Australopithecines
Small, two-legged, apelike creatures live in East and South Africa. They mainly eat fruit and meat and may use primitive bone tools.

4 MYA

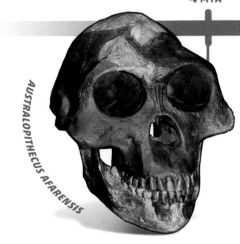

AUSTRALOPITHECUS AFARENSIS

CLOVIS POINT

c. 9000 BCE
Wheat crops
Domesticated strains of barley, emmer, and einkorn wheat are grown for the first time, in the Zagros mountains of western Iran.

c. 10,000 BCE
Göbekli Tepe
A ritual mound is built by Neolithic peoples in Anatolia, Turkey. It contains T-shaped stone pillars in massive circles.

c. 18,000 YA
First pottery
Pottery bowls are made in Jiangxi, China. They are molded by hand—the potter's wheel will not appear until around 3500 BCE, in Mesopotamia.

EINKORN

c. 9700 BCE
Ice Age
The last major Ice Age comes to an end and the glaciers retreat across Siberia, northern Europe, and North America.

c. 12,000–13,000 YA
Clovis points
Across North America, sharp points are shaped from flint and other minerals. They are affixed as weapons to the ends of javelins, arrows, and darts.

c. 24,000–10,000 YA
Crossing over
People cross what was then a land bridge between Siberia and Alaska, and begin to settle in North America. They later migrate southward into Central and South America.

c. 7300 BCE
Settlements
Permanent farming towns are widespread throughout West Asia. One of the largest early towns is 'Ain Ghazal.

c. 7100 BCE
Çatalhöyük
A large settlement flourishes at Çatalhöyük in Anatolia, Turkey. The town is home to around 7,000 people with their houses packed tightly together.

FLAX

c. 6500 BCE
Cultivating rice
Oryza sativa, or Asian rice, is grown in the Yangtze River valley in China. Rice-growing slowly spreads to other countries nearby.

PLASTER STATUE FROM 'AIN GHAZAL

c. 7000 BCE
Textiles
Fibers from the flax plant are used to make textiles in the Levant.

RECONSTRUCTION OF ÇATALHÖYÜK

2.4 MYA
Homo habilis
In East Africa, *Homo habilis* appear. They make primitive tools to butcher and skin animals and to cut wood.

PRIMITIVE HAND AX

c. 300,000 YA
Homo sapiens
The first *Homo sapiens*—modern humans—begin to emerge from the descendants of *Homo erectus* that remained in Africa.

c. 100,000 YA
Out of Africa
Homo sapiens begin to leave Africa and move slowly into West Asia. A more substantial migration along the southern Asian coast begins around 70,000 years ago.

2 MYA
Homo erectus
The first *Homo erectus* emerge in Africa, then slowly disperse across Europe and Asia. These people are the first to have a recognizably human body shape.

HOMO ERECTUS

CAVE PAINTING IN SULAWESI

c. 70,000 YA
Wearing clothing
People begin to wear clothes to keep themselves warm.

c. 45,000 YA
Cave art
People begin to make simple drawings of animals and stencils of their hands on cave walls in Spain, France, and Sulawesi in Indonesia.

c. 65,000 YA
Into Australia
People from southeast Asia reach Australia, first by sailing the distance on small rafts and later by crossing the land bridge from New Guinea.

c. 40,000 YA
Early carvings
Europeans carve figurines, flutes, and tools from mammoth tusks, antler, and bone.

c. 40,000 YA
Neanderthals
Homo neanderthalensis, the closest relatives of modern humans, die out in Europe.

TOMB PAINTING SHOWING CATTLE

STANDING STONES IN CARNAC

c. 6000 BCE
Farm animals
Goats, sheep, and pigs are domesticated in West Asia and India.

4000 BCE

c. 6200 BCE
Copper
People living in Çatalhöyük use heat combined with intense hammering to create jewelery and other items out of copper.

c. 4500 BCE
The plow
In the Balkans, people use plows to break up the ground. New farming techniques slowly spread across Europe.

c. 4300 BCE
Megalithic tombs
Huge stone tombs are built in Brittany, France, and stone circles are erected in Carnac, France.

HUMANS EVOLVE

Our species, *Homo sapiens*, evolved in Africa around 300,000 years ago. We are the only remaining member of a group called hominins. Hominins evolved from African apes around six million years ago, when one group of apes began to walk upright.

▶ **HOMININ EVOLUTION**
Hominins changed over time, evolving into new species. They grew taller, lost their ape body hair, and developed increasingly bigger brains. These two skulls compare *Australopithecus afarensis*—one of the earliest hominins to be discovered—with a 30,000-year-old *Homo sapiens*.

Lucy's skull had to be reconstructed from fragments.

This artist's reconstruction of Lucy shows what she might have looked like when she lived.

Big teeth helped chew roots and leaves.

AFRICA

EAST AFRICAN HOMELAND
Most of the earliest hominin species evolved in East Africa. The red area on this map shows where Lucy's species and others in the same group, known as Australopithecines, lived 4 million years ago.

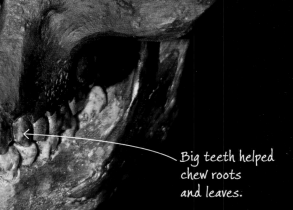

Longer arms helped *Australopithecus afarensis* climb trees.

LUCY
This is the face of a female *Australopithecus afarensis*, nicknamed Lucy when her skeleton was found in 1974. Lucy lived in East Africa 3.2 million years ago. She walked upright, but her brain was the size of a chimp's.

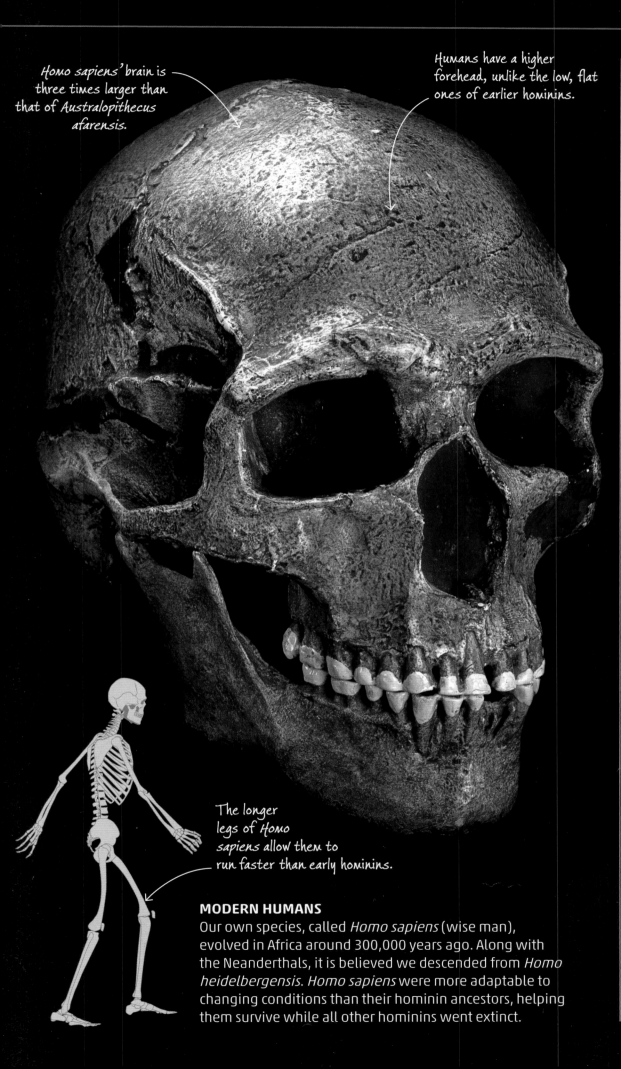

Homo sapiens' brain is three times larger than that of *Australopithecus afarensis.*

Humans have a higher forehead, unlike the low, flat ones of earlier hominins.

The longer legs of *Homo sapiens* allow them to run faster than early hominins.

MODERN HUMANS

Our own species, called *Homo sapiens* (wise man), evolved in Africa around 300,000 years ago. Along with the Neanderthals, it is believed we descended from *Homo heidelbergensis. Homo sapiens* were more adaptable to changing conditions than their hominin ancestors, helping them survive while all other hominins went extinct.

HUMAN RELATIVES

Homo sapiens and our closest hominin relatives all belong to the group Homo (man). Some of these species, such as the Neanderthals, existed at the same time as modern humans, but they all have died out.

HOMO ERECTUS

Homo erectus (upright man), c. 1.9 million years ago, were the first hominins as tall as modern humans. They learned to control fire, made stone axes, and moved out of Africa into Asia.

HOMO HEIDELBERGENSIS

Homo heidelbergensis, c. 700,000 years ago, were the first hominins to build shelters, which were made from wood, and to hunt large animals using spears. They were the first to move into Europe.

HOMO NEANDERTHALENSIS

Descended from *Homo heidelbergensis*, Neanderthals spread across Europe and western Asia c. 400,000 years ago. They wore animal skin clothing and buried their dead.

TOOLS DEVELOP

Learning to use tools was a huge step forward in human development. The first simple stone choppers, used from around 3.3 million years ago, made it easier to butcher meat and dig up roots. As tools advanced, humans moved from being scavengers to skilled hunters. Tools also enabled people to catch fish, build shelters, and make clothes.

Flint is a type of rock that often has a black core.

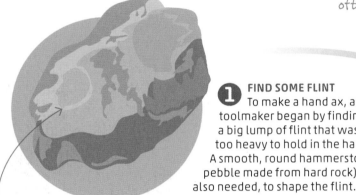

Unworked lump of flint

1 FIND SOME FLINT
To make a hand ax, a toolmaker began by finding a big lump of flint that was not too heavy to hold in the hand. A smooth, round hammerstone (a pebble made from hard rock) was also needed, to shape the flint.

2 ROUGHLY SHAPE
The toolmaker shaped the tool by striking the flint with the hammerstone and chipping away large flakes. Razor sharp, the flakes themselves were often used as cutting and scraping tools.

Flakes struck from the flint core were very sharp.

▶ STONE AGE TOOLS

Stone tools were so important that the earliest and longest period of prehistory is called the Stone Age. The longest-lasting tool was the leaf-shaped flint hand ax, invented by *Homo erectus* (see pages 12–13) around 1.76 million years ago. It was made in the same way for the next million and a half years. This step-by-step sequence shows how a hammerstone would have been used to shape a simple piece of flint into a sharp hand ax.

The hammerstone is round, smooth, and easy to hold.

HANDY MAN
The first stone tools were smooth river stones that were shaped into crude choppers. Roughly 2.4 million years ago, *Homo habilis* (handy man) were using this type of tool for digging, cutting plants, cracking nuts, and butchering animals.

HUNTING WITH SPEARS
Early humans were scavengers, but better tools allowed them to become active hunters. More than 300,000 years ago, *Homo heidelbergensis* were using sharpened wooden spears to hunt big dangerous animals, such as elephants.

A hammer of antler or bone was used to hone the sharp edges.

❸ SHARPEN EDGES
When the ax had been roughly shaped with the hammerstone, the toolmaker used a softer hammer, made of antler or bone. This could be used in a more controlled way, producing thinner flakes and refining the shape of the hand ax.

The toolmaker left one edge blunt so it was safe to hold.

❹ FINISHED TOOL
The finished ax had a broad base, and was easy to hold in the hand. This was a general-purpose tool, used for butchering meat, scraping animal hides, digging, and chopping wood.

Sewing needle

Barbed harpoons were used to catch fish.

BONE-CARVED TOOLKIT
Around 40,000 years ago, modern humans made a wide range of tools using carved bone and antler. With a bone needle, they could sew clothing, which helped them keep warm in cold climates.

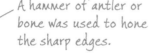

HUMANS MIGRATE OUT OF AFRICA

▶ **FOSSIL FOOTPRINT**
Little trace remains of the earliest human journeys. This 20,000-year-old human footprint from Lake Mungo in southeast Australia is a rare and lucky piece of evidence. By the time this footprint was made, people had been living in Australia for at least 45,000 years.

Around 100,000 years ago, *Homo sapiens* (modern humans) moved out of their African homeland and crossed into Asia. At first, they kept to the warm south, often following coasts, which were rich in food resources. Later they traveled north to the colder climates of Europe and northern Asia, and eventually crossed into the Americas. Traveling mostly on foot, and later by boat, humans eventually settled every inhabitable part of our planet.

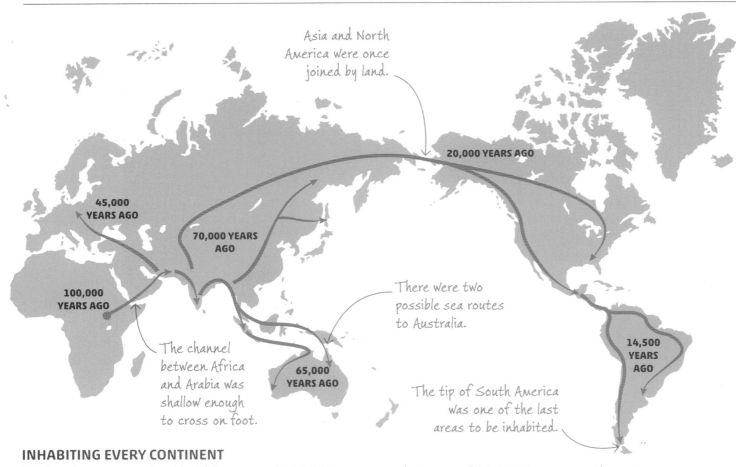

Asia and North America were once joined by land.

20,000 YEARS AGO

45,000 YEARS AGO

70,000 YEARS AGO

100,000 YEARS AGO

There were two possible sea routes to Australia.

The channel between Africa and Arabia was shallow enough to cross on foot.

65,000 YEARS AGO

14,500 YEARS AGO

The tip of South America was one of the last areas to be inhabited.

INHABITING EVERY CONTINENT

Modern humans evolved in Africa around 300,000 years ago, but around 100,000 years ago they began to spread around the globe. At this time in prehistory, Earth's climate was much colder and drier than it is today. The water locked up in large ice sheets at the poles created low sea levels. These allowed *Homo sapiens* to walk from East Africa to Arabia and later cross a land bridge from Asia to the Americas. Humans eventually populated every continent except Antarctica.

JOURNEY TO AUSTRALIA

It took humans thousands of years to migrate to Australia from Africa. Most of this journey was done on foot, but they also crossed open water on boats. Along the way, they encountered the descendants of other hominins who had left Africa in earlier waves of migration.

ON FOOT

Favorable climate conditions opened up the route out of Africa, making it easier for humans to follow herds of animals or search for new sources of food. Over many generations they traveled farther afield, eventually reaching Australia.

CROSSING WATER

People settling in Australia would have had to make open-sea journeys. However, at this time sea levels were lower, so the distance between southeast Asia and Australia was much shorter. The light green on the map at left shows the land above sea level at the time of the first human migrations.

Pacific Ocean

Australia

Footprint found at Lake Mungo, southeast Australia

MEETING RELATIVES

Modern humans met and interbred with hominins that were already living in other parts of the world. The Neanderthals in Europe and western Asia had evolved from the earlier migrations of *Homo heidelbergensis* hundreds of thousands of years earlier.

EARLY HUMANS
MAKE FIRE

By roughly a million years ago, our *Homo erectus* ancestors were controlling fire. First they used naturally occurring fires—usually lit by lightning strikes—but they eventually learned to make fire themselves. Controlling fire was a pivotal step in human history. Using its warmth and light, humans were able to survive in harsher environments, while a diet of cooked meat boosted our brain power.

▶ MAKING FIRE

Striking flint against a rock or rubbing sticks together can create enough friction to make a spark and start a fire. The first human fire-makers may have simply rotated a stick between their palms. But later prehistoric people are known to have used the bow drill, a tool that makes this task easier.

1 CREATING A SPARK

The bow drill rests on a nest of dry moss, leaves, or grass—material that will ignite easily. By drawing the bow rapidly back and forth, the fire-maker creates friction. Hot dust produced by the friction forms a hot, glowing ember, which drops onto the flammable material below.

A piece of wood or bone was placed on top to hold the spindle in place.

The rotating spindle produces friction.

BOW

SPINDLE

FIREBOARD

BOW DRILL

A bow drill consists of an upright stick called a spindle, which is placed on a plank of wood, called the fireboard. Drawing the bow back and forth makes the spindle rotate rapidly, creating friction between the spindle and the fireboard.

The notch in the board allows the burning ember to drop down into the tinder—a nest of flammable dry grasses.

THE FIRST FIRES

Homo erectus first learned to be unafraid of natural fires, caused by lightning strikes, which are common in the African bush. They collected and preserved smoldering wood to build their first fires. The first evidence of controlled fire-use dates to around one million years ago.

SOCIAL GATHERING

Fire would have kept early humans warm at night, and provided protection against wild animals. But gathering around the fire may also have been important for social bonding, even encouraging the development of language.

EASIER DIGESTION

Food that was cooked was much easier to eat and digest. Unlike their ape ancestors, early humans no longer had to spend hours each day chewing. Their teeth and guts grew smaller, and the extra energy from cooked meat allowed the growth of bigger brains.

2 BUILDING THE FLAMES
Once the tinder nest began to smoke, the fire-maker picked it up and gently blew on it until it burst into flames. When the flames were strong enough, the fire could be built up using smaller sticks first and then larger pieces of wood.

ART BEGINS

Around 45,000 years ago, our ancestors began to make art. Inside dark caves they drew pictures of animals and painted around their hands to leave their mark. We do not know exactly why people began to make these pictures, but it may have been a means of sharing stories, marking a special place, connecting with their community, or a way of reaching out to those who would come after them. Whatever the reason, it shows a great leap forward in human imagination, creativity, and self expression.

▶ CAVE OF HANDS

While the earliest examples of cave painting are from 45,000 years ago, people continued to make the same type of art for thousands of years. This cave in Santa Cruz, Argentina, is filled with painted hands. Men, women, and children made these marks over a period of 8,000 years starting from around 7300 BCE. Similar hand stencils have been found across the world. Making a hand stencil was early peoples' way of marking their presence in a special place. The people who made these may have felt connected to all those who had been there before them.

PAINTING FROM MEMORY
When people began painting animals around 45,000 years ago, it showed a leap in human brain function. Drawing from memory requires abstract thinking—the ability to imagine things not physically present.

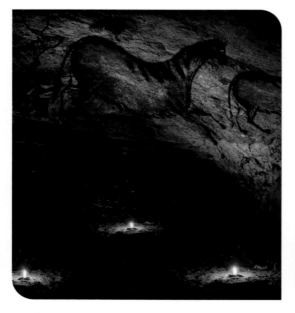

FLICKERING LIGHT
The deep caves where the earliest art is found were special places, not places where people lived. The paintings were viewed by lamplight, which would create the illusion that the animals were moving and alive.

CREATING HANDPRINTS

Cave art was produced using natural pigments—colors found in nature. Charcoal was used for black, chalk for white, and different types of earth could make shades of brown. The handprints seen here were made with a pigment called red ocher. The artists made the prints by blowing paint onto the wall to leave the outline of their hands.

The artist stirs the paint with a stick.

1 MIXING PIGMENT The first step was to make the paint by mixing the red ocher with water or saliva. This might have been done in a stone vessel or a shell.

The hollow tubes were placed end to end.

2 SETTING UP The artist probably sprayed the paint through a pair of hollow reeds or bird bones. They placed one of these in the pigment, and the second across the top of the first.

Blowing the paint created a spray-paint effect.

3 BLOWING THE PAINT With one hand placed on the wall, the artist then blew through the upper tube. This drew the paint up through the lower tube and sprayed it onto the wall, leaving an outline of the artist's hand behind.

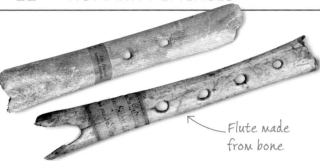

Flute made from bone

MAKING MUSIC

The oldest-known musical instruments are flutes made of bone and ivory. They may have accompanied dances, or been used in ceremonies or while socializing around a fire. These 32,000-year-old flutes were found in France.

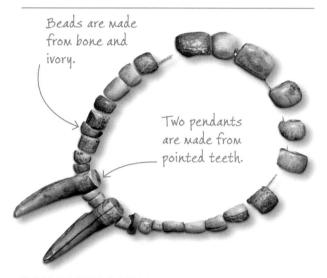

Beads are made from bone and ivory.

Two pendants are made from pointed teeth.

DECORATIVE ORNAMENT

It was common for people at this time to wear jewelery, such as the necklace above from Skara Brae in Orkney, Scotland. Jewelery was made using bones, teeth, shells, and ivory, and was often worn as necklaces or bracelets.

BURIAL OF THE DEAD

Around this time, people started burying their dead, often with valuable offerings. The skeleton above, found in Italy, was buried with ivory beads. This could indicate a belief in an afterlife where these ornaments would have been useful.

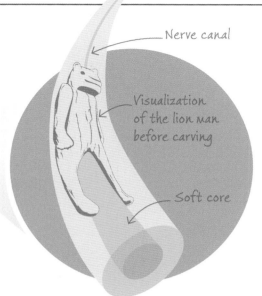

Nerve canal

Visualization of the lion man before carving

Soft core

CARVING THE MAMMOTH TUSK

It is thought to have taken around 400 hours to make the lion man, which was carved from hard mammoth ivory using simple stone tools. The artist would have had to carefully plan the carving. Its shape tapers with the curve of the tusk, and the legs were carved to either side of the soft pulp at the tusk's center.

◄ LION MAN

Discovered in a German cave in 1939, this figurine depicts a man with the head of a lion. Standing 12 in (30 cm) tall, it was carved 40,000 years ago from the tusk of a mammoth. Its exact purpose is unknown, but it shows the ways in which people were using their imaginations to understand and share ideas about the world around them.

CULTURE
EMERGES

Around 45,000 years ago, our hunter-gatherer ancestors were spending their time searching for food and trying to survive. However, evidence they've left behind shows they were also creating art, telling stories, making music, and sharing customs, such as caring for their dead. Collectively, these activities make up the earliest-known culture.

CAVE LION
The head of the lion man is modeled on the cave lion, an extinct species of lion that lived in Europe and Asia during the time the figurine was carved. Cave lions were larger than their modern cousins, and would have been the fiercest predators living at this time.

The head is facing forward, with the ears pricked up and alert.

The carving was found fractured into 200 fragments.

The surface was worn smooth from repeated handling over many years.

TAKING SHELTER

Building shelters allowed humans to settle in every inhabitable part of the world. The earliest structures were built with various different materials, but they always served an important purpose. They may have offered shelter from the weather, provided warmth and a safe place to sleep at night, or given people a place to gather together.

▶ **MAMMOTH HUT**
During the last Ice Age, around 15,000 years ago, hunters on the cold, treeless plains of eastern Europe and northern Asia built their shelters from mammoth bones and hides. Only the bones of these structures survive, but this reconstruction shows how they are thought to have looked.

HUNTING MAMMOTH
Mammoths provided hunters with everything they needed to survive, including meat; skins for clothing; and dung, which could be burned for fuel. People even made spears from mammoth tusks.

Mammoth hides kept out the wind and rain.

▶ **BUILDING MATERIALS**
Around the world, people built shelters with whatever material was locally available. Early houses were often round, a shape that is easier to construct.

STONE
In treeless Orkney, Scotland, 5,000 years ago, early farmers used local stone, which naturally forms flat slabs, to build houses and furniture.

MUDBRICK AND STONE
In hot, dry countries, people often used sun-dried mudbrick, as in this reconstruction of a farmer's house from Cyprus 9,000 years ago.

TIMBER
Japanese houses from the Jomon period 16,000 years ago were made from wood and had thatched roofs, such as the above reconstruction.

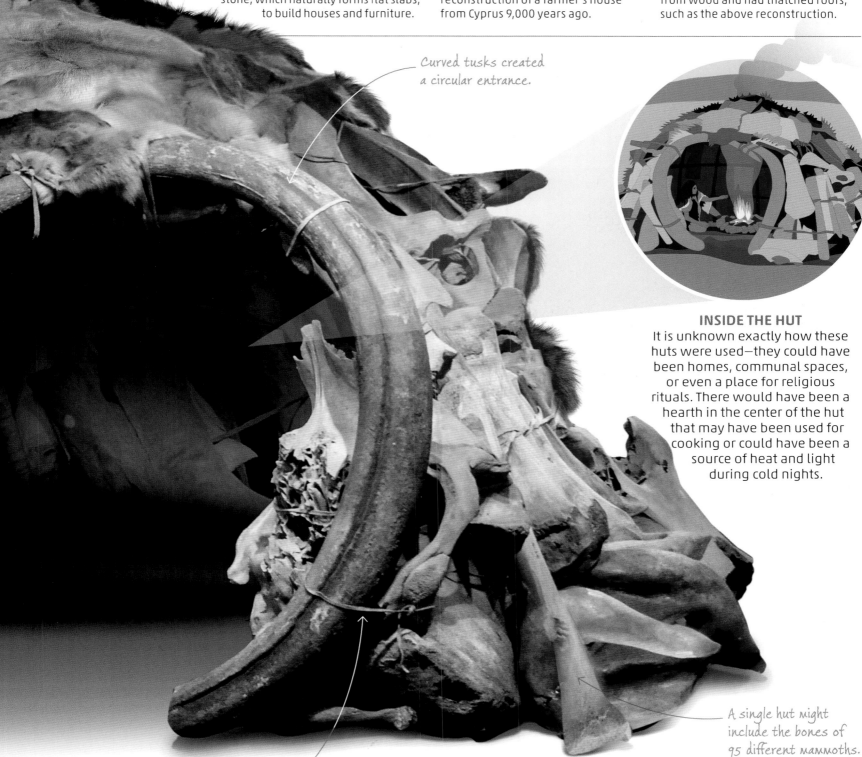

Curved tusks created a circular entrance.

INSIDE THE HUT
It is unknown exactly how these huts were used—they could have been homes, communal spaces, or even a place for religious rituals. There would have been a hearth in the center of the hut that may have been used for cooking or could have been a source of heat and light during cold nights.

A single hut might include the bones of 95 different mammoths.

Bones were lashed together with cords made from mammoth hide.

FARMING
CHANGES EVERYTHING

For most of prehistory, people lived as hunter-gatherers, moving from place to place in search of wild foods.
Everything changed around 10,000–9000 BCE when people began to store and sow seeds, and control the breeding of animals. This new lifestyle led people to settle in one place. As the food supply grew, the human population rose dramatically.

▼ DOMESTICATING WHEAT
Bringing animals and plants under human control is called domestication. Animals and plants were both changed by this, as a result of human selection. Wheat was the first plant to be domesticated. People selected plants with bigger grains that stayed longer on the plant, because they were easier to harvest. Farming could feed many more people but was a harder way of life, as caring for crops took up much more time and effort than hunter-gathering.

THE FERTILE CRESCENT
The first farmers lived in the Fertile Crescent, which stretches from Egypt to Mesopotamia. The region had a good source of wild food plants, including wheat and pulses. Farming was later invented in other parts of the world, such as China, where people grew rice and millet.

SHATTER-RESISTANT WHEAT
Wild wheat has heads that shatter (fall off the plant) when ripe, releasing seeds to be spread by the wind. Early farmers cultivated the plants that did not shatter easily. Eventually they created a wheat whose grains could no longer be spread by the wind, allowing them to harvest the grain for food.

DOMESTICATED WHEAT

WILD WHEAT

KEY
■ Fertile Crescent

Mediterranean Sea

Mesopotamia

ASIA

EGYPT

Persian Gulf

AFRICA

Red Sea

Arabian Peninsula

DOMESTIC GOATS

Early farmers also began breeding animals, which provided regular supplies of animal products such as milk and hides. Wild goats had long, sharp horns, but the individuals farmers bred from had downward-pointing horns, which were safer to handle.

POOR NUTRITION

Farmers ate a more limited and less healthy diet than hunter-gatherers. People lived on a few staple crops that lacked vitamins and minerals. Unleavened bread, made using ground wheat flour, would have been a regular part of their diet.

SETTLING DOWN

Farmers had to live close to the fields where they grew their crops. They began to settle down in villages, at first in family groups. As the population rose, more people settled down and the villages grew in size.

Wheat grains cling to the plant until they are harvested.

GRINDING WHEAT

Wheat grains had to be ground to make flour. Early farmers used a saddle quern to do this, pushing the upper stone backward over the flat lower stone. This was grueling, hard work, and often led to diseases in the joints.

Modern wheat could not survive without humans to plant it.

BUILDING THE FIRST TOWNS

The shift to farming meant more food was being produced, which could feed more people. This led to larger groups of people living together in one place. By 7300 BCE, villages in the Fertile Crescent had grown into the world's first towns. The earliest were Çatalhöyük in Turkey and 'Ain Ghazal in Jordan. Both began as farming settlements, but as they got bigger people began to take more specialized roles, and crafts and trade took off.

▼ **THE FIRST TOWNSPEOPLE**
Not much is left of the first towns besides the foundations of the houses and various artifacts such as figurines, stone tools, and bits of pottery. One of the most stunning discoveries was made at 'Ain Ghazal, where archaeologists discovered more than 30 half-life-size human statues, which may have represented the ancestors of the people living there.

The head was formed around a central post built of reeds wrapped with twine.

The head was shaped using lime plaster.

Reeds were collected from the river.

REED FRAME
The 'Ain Ghazal statues were made with a framework of reeds, tied into bundles. This framework was covered with lime plaster. The artists carefully modeled the faces, while leaving the bodies roughly shaped without limbs. This suggests that they may have worn clothes and wigs or headdresses.

BUSTLING TOWN

'Ain Ghazal was founded on the side of a valley above the Zarqa River in what is now Jordan. At its peak, it had a population of 2,500 people, living in closely packed rectangular houses made of timber posts with mudbrick walls and flat roofs. House sizes varied, suggesting that some people were wealthier than others.

The Zarqa River provided water for the farmers' fields nearby.

THE FIRST SETTLEMENTS

The earliest settlements were founded in the well-watered Fertile Crescent (see page 26), where the soil was rich in nutrients and the first farmers could easily grow crops. Living together was a new way of life, so each town developed differently, with unique house styles, art, and religious beliefs.

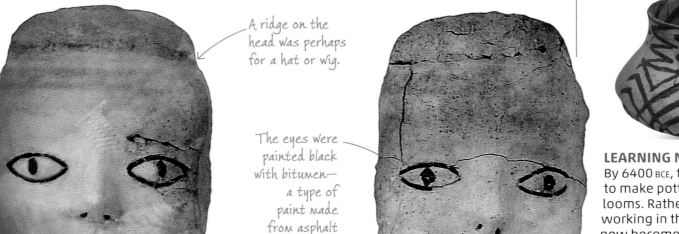

A ridge on the head was perhaps for a hat or wig.

The eyes were painted black with bitumen— a type of paint made from asphalt or coal tar.

Some statues have double heads.

Decorated pot from Çatalhöyük

LEARNING NEW SKILLS

By 6400 BCE, the townspeople had learned to make pottery and weave textiles on looms. Rather than spending all their time working in the fields, some people could now become specialized craftworkers. Making blade tools was another skilled craft.

TRADE BEGINS

The rise of skilled craftspeople sparked the birth of trade. People traded goods such as obsidian—a shiny black glass. In Çatalhöyük they crafted tools like these obsidian arrow heads, and traded them with people from other towns.

MYSTERIOUS MEGALITHS

Dated as early as 4500 BCE, the Carnac stones in Brittany, France, form the largest megalithic site in the world. Spreading over an area of 100 acres (40 hectares), the Carnac stones' site is made up of more than 2,800 standing stones, some of which stand up to 13 ft (4 m) tall. The stones were cut from local granite outcroppings, but exactly how prehistoric peoples transported these stones is a mystery, as is their function. They may have been religious monuments or used during rituals. Some people believe they are aligned with the stars and served an astronomical purpose.

Civilization began as more and more people started living alongside each other in the **first cities**. This new way of life drove the invention of **writing**—marking the start of recorded **history.** Other advances followed thick and fast: improved **metalworking** forged better tools and the **wheel** brought a revolution in **transportation. Empires expanded**, **trade networks** were established, and **money** was invented.

CIVILIZATION BEGINS

TIMELINE OF THE ANCIENT WORLD

The first cities were built in Mesopotamia, in West Asia, around 6,000 years ago. Soon after, civilization developed in Egypt and, independently, in the Indus Valley, China, and Mesoamerica. The Bronze Age and, later, the Iron Age spread across Europe, which by the end of the period had produced influential civilizations in ancient Greece and Rome.

c. 3500 BCE
The wheel
The wheel is invented in Mesopotamia. First used for making pottery, it is later adapted there and in eastern Europe to make the first wheeled carts.

4000 BCE

c. 4000 BCE
First cities
The world's first cities are built in Sumer in Mesopotamia. One of them, Uruk, has around 40,000 residents at its peak in 3100 BCE.

RECONSTRUCTED ISHTAR GATE IN BABYLON

c. 1000 BCE
Phoenician commerce
The first Phoenician colony is founded at Kition in Cyprus. It is the first of many around the Mediterranean, forming a profitable trading empire.

c. 1200 BCE
The Iron Age begins
The working of iron to make weapons and tools begins in West Asia and spreads slowly across Europe, Asia, and Africa.

c. 1250 BCE
The Olmecs
The Mesoamerican Olmec people build ceremonial centers with pyramid-shaped earth mounds and create huge stone sculptures of their gods and leaders.

OLMEC STONE HEAD

934 BCE
Neo-Assyrian Empire
The Neo-Assyrian Empire dominates West Asia, even capturing Egypt in 671 BCE.

c. 1200 BCE
Mycenaean civilization ends
The Mycenaean civilization of ancient Greece began around 1650 BCE. It comes to a sudden end after it is attacked by the Sea Peoples, a seafaring group that also attacks Egypt.

ALEXANDER FIGHTING THE PERSIANS AT ISSUS

336–323 BCE
Alexander the Great
Alexander of Macedonia carves out a massive Greek empire that stretches from Greece and Egypt to the borders of India, conquering the mighty Persian Empire in the process.

WOLF FEEDING ROMULUS AND REMUS

c. 900 BCE
Greek city-states
The first city-states in Greece are founded in Sparta and by the eastern Aegean Sea. They become centers of political power, commerce, and cultural life.

559 BCE
Achaemenid Empire of Persia
Under the rule of Cyrus the Great, the Persian Empire begins to expand, becoming the largest empire in the world so far.

753 BCE
The founding of Rome
According to legend, the city of Rome is founded by the twins Romulus and Remus, who were fed milk by a wolf after their royal uncle ordered them to be left to die.

c. 563–483 BCE
Life of the Buddha
Gautama Buddha rejects his old life and begins to teach a new way of life, which becomes Buddhism. Ashoka the Great of India spreads the new religion.

THE PARTHENON, ATHENS

508 BCE
Democracy
After various false starts, the Greeks of Athens establish the world's first democracy.

230–221 BCE
Unification of China
During the reign of King Zheng of Qin, China is unified for the first time. Zheng takes the title Qin Shi Huang, "First Emperor."

MINOAN
BRONZE BULL
LEAPER

c. 3100 BCE
Unification of Egypt
Narmer (also known as Menes),
ruler of Upper Egypt, conquers
Lower Egypt and unites the
country for the first time.

c. 2686–2181 BCE
**The Old Kingdom
of Egypt**
Egyptian civilization
flourishes. The great
pyramids are built at
Giza, and Egyptian
influence extends up
the Nile into Nubia.

3400–3200 BCE
First writing
The first pictograph writing
systems slowly develop in
Mesopotamia and Egypt.

c. 3300 BCE
The Bronze Age begins
People begin to use bronze to make tools and weapons
in West Asia and Greece. Bronze, an alloy of copper and tin,
is harder and more durable than earlier metals.

THE SPHINX AND GREAT PYRAMID

c. 1500 BCE
Bantu peoples
Bantu peoples from western
Africa have moved south
into the Central African
rainforests, reaching the
Great Lakes by 1000 BCE.

1792–1750 BCE
King Hammurabi
Hammurabi, ruler of
Babylon, conquers most
of Mesopotamia. The
law code of Hammurabi,
written around 1750 BCE, is
the most comprehensive
legal text in West Asia.

c. 2600 BCE
Indus Valley civilization
The cities of Harappa and Mohenjo-Daro
are built by a civilization in the Indus
Valley. The cities have mudbrick walls
and streets laid out on a grid pattern.

HARAPPAN SEAL

c. 1766 BCE
Shang China
The Shang dynasty is founded
by King Tang. Its pictographic
script is the forerunner of
modern Chinese alphabets.

c. 2000 BCE
Minoan civilization
Europe's first cities are
developed by the Minoans on
the Greek island of Crete. The
Minoans trade olives, wool, and
other farmed products across
the Mediterranean.

2334–2279 BCE
Sargon the Great
The ruler of Akkad, Sargon the Great,
founds the world's first empire, centered
on Agade in southern Mesopotamia.

GUPTA COIN

c. 33 CE
Christianity is founded
This is the traditional date for
the death of Jesus Christ,
founder of Christianity.

400 CE

27 BCE
Roman Empire
Augustus, nephew of Julius
Caesar and ruler of Rome,
establishes a hereditary empire.
He called himself *princeps* (first
citizen) and his successors were
known as *imperator* (emperor).

STATUE OF
AUGUSTUS

313 CE
Christian Rome
Roman Emperor
Constantine the Great
begins to move toward
Christianity. He issues
an edict tolerating
the Christian religion,
and later converts.

380–414 CE
The Gupta Empire
Chandragupta II rules the Gupta
Empire, which dominates North
and East India. The Guptas are
devout Hindus, and the great
Hindu epics *Ramayana* and
Mahabharata reach their
final form around this time.

NEW DIET

Pottery led to a richer and tastier diet. People could now boil and fry foods and make stews. They fermented grapes and grains to make wine and beer. Milk was made into various dairy products, such as cheese, which could be stored and was easier to digest.

DECORATED POTS

Some of the oldest pots were decorated, at first with patterns scratched onto the clay, and later colored with glazes. This 5,000-year-old pot, made by the Jomon people of Japan, is a cooking vessel, with holes for hanging over a fire. Created by hand, it was made by building up the vessel from the bottom with coil upon coil of soft clay. When dry, it was fired at a low heat, perhaps in a bonfire.

POTTERY AND TRADE

Pottery made it easy to trade goods, often over long distances. The Phoenicians, Greeks, and Romans all used amphorae—tall pots with two vertical handles—to transport foodstuffs such as wine and oil across the seas in merchant ships.

POTTERY
IS INVENTED

The invention of pottery was a key moment in early human history. For most of prehistory, people lived as mobile hunter-gatherers, using baskets or leather bags to carry food and drink. It was only after they settled down that they started making pottery, which is too heavy and fragile for life on the move, by moulding clay and baking it in a fire. Pots were useful for carrying liquids and cooking, and decorated pottery gave people a way to display status. With a wheel, pots could be mass produced.

TURNTABLE WHEEL

This potter uses a long stick to set a turntable wheel rapidly spinning. When it reaches the desired speed, the potter will then bend down to shape the clay into a pot.

The potter uses one hand to drip water over the clay, keeping it soft, while using the other hand to shape the clay into a pot.

▼ POTTER'S WHEEL

The potter's wheel was invented in Mesopotamia around 3500 BCE—a few hundred years before wheels were used for transportation. The potter's wheel began as a turntable, moved slowly by hand. Later, a fast wheel turned by a stick was developed, which allowed pots to be "thrown" and produced rapidly on a large scale. This wheel is from Karnataka in India.

The fast-spinning wheel allows a pot to be made in minutes.

The clay must be centered or it will fly off to the side.

THE BRONZE AGE
BEGINS

The invention of metalworking was one of the most important technological advances in history. Metals can be moulded into sharp-edged tools and weapons and used to cast beautiful objects. The first metal tools were made with copper, which is soft, but around 3500 BCE, metalworkers in West Asia added tin to copper, creating a harder metal, bronze. This marked the beginning of a new age.

▶ BRONZE TOOLS
Unlike stone tools, which break easily, bronze tools could be molded, hammered into new shapes, and sharpened when they grew blunt. Some of the earliest bronze tools were axes, made by pouring the molten metal into one-sided stone or pottery molds.

Molten bronze, heated to around 1740°F (950°C) is poured into the mold.

1 MIXING METALS
To make bronze, nuggets of copper and tin are placed in a pottery dish called a crucible. This can then be heated over a fire until the two metals melt and combine.

The blade has a wide, curved cutting edge.

5 **AX HANDLE**
The ax head has now been fitted into a wooden handle. As casting improved, people made ax heads that fitted neatly over the handle.

Newly cast bronze resembles gold. As the metal ages, it will become duller.

4 **AX HEAD**
Once it has cooled, the ax head can be pried out of the mold and its edge sharpened. It is not just a practical tool, but also a beautiful object.

TRADE IN METALS
Demand for copper and tin, both rare metals, created long-distance trade. Between 2000 BCE and 1500 BCE, the eastern Mediterranean was dominated by the Minoans, a seafaring civilization in Crete, who may have traded tin from as far away as Cornwall in Britain.

3 **COOLING IN THE MOLD**
The one-sided mold is filled to the top. As the metal cools, its color changes from red hot to reddish gold.

STATUS SYMBOL
Bronze allowed people to fasten their clothes in new ways, using brooches and pins. Only the richest people could afford bronze brooches, so they were a new way of displaying wealth and status. The brooch pictured here was found in Central Europe and dates from around 1500 to 1200 BCE.

Molten bronze glows brightly.

2 **POURING THE MOLTEN METAL**
Once the metal has melted, the crucible is carefully lifted from the heat source and the molten metal is poured into the mold.

Lengths of bronze wire, twisted into shape

BRONZE AGE CHINA
The new metal was also invented in China, where the Bronze Age began around 1700 BCE during the Shang dynasty. Chinese bronze casters used pottery molds, in several sections, to make elaborate ritual objects. At Sanxingdui, people created sculptures with masklike faces, perhaps showing ancestors or gods.

WARRIOR SOCIETY
In Europe, the Bronze Age began in around 2200 BCE. It created a society dominated by wealthy, aristocratic warriors. People built burial mounds for rich individuals, who were often buried with weapons and armor. The invention of a hard metal allowed people to make a new weapon, the sword. Bronze was also beaten into sheets, and hammered to make helmets and shields.

Bronze swords have central ridges for strength.

The bronze face is decorated with gold leaf.

▶ THE WHEEL REVOLUTION

The very first wheel, invented in Mesopotamia around 3500 BCE, was nothing to do with transportation—it was used for making pottery (see pages 36-37). It was not until around 300 years later that the first wheeled vehicles came into existence. But once this revolution had taken place, wheels advanced over the next 2,000 years from heavy, solid wood to light, spoked wheels with strong iron rims.

A long peg stops the wheel falling off the axle.

The wheel turns around an axle—a long rod running through its middle.

Although this wheel looks simple, it took great skill to build the first one, and bronze tools to carve the wood.

Replica early wheel

The wheel is made of several planks of wood.

Wooden pegs hold the sections together.

THE WHEEL IS INVENTED

One of the most important inventions of all time, the wheel led to a transportation revolution, as farmers carted food, and warriors went to war on wheeled chariots. The earliest-known cart wheels, from around 5,000 years ago, were found in eastern Europe and West Asia, but the new technology soon spread.

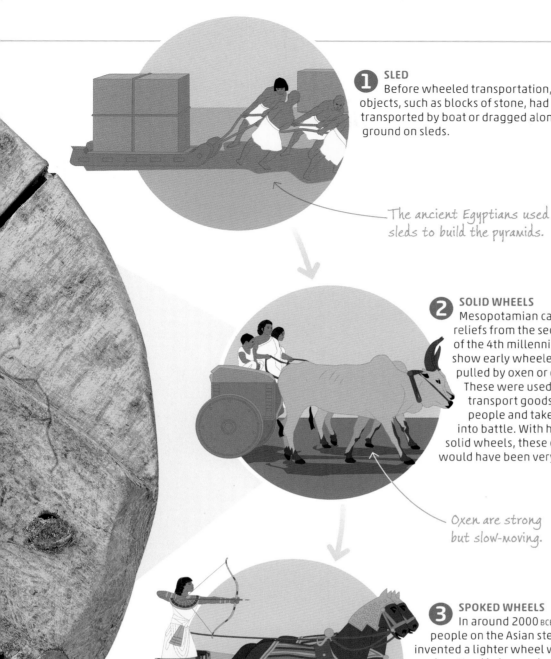

① SLED
Before wheeled transportation, heavy objects, such as blocks of stone, had to be transported by boat or dragged along the ground on sleds.

The ancient Egyptians used sleds to build the pyramids.

② SOLID WHEELS
Mesopotamian carved reliefs from the second half of the 4th millennium BCE show early wheeled carts, pulled by oxen or donkeys. These were used to transport goods and people and take warriors into battle. With heavy, solid wheels, these carts would have been very slow.

Oxen are strong but slow-moving.

③ SPOKED WHEELS
In around 2000 BCE, people on the Asian steppes invented a lighter wheel with spokes. Used in horse-drawn chariots, the spoked wheel revolutionized warfare, allowing rapid movement on a battlefield. By 1500 BCE, war chariots had spread across Asia and Europe, from China to Britain.

Egyptian pharaohs went to battle in two-wheeled chariots.

④ IRON-RIMMED WHEELS
By 1000 BCE, Celtic people in Europe were fitting iron rims around their wheels, which made them much stronger. Wheel design did not change again until the 19th-century invention of tires and metal spokes.

Strips of iron were added to wooden wheel rims.

WATERWHEELS
An ancient Greek invention, waterwheels are turned by flowing water. They can be used to grind grain by rotating a millstone. Wheels like these in Syria were described by the Romans. They lift water from the low-lying Orontes River onto fields above.

GEARED MECHANISMS
Gears—wheels with teeth that allow them to interlock—are machines that transmit or control movement. This is a reconstruction of a 2,000-year-old Greek device, known as the Antikythera mechanism, used to track the calendar.

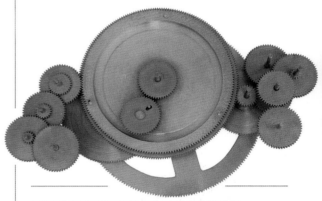

MESOAMERICAN WHEELED TOYS
Although the wheel was invented in Mesoamerica, it was only used for small, pull-along toys. Mesoamerican people never developed wheeled transportation, probably because they had no domesticated animals big enough to pull carts. People had to carry loads on their backs.

Pottery dog toy with wheels

THE FIRST CITIES

The world's first cities were built around 6,000 years ago in southern Mesopotamia, in a land originally called Sumer. Mesopotamia means "the land between the two rivers"—the Tigris and the Euphrates, which flow through present-day Iraq. The Sumerians invented kingship and organized religion, with priests and temples. They came up with writing and wrote the first law codes. The region also saw the world's first armies and empires.

WARS AND EMPIRES

When they first developed, the cities of Mesopotamia were separate city-states, each with its own ruler. As time went on, the cities began to rival each other and went to war in order to gain more power. Around 2350 BCE, King Sargon of Akkad, in northern Mesopotamia, conquered Sumer, creating the world's first empire.

A bronze head of Sargon, damaged by a later invader

▼ RELIGIOUS RULE

Every city was ruled by a king on behalf of the local god, who was worshipped in a tall, stepped temple called a ziggurat. This was the administrative center of the city. The ziggurat of Ur was built around 2100 BCE and partly rebuilt in the 1980s. On the far right is an impression of how it might have looked originally.

Farmlands watered by irrigation feed the city.

Sailboats carry trade.

The river brings water to the city.

THE HEART OF THE CITY

The ziggurat lay at the heart of the city, in a temple complex where grain was stored and distributed to the people. The city was built on big harvests, made possible by irrigation – management of the water from rivers that flooded each year. This required social organization, as people had to work together, digging canals, dykes, and reservoirs.

KINGS MAKE LAWS

In cities, large numbers of people who did not know each other had to learn to live together peacefully. To resolve disputes between people, Mesopotamian kings created the first law codes. The most famous is the code of Hammurabi of Babylon, written in 1790 BCE. One of his laws declares, "If a man put out the eye of another man, his eye shall be put out."

Hammurabi receives his laws from Shamash, the god of justice.

Flowers of gold from Iran

Blue lapis lazuli from Afghanistan

Red carnelian beads from India

TRADE AND CRAFTS

Mesopotamia lacked almost all raw materials. From an early date, there was long-distance trade. Cities exported barley, dates, textiles, and handicrafts, and imported stone, timber, metals, gemstones, and ivory. This headdress and beadwork belonged to Queen Puabi, who ruled Ur in 2600 BCE. It is made from imported gold, carnelian, and lapis lazuli.

A shrine held a statue of Nanna, the moon god, later renamed Sin.

The ziggurat is built of mud bricks.

Trees and plants may have been planted on the terraces.

WRITING
MAKES HISTORY

People started to write as civilizations became more complex. At first, writing allowed people to make a note of farming and trade deals. As writing became more advanced, it was also used to express ideas and tell stories. This marked the beginning of history—from this point onward we can read accounts of how people lived, written in their own words.

The tablet is written from left to right and top to bottom.

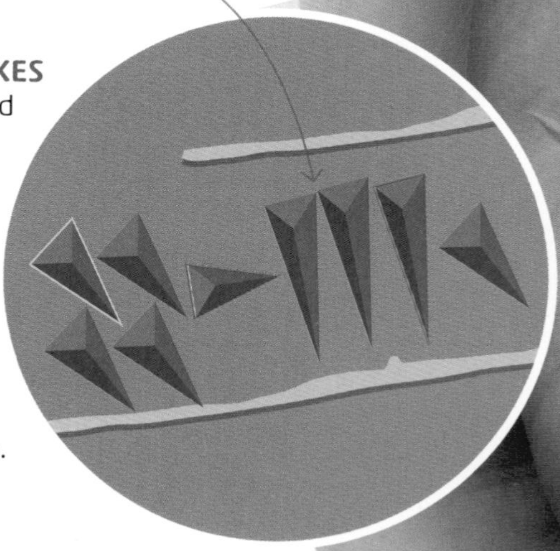

Strokes are grouped together to make words.

THREE STROKES

Three basic strokes are used for wedge-shaped writing: diagonal (highlighted in yellow), horizontal (red), and vertical (blue). The strokes shown here make the sound "mush", which means "serpent" in the language of the Hittites, who lived in what is now Turkey 3,000 years ago.

▶ WEDGE-SHAPED WRITING

Invented in Mesopotamia around 3200 BCE, some of the earliest writing was known as cuneiform. This means "wedge-shaped." It was written in wet clay using a reed with a wedge-shaped tip. At first, this writing used picture signs, which stood for both sounds and ideas. Over time, these were simplified into lines, which could be written quickly on the clay.

RECORD-KEEPING

People first used writing for commercial transactions. It allowed them to make a note of property, debts, and taxes. To read and write in Mesopotamia, people had to learn hundreds of different signs. Educated scribes, who were always men, had a high status in society.

A scribe records the size of a harvest for tax purposes.

The soft clay is easy to write on, but tablets can be baked hard for storage.

The writing tool is made from a reed with a wedge-shaped tip.

SACRED SPELLS

The ancient Egyptians believed that writing had been invented by the god Thoth and had magical power. They called their writing "the words of the gods" and used it to write spells on tomb and temple walls from around 3300 BCE. Hieroglyphics, the Greek name, means "sacred signs."

ALPHABET RULES

Around 1500 BCE, people in Canaan, east of Egypt, adapted Egyptian hieroglyphs to create a simple system with just 22 sound signs—the first alphabet. Spread by the Phoenicians (see page 57), it was then expanded by the ancient Greeks and Romans. For the first time, ordinary people could learn to read and write.

Roman woman with a writing tablet

ORACLE BONES

The oldest surviving Chinese writing is found on oracle bones from the Shang dynasty (c. 1600 BCE). Shang rulers used these to ask advice from their ancestors. Questions were written on turtle shells and ox bones, which were then heated until they cracked. The cracks were interpreted to provide the answers.

As in modern Chinese, each symbol stands for an idea.

A KINGDOM RISES ON THE NILE

More than 5,000 years ago, a great kingdom emerged on the banks of the Nile. Lasting more than 3,000 years, Egypt became one of the ancient world's richest civilizations. It was known to its people as Kemet, meaning "black land," because of the rich, black soil left by the annual flooding of the Nile. The kingdom built its success on this fertile land, using new farming methods to increase yields and build great wealth.

▼ OX-DRAWN PLOW

The ancient Egyptians were among the first people to use ox-drawn plows. These enabled them to sow seeds over a large area, massively increasing the amount of crops that they could grow. Farmers producing more food meant that people were able to spend time on other activities. Egyptians believed they had to farm the fields in the afterlife, and so were often buried with tomb models such as this.

THE NILE FLOOD CYCLE

The ancient Egyptians relied on the annual flood cycle of the Nile for fertile soil to grow crops. They believed the gods were responsible for the seasons, which they named Akhet, Peret, and Shemu, setting their calendar by the onset of the floods.

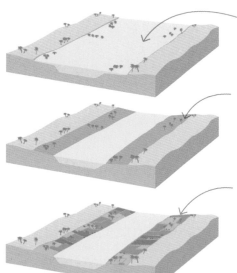

During Akhet, heavy rains at the Nile's source would cause it to flood.

During Peret, the waters receded to reveal a layer of silt, in which barley and wheat were sown.

During Shemu, crops were harvested and seeds gathered for the following year.

Two oxen were harnessed to the draft pole, which the farmer steered with a handle.

EGYPT'S MOTHER GODDESS

Widely worshipped by the ancient Egyptians, Hathor was known as the mother goddess of Egypt. The annual flooding of the Nile was seen as her blessing to the land.

Hathor is shown as a woman with cow ears. She was associated with a divine cow who was believed to make the Nile flood.

PLOWING A FURROW

The hook-shaped wooden plow is used to make a long, narrow trench, known as a furrow, in the ground. A farmer walks behind the two oxen that pull the plow, sowing wheat or barley seeds.

THE KINGDOMS OF EGYPT

The ancient Egyptians built their kingdom in the narrow strip of land along the Nile, protected from invasion by the surrounding desert. Egypt's long history is broken into three periods, or kingdoms, interspersed with periods of disunity. This map shows how the land controlled by Egypt grew over these three time periods.

KEY
- Old Kingdom (c.2649–2150 BCE)
- Middle Kingdom (c.2030–1640 BCE)
- New Kingdom (c.1550–1070 BCE)

Mediterranean Sea

Nile Delta

Giza ● Memphis

LOWER EGYPT

Valley of the Kings ● Thebes

Western Desert

UPPER EGYPT

Red Sea

Abu Simbel ●

Eastern Desert

NUBIA

Nile

Nebamun, an Egyptian scribe, is hunting with his wife Hatshepsut and their daughter.

Cats were often brought on hunting trips, helping to catch birds.

HUNTING AND FISHING

As well as providing rich farmland, the Nile was host to a variety of wildlife, including geese and ducks. Pharaohs and nobles hunted these in the river marshes, from boats made of papyrus reeds. Egyptian fishermen also used large nets, placed between their boats, to catch fish.

The oxen helped trample the seeds into the soil.

PHARAOHS
RULE ANCIENT EGYPT

Linen strips are wrapped around every part of the body and painted with resin to glue them together.

The ancient Egyptians were the first people to believe their rulers were god-kings. Called pharaohs, these divine rulers were thought to be responsible for maintaining cosmic balance and harmony, so ensuring the prosperity of the kingdom, even after their death. Mummification was believed to guarantee the safe travel of their souls to the afterlife.

1 WASHING THE DEAD BODY
An embalmer washes the pharaoh's body with sweet palm wine and rinses it with water from the River Nile. He sticks a long hook up the nose to smash the brain and pull it out, discarding it as a useless organ.

Dried organs were stored in canopic jars for the afterlife.

▶ TUTANKHAMEN'S MUMMY
The boy king Tutankhamen was about 19 years old when he died in 1324 BCE. He was mummified and buried in an elaborate tomb with all the possessions, including board games and clothes, that he would need in the afterlife.

This amulet represents the falcon-headed sky god Horus.

A scarab beetle inscribed with a spell covers the heart of Tutankhamen.

2 REMOVING ORGANS
The embalmer cuts a slit in the body and removes the internal organs. The liver, lungs, stomach, and intestines are packed in a mineral salt called natron to dry them out. The heart is left in the body as it is believed to hold intelligence and emotions.

3 DRYING AND STUFFING
The embalmer covers the body with natron to dry it out. After 40 days, he washes the body again with Nile water and stuffs it with herbs so it looks lifelike, then rubs scented oils in to keep the skin elastic.

Embalming fluids were preserved and buried with the body.

4 WRAPPING WITH LINEN
Embalmers wrap each part of the preserved body with long strips of linen, placing magical charms called amulets between the layers to protect the pharaoh on his journey to the afterlife.

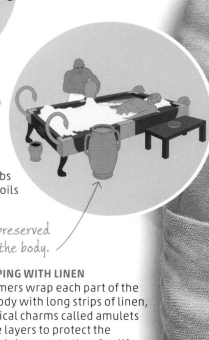

The vulture goddess Nekhbet and cobra goddess Wadjet, patrons of Upper and Lower Egypt, protect the pharaoh.

Tutankhamen is shown wearing the striped head-cloth typically worn by pharaohs.

LIGHT-HEARTED PHARAOH

After death, the pharaoh would travel through the underworld to an afterlife. But in order to reach this paradise, his heart needed to be pure. The jackal-headed god Anubis would weigh the heart against the feather of truth. If heart was lighter than feather, Osiris, god of the underworld, would allow the soul to pass. But if the heart was heavier, it would be eaten by the crocodile-headed goddess Ammit and the soul would cease to exist.

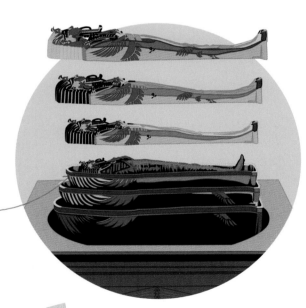

The inner coffin is gold and the outer ones are gilded wood.

6 STACKING COFFIN CASES
Three coffin cases and a stone sarcophagus encase the mummy. Placed inside three more gilded sarcophagi in a painted tomb chamber, the stacked coffins were meant to ensure a smooth transformation from human to god.

5 GOLD DEATH MASK
A death mask preserves the pharaoh's likeness. Made of 22 lb (10 kg) of beaten gold, it is inlaid with lapis lazuli, turquoise, and carnelian. Ancient Egyptians believed that the skin of the gods was made of gold.

NUBIA
RIVALS EGYPT

The land of Nubia lies on the banks of the Nile River south of Egypt. From around 2500 BCE, it was home to some of the earliest civilizations in Africa, the kingdoms of Kush. Egypt invaded Nubia repeatedly, but the Nubians fought back and even took over Egypt in the 8th century BCE, briefly ruling the two lands as one.

▼ LAND OF THE BOW
The Egyptians called the Nubian region Ta-Seti, "the land of the bow"—a reference to the skilled Nubian archers. They were known for dipping their arrows in poison and shooting them through their enemy's eye. When under Egypt's rule, Nubians also served in the Egyptian army. This model of Nubian archers was found in an Egyptian tomb from around 2000 BCE.

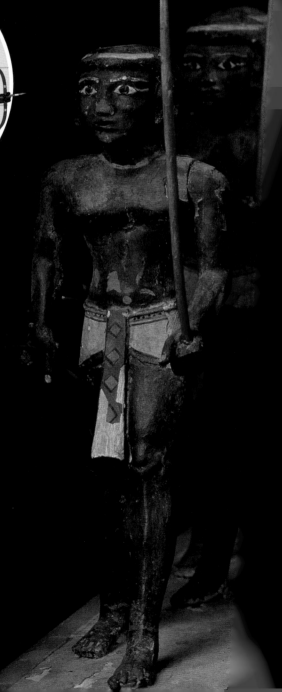

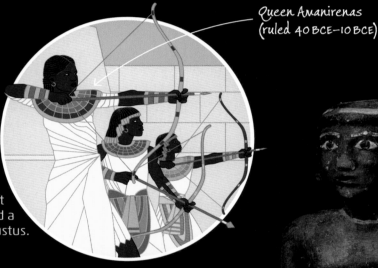

Queen Amanirenas
(ruled 40 BCE–10 BCE)

WARRIOR QUEEN
There were many warrior queens in Nubia, where women as well as men fought as archers. In 25 BCE, Amanirenas, Queen of Meroë, led an army against the Romans then occupying Egypt. The fierce warrior queen lost an eye in battle, but returned having captured a bronze statue of the Roman Emperor Augustus.

Carved head of Taharqa

TRADING PARTNERS
Although rivals, Egypt and Nubia had a fruitful trading relationship along the Nile. Along with natural resources such as gold, Nubia had access to goods, including ebony, ivory, and animal pelts, from the African interior. It traded these for Egyptian goods such as olive oil.

NUBIAN PHARAOHS
In 747 BCE, the Nubians invaded Egypt and established a dynasty that ruled over the two kingdoms for nearly 100 years. The joint kingdom's most prosperous period was under Pharaoh Taharqa, who ruled from 690 to 664 BCE. He restored Egypt's temples and built pyramids in Nubia.

KUSHITE KINGDOMS

In ancient times, Nubia was dominated by a series of kingdoms, known as the kingdoms of Kush. Each had a different capital. The earliest was Kerma. In time, this was eclipsed by Napata, which had a fierce rivalry with Egypt. The last Kushite kingdom was Meroë. It was defeated in 350 CE by a new regional power, Aksum.

THE KINGDOM OF AKSUM

In the 4th century, a powerful kingdom emerged in what is now Ethiopia, called the Kingdom of Aksum. It lay on trade routes between India and Rome and this made it rich. Ezana, its most famous king, adopted Christianity in 333 CE, recording his conversion on a stele (stone monument) known as the Ezana stone. He later conquered Meroë.

Aksum was one of the first African civilizations to mint gold coins.

EPIC STRUGGLE

Written in the ancient language of Sanskrit between 500 BCE and 100 BCE, the *Ramayana* is one of the oldest poems in the world. Along with other sacred Hindu texts, it gives an insight into the beliefs of ancient India. In an epic struggle between good and evil, the hero Rama is on a journey to rescue his abducted wife, Sita, from the wicked demon-king, Ravana. This page from a 17th-century manuscript shows an army of monkeys on their way to free Sita from Ravana. Rama, in blue, is riding on the Hindu monkey god Hanuman, while his loyal brother Lakshmana follows behind him.

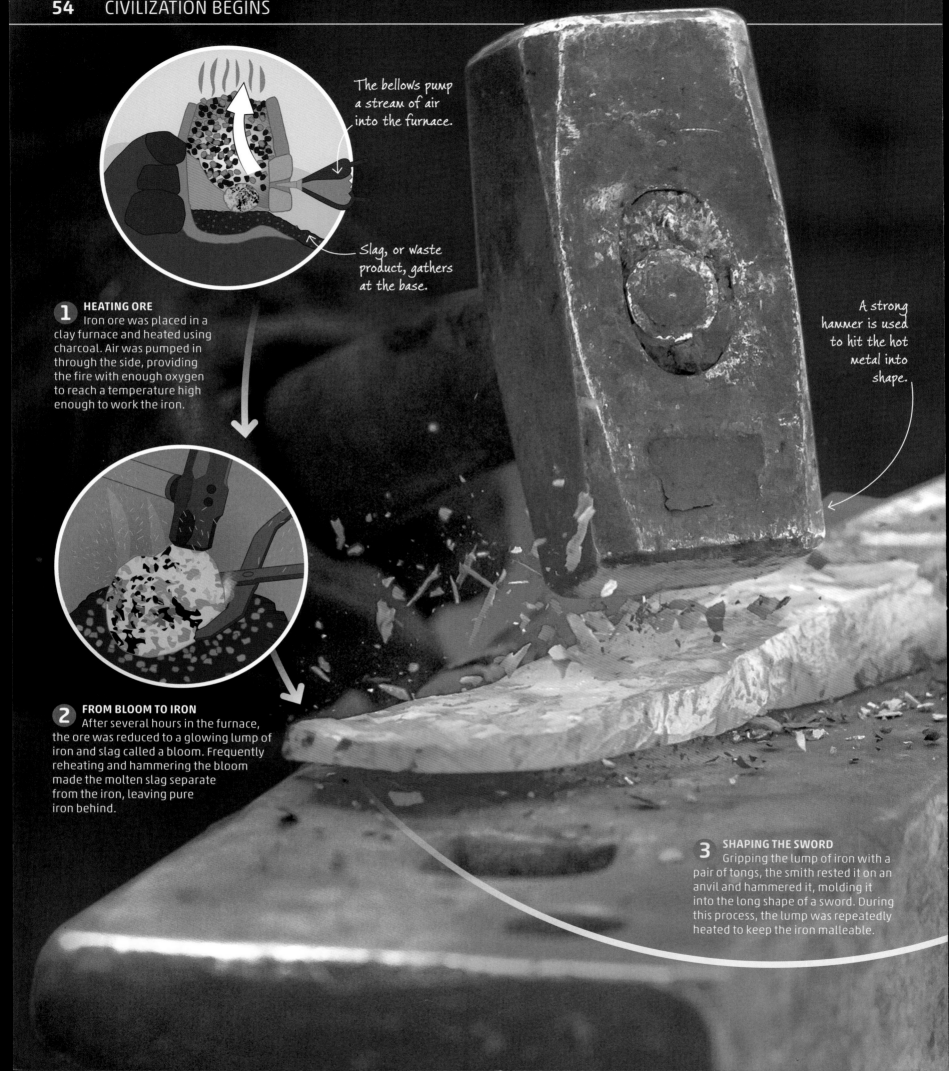

The bellows pump a stream of air into the furnace.

Slag, or waste product, gathers at the base.

1 HEATING ORE
Iron ore was placed in a clay furnace and heated using charcoal. Air was pumped in through the side, providing the fire with enough oxygen to reach a temperature high enough to work the iron.

A strong hammer is used to hit the hot metal into shape.

2 FROM BLOOM TO IRON
After several hours in the furnace, the ore was reduced to a glowing lump of iron and slag called a bloom. Frequently reheating and hammering the bloom made the molten slag separate from the iron, leaving pure iron behind.

3 SHAPING THE SWORD
Gripping the lump of iron with a pair of tongs, the smith rested it on an anvil and hammered it, molding it into the long shape of a sword. During this process, the lump was repeatedly heated to keep the iron malleable.

THE IRON AGE BEGINS

Iron is the most common metal on Earth, yet it was the last to be worked. It is not usually found in its pure form, but locked up in rock known as iron ore. Very high temperatures are needed to free iron from its ore, in a process known as smelting. The technique was first developed in West Asia in around 1550 BCE and, after 1200 BCE, spread across Asia, Europe, and, later, Africa.

◄ FORGING A SWORD

Unlike a bronze sword, an iron sword could not be cast in a mold. It had to be forged—heated and hammered into shape by a smith. Iron weapons were sharper and stronger than those made of bronze, and led to the development of many fierce warrior societies, such as the Celts (see pages 80–81).

4 SHARPENING THE BLADE
The finished sword was sharpened by pushing it backward and forward over a whetstone. Sometimes oil or water was poured onto the stone to reduce friction. One of the advantages of iron swords was that the hard metal did not go blunt as fast as softer bronze.

Whetstones were made from hard, fine-grained stones, such as schist.

SKY METAL

Before people learned to smelt iron, the only way to get pure iron was from meteorites, rocks that fall to Earth from outer space. The Egyptians called iron "metal from heaven" and valued it more highly than gold. Around 1323 BCE, Pharaoh Tutankhamen was buried with this dagger made from meteoric iron.

Iron blade

TOUGHER TOOLS

Iron made work easier for people because it could be made into cheap, everyday tools. It was widely used to make picks, pincers, hammers, chisels, and saws. Iron nails helped people build ships, and iron-tipped plows were more effective than the previous wooden ones.

PICK HEAD

BLACKSMITH'S PINCERS

FORESTS FOR FUEL

Iron-working required vast amounts of charcoal, made by slowly burning wood to dry it out. This led to many more trees being chopped down—a feat made easier by sharp iron tools—changing the natural landscape of many countries forever.

PHOENICIANS
SAIL THE SEAS

The Phoenicians were the greatest navigators in the ancient world. From their base in what is now Lebanon they sailed throughout the Mediterranean, trading products such as glassware and dye, and goods from other lands. Their voyages linked Mediterranean worlds together—spreading art, ideas, and their alphabet.

SEAFARERS
The Phoenicians' sturdy ships were built of cedar wood from the forests of Lebanon. As well as their Mediterranean voyages, Phoenician sailors explored the Atlantic coast of Europe and, in around 600 BCE, they may have made the first journey around the whole of Africa.

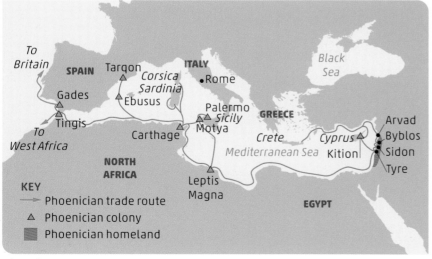

To Britain
SPAIN
Tarqon
Corsica
Sardinia
ITALY
Rome
Black Sea
Gades
Ebusus
Palermo
Sicily
GREECE
Arvad
Byblos
Tingis
Carthage
Motya
Crete
Cyprus
Sidon
To West Africa
Mediterranean Sea
Kition
Tyre
NORTH AFRICA
Leptis Magna
EGYPT

KEY
→ Phoenician trade route
△ Phoenician colony
▨ Phoenician homeland

MASTERS OF THE MEDITERRANEAN
Based in an area of present-day Lebanon, the Phoenicians had a number of important coastal cities, including Tyre, Byblos, and Sidon. These key ports allowed them to expand their reach from the 10th century BCE onward—founding trading stations across the Mediterranean. One of these, Carthage, later became the center of a great empire. Others, such as Cadiz in Spain and Palermo in Sicily, are major cities today.

▼ THE ART OF GLASSMAKING

Phoenician cities were craft centers, producing carved ivory, textiles, and metalwork. The city of Sidon was famous for its glassmakers, and may have been the source of these glass beads, decorated to look like faces. Much like the craftsmen who made them, these tiny treasures sport dark hair and thick beards.

1 GLASS FURNACE
The Phoenicians made glass by heating sand and plant ashes together in a furnace. By adding various minerals, they produced different colored glass. Blue glass was made with cobalt, while red came from copper.

2 MAKING A BEAD
To make a decorative bead, a glassmaker wound molten glass around the end of a rod. He painted the features on the surface with different colored molten glass.

Drops of yellow glass form earrings.

The white glass lips are colored with added tin.

3 DETAILED DESIGNS
The finished beads bore intricate, colorful faces and were often worn on necklaces. Beads like these have been found across the Mediterranean.

PRICEY PIGMENT
The most expensive Phoenician product was a purple dye, called Tyrian purple, made from the *Murex trunculus* sea snail. It took 12,000 snails to produce enough dye for the hem of a robe.

Each symbol was a consonant, such as this "h."

SPREADING THE ALPHABET
The Phoenicians' lasting legacy is their alphabet, which they introduced to Europe. Made of 22 signs, it was copied and adapted by the Greeks and the Romans, and is the basis of the words you are reading here.

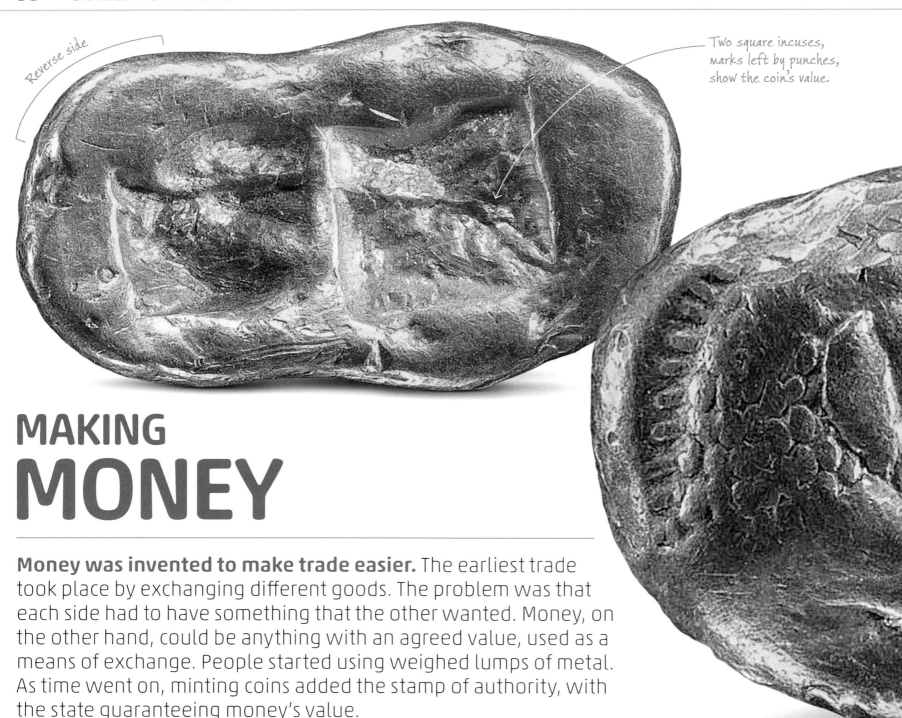

Reverse side

Two square incuses, marks left by punches, show the coin's value.

MAKING
MONEY

Money was invented to make trade easier. The earliest trade took place by exchanging different goods. The problem was that each side had to have something that the other wanted. Money, on the other hand, could be anything with an agreed value, used as a means of exchange. People started using weighed lumps of metal. As time went on, minting coins added the stamp of authority, with the state guaranteeing money's value.

COWRIE SHELLS
The earliest Chinese money, 3,500 years ago, was cowrie shells. These were highly valued because they were rare, easy to carry, and long-lasting. In Chinese writing, the sign for money is a cowrie shell.

TOOL-SHAPED MONEY
Coins in China began with bronze models of cowrie shells. From around 600 BCE, kings issued coins shaped like spades and knives. The First Emperor replaced these tool-shaped coins with round ones with a square hole in the middle, representing heaven and earth.

POLITICAL COINS
Issuing coins showed a ruler's authority. Roman emperors used coins to promote their public image and spread news. One side carried a portrait, while the other boasted of an achievement.

Imperial gold coin of Emperor Hadrian (r. 117–138 CE)

▼ COIN OF CROESUS

This is one of the earliest coins, made in 550 BCE. It was issued by King Croesus of Lydia, in what is now Turkey. In a process known as minting, the Lydians stamped coins with symbols that guaranteed their weight and value.

The lion and the bull were royal emblems.

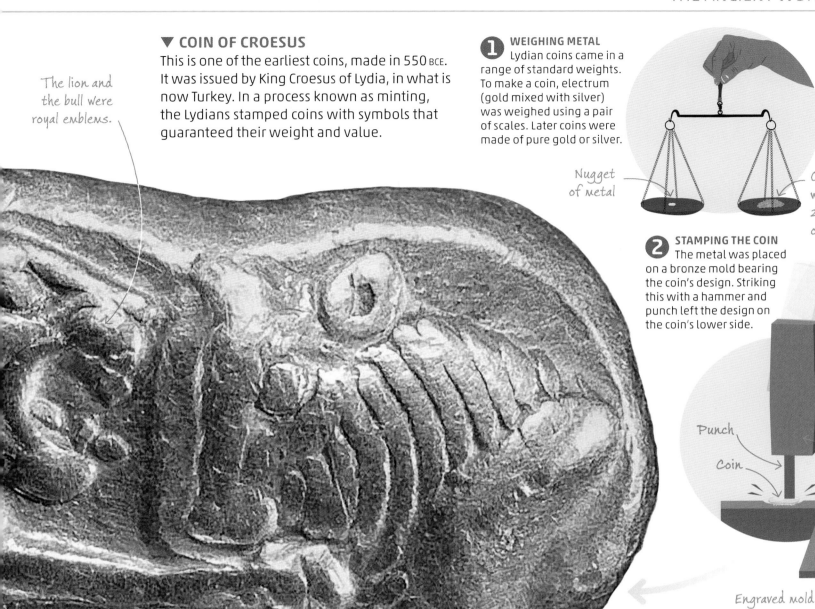

Front side

1 **WEIGHING METAL**
Lydian coins came in a range of standard weights. To make a coin, electrum (gold mixed with silver) was weighed using a pair of scales. Later coins were made of pure gold or silver.

Nugget of metal

One coin weighed 220 grains of wheat.

2 **STAMPING THE COIN**
The metal was placed on a bronze mold bearing the coin's design. Striking this with a hammer and punch left the design on the coin's lower side.

Punch

Hammer

Coin

Engraved mold

3 **THE FINISHED COIN**
King Croesus' coin carried the lion and bull on one side and marks left by punches on the other. The shape of the coin was unimportant: the punch marks guaranteed its value.

RELIGIOUS MESSAGE

From the 7th century CE, the caliphs who ruled Islamic states were leaders of a religious community as well as a state. They used coins to spread the message of Islam. This coin declares, "There is no god but Allah."

Gold dinar minted in 780 CE during the reign of Caliph Al-Mahdi

BANKNOTES

Paper money originated in China, around 900 CE, when merchants started trading in receipts for money to avoid having to carry huge quantities of heavy coins. In the 1120s, the government took over the system and issued the first printed banknotes.

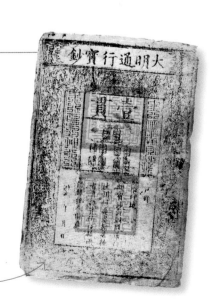

Banknote dating to the Ming dynasty (1368-1644)

PERSIA BECOMES A
SUPERPOWER

In the 6th century BCE, a king called Cyrus the Great founded the Persian Empire. At its height, it spanned three continents, and became the most powerful empire in the ancient world. In order to control this vast realm, Persian kings divided the land into provinces, governed by local rulers. The empire survived for more than 200 years before it was conquered by Alexander the Great in 331 BCE.

THE FIRST MAIL
The Persians created the first postal system. Official messengers, riding in relay, could travel the length of the Royal Road in just nine days. They waited with fresh horses at stations spaced a day's ride apart.

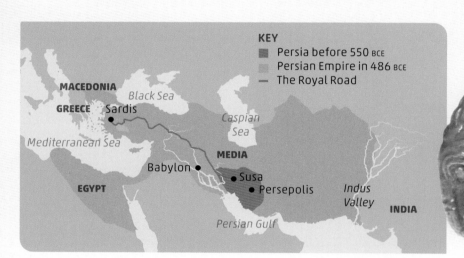

KEY
■ Persia before 550 BCE
■ Persian Empire in 486 BCE
— The Royal Road

MACEDONIA
Black Sea
GREECE Sardis
Caspian Sea
Mediterranean Sea
MEDIA
Babylon ●
● Susa
EGYPT
● Persepolis
Indus Valley
INDIA
Persian Gulf

THE ROYAL ROAD
The empire reached its greatest extent under Darius the Great (ruled 522–486 BCE). Darius built the 1,550-mile (2,500-km) Royal Road linking Susa (in modern Iran) to Sardis (in modern-day Turkey). The road was used for government, communications, and trade.

KING OF KINGS
Darius divided the empire into more than 20 provinces, called satrapies, each with its own satrap (governor). The satraps kept law and order and collected taxes on behalf of the king. Darius also founded a new capital, Persepolis, where he built a huge palace, later extended by his son Xerxes I. In 330 BCE, Persepolis was burned to the ground by Alexander the Great.

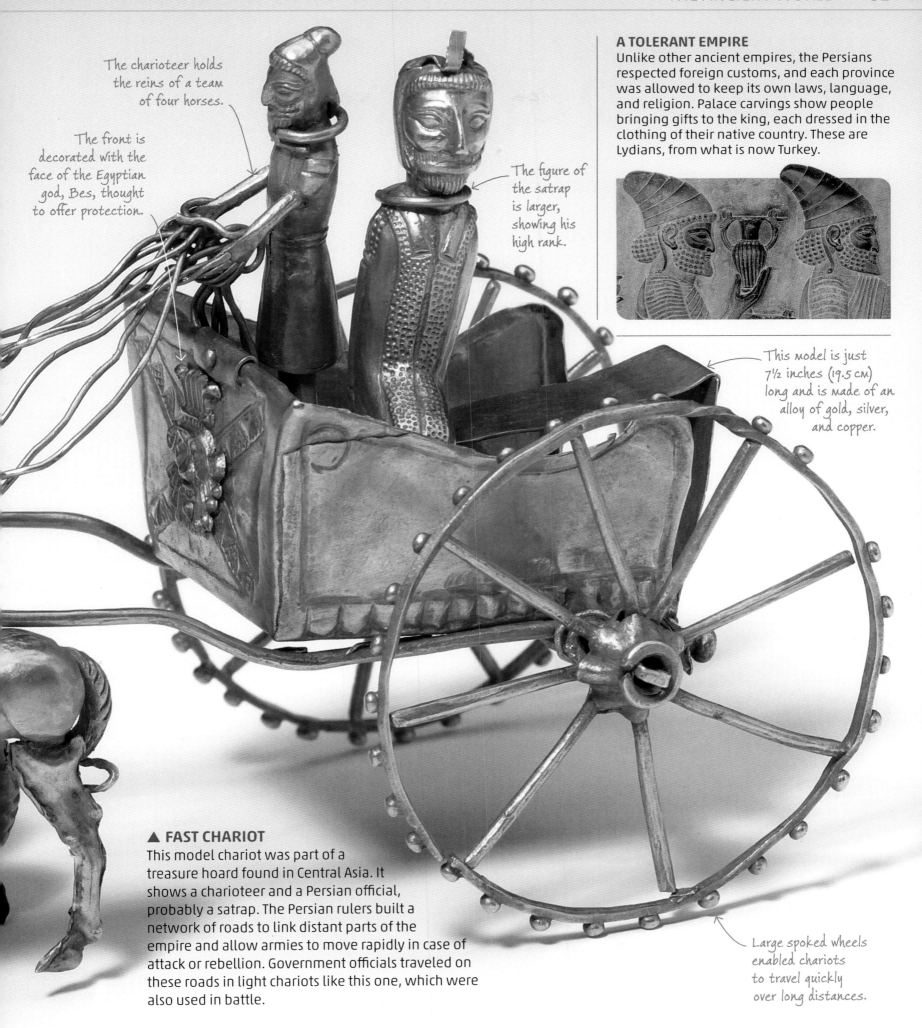

The charioteer holds the reins of a team of four horses.

The front is decorated with the face of the Egyptian god, Bes, thought to offer protection.

The figure of the satrap is larger, showing his high rank.

A TOLERANT EMPIRE
Unlike other ancient empires, the Persians respected foreign customs, and each province was allowed to keep its own laws, language, and religion. Palace carvings show people bringing gifts to the king, each dressed in the clothing of their native country. These are Lydians, from what is now Turkey.

This model is just 7½ inches (19.5 cm) long and is made of an alloy of gold, silver, and copper.

▲ FAST CHARIOT
This model chariot was part of a treasure hoard found in Central Asia. It shows a charioteer and a Persian official, probably a satrap. The Persian rulers built a network of roads to link distant parts of the empire and allow armies to move rapidly in case of attack or rebellion. Government officials traveled on these roads in light chariots like this one, which were also used in battle.

Large spoked wheels enabled chariots to travel quickly over long distances.

THE BIRTH OF
DEMOCRACY

Democracy was born in Athens more than 2,500 years ago. Meaning "rule by the people," it inspired the system of government that most countries have today. In the 6th century BCE, every city in ancient Greece was a separate state, with its own government and laws. Generally, in these city-states, only the richest citizens held power. But in Athens, every male citizen had an equal role in government.

▼ DEMOCRACY MACHINE

In Athens, public officials were chosen by drawing lots, using a machine called a *kleroterion*. This was used to select men to serve on the *boule*, a council of 500 men which ran the day-to-day government of the city. The *kleroterion* was also used to pick jurors to judge law cases.

A kleroterion as it would have looked

A remnant of a 3rd-century BCE kleroterion

WARRING CITY-STATES

Greek city-states often went to war with each other, as shown on this vase. The most warlike was Sparta. It was an oligarchy, meaning "rule by the few." Two kings, five high councillors, and 28 old men made political decisions. Spartan men were full-time soldiers who spent all their time training.

WOMEN'S LIVES

Only men played a role in politics in ancient Greece. Athenian women spent most of their time at home, spinning and weaving and caring for children. In contrast, Spartan women took part in sports, such as running races. The aim was to make them as fit as the men.

Bronze model of a Spartan girl running

CASTING OUT

The Athenians invented a system to stop any individual becoming too powerful and threatening the democracy. This was called ostracism, a word we still use today to mean public shunning. Citizens would write the name of a man they saw as a threat on a piece of pottery called an *ostrakon*. If more than 6,000 people wrote his name on an *ostrakon*, the man was exiled for 10 years.

ATHENIAN ASSEMBLY

Every big decision in Athens was made by voting in an assembly of citizens. Every citizen had the right to speak and vote, and 6,000 had to be present for a decision to be binding. Women, enslaved people, and foreign-born inhabitants were not citizens.

The assembly was held beneath the Acropolis (high city).

This ostrakon carries the name of Themistocles, a famous general who was cast out for his arrogance.

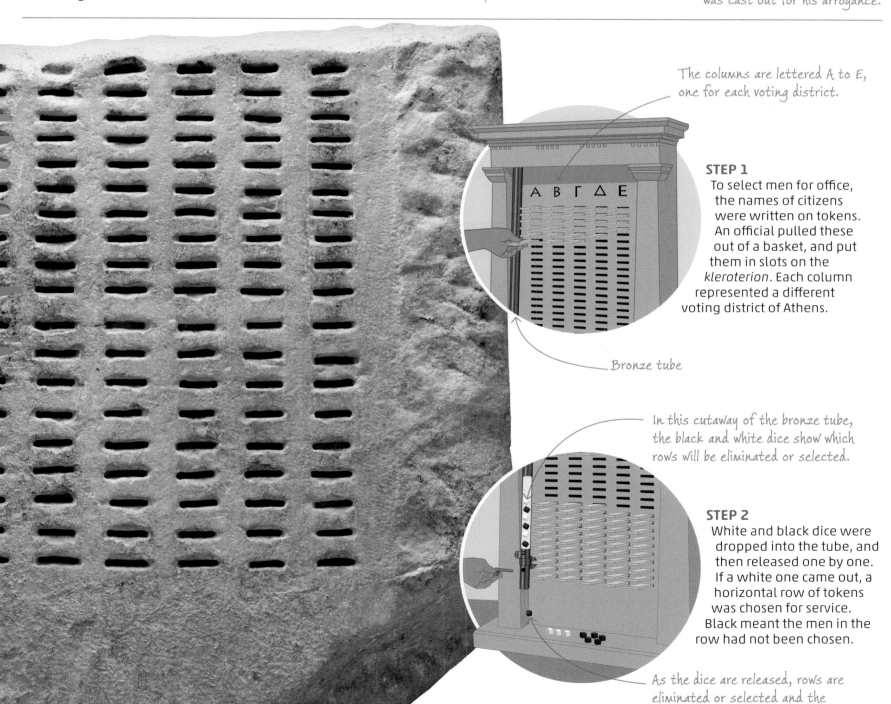

The columns are lettered A to E, one for each voting district.

STEP 1

To select men for office, the names of citizens were written on tokens. An official pulled these out of a basket, and put them in slots on the *kleroterion*. Each column represented a different voting district of Athens.

Bronze tube

In this cutaway of the bronze tube, the black and white dice show which rows will be eliminated or selected.

STEP 2

White and black dice were dropped into the tube, and then released one by one. If a white one came out, a horizontal row of tokens was chosen for service. Black meant the men in the row had not been chosen.

As the dice are released, rows are eliminated or selected and the tokens are removed row by row.

ANCIENT GREEK MYTHS

The ancient Greeks made sense of their world through stories, called myths. These stories of gods, monsters, and heroes were told to explain the origin of humans and the world they lived in. Passed down from generation to generation, these much-loved tales were the basis of poems and plays and were often illustrated on vases and other items of pottery. Many Greek myths, such as the story of the Trojan Horse, are still told today.

GREEK SOLDIERS EMERGE
While the Trojans slept, the Greeks crept out of their hiding place. They threw open the gates of Troy to let the Greek army into the city.

The soldiers waited until dark before climbing out of the horse.

▶ THE TROJAN HORSE

One of the most famous Greek myths tells the story of an ancient war between the Greeks and the city of Troy, in modern-day Turkey. According to legend, the Greek army besieged Troy for 10 years before capturing the city with a clever trick. The Greeks pretended to sail away, leaving behind a wooden horse as a peace offering. The Trojans dragged the horse into their city, not realizing that it concealed Greek soldiers inside.

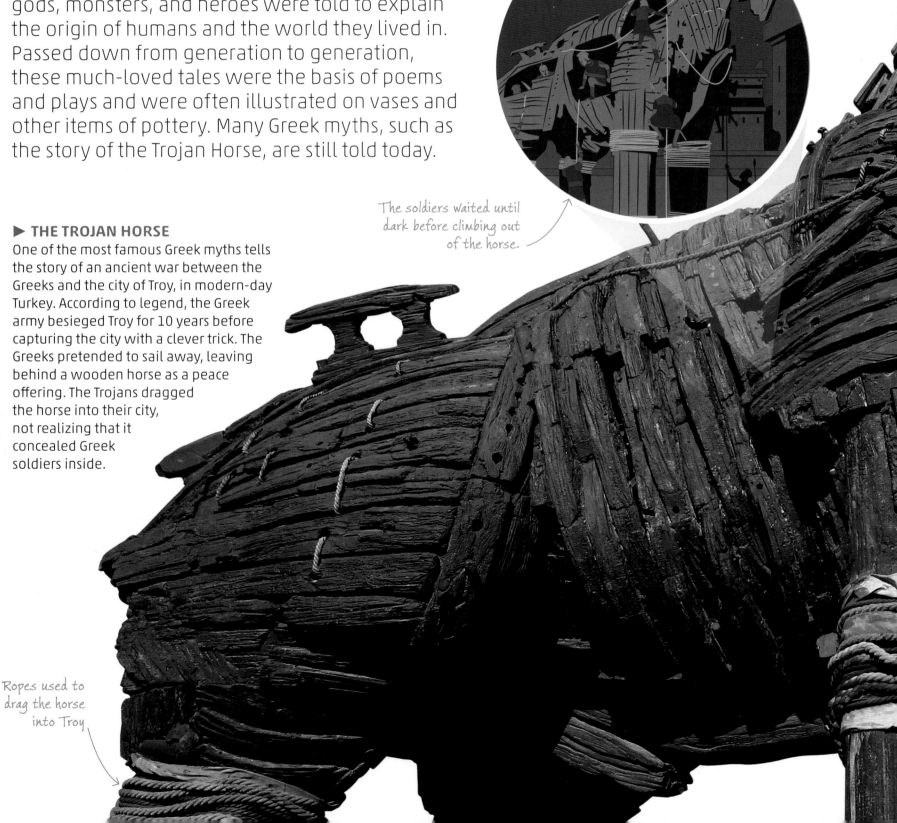

Ropes used to drag the horse into Troy

Full-size, modern replica of the Trojan horse

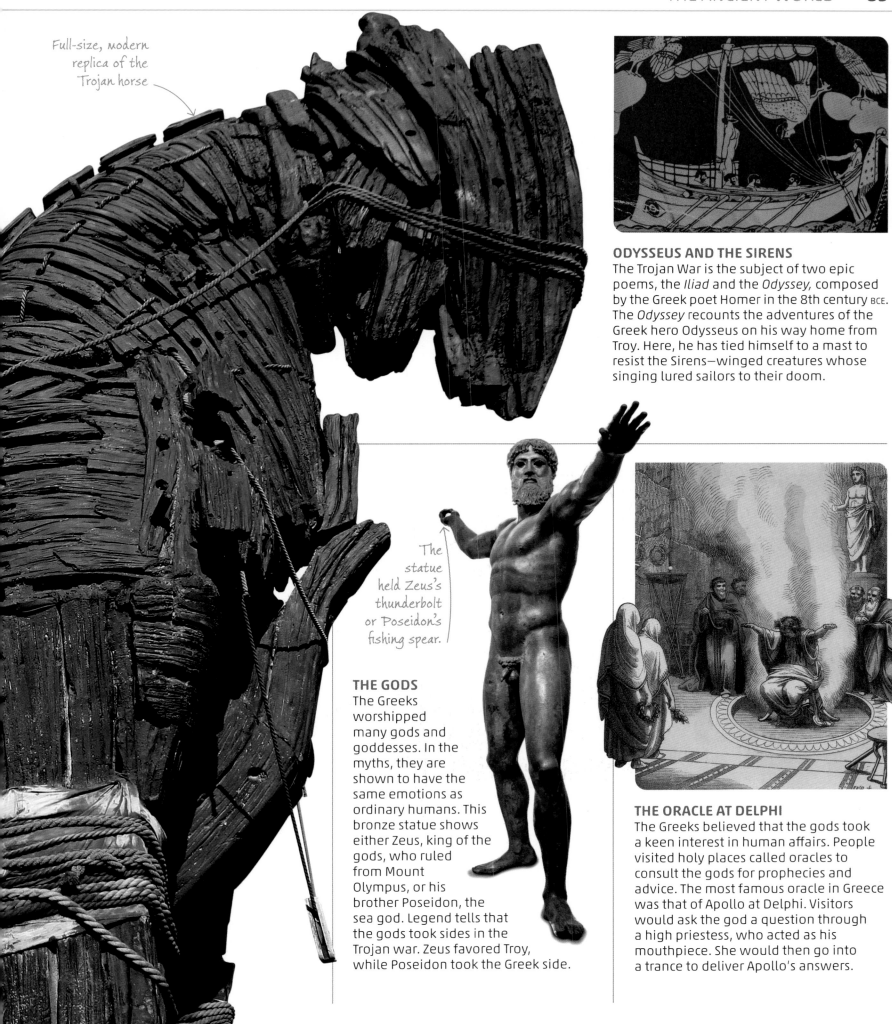

ODYSSEUS AND THE SIRENS
The Trojan War is the subject of two epic poems, the *Iliad* and the *Odyssey,* composed by the Greek poet Homer in the 8th century BCE. The *Odyssey* recounts the adventures of the Greek hero Odysseus on his way home from Troy. Here, he has tied himself to a mast to resist the Sirens—winged creatures whose singing lured sailors to their doom.

The statue held Zeus's thunderbolt or Poseidon's fishing spear.

THE GODS
The Greeks worshipped many gods and goddesses. In the myths, they are shown to have the same emotions as ordinary humans. This bronze statue shows either Zeus, king of the gods, who ruled from Mount Olympus, or his brother Poseidon, the sea god. Legend tells that the gods took sides in the Trojan war. Zeus favored Troy, while Poseidon took the Greek side.

THE ORACLE AT DELPHI
The Greeks believed that the gods took a keen interest in human affairs. People visited holy places called oracles to consult the gods for prophecies and advice. The most famous oracle in Greece was that of Apollo at Delphi. Visitors would ask the god a question through a high priestess, who acted as his mouthpiece. She would then go into a trance to deliver Apollo's answers.

▼ WARRIOR KING

A brilliant general, Alexander spent 11 years in Asia on military campaigns, and never lost a battle. As well as conquering the Persian empire, he also invaded India and won battles against a vast Indian army that fought with war elephants. This relief shows him defeating the Persians at the Battle of Issus in 333 BCE. Alexander died 10 years later, at the age of just 32, and the vast empire that he had built broke up.

FEARSOME ARMOR

Alexander wore a helmet in the shape of a lion's head, to remind people of the legendary hero Hercules. Macedonian kings claimed to be descendants of Hercules, who killed a monstrous lion and then wore its skin as armor.

The statue once held a metal spear. Alexander would have fought with a wooden spear tipped with iron.

Alexander's horse, Bucephalus, was a large black stallion, which he tamed at the age of 12. When the horse died, Alexander named a city after him.

ALEXANDER THE GREAT

Winning his first battle at 16 years old, and becoming king at 20, Alexander of Macedon was a legendary leader. His father, Philip, King of Macedon, had unified the Greek city-states. Alexander set out to conquer the Persian empire and in 334 BCE, he led an army into Asia. His influence spread Greek culture from Egypt to Afghanistan.

A Persian cavalry soldier is depicted falling under the might of Alexander's horse.

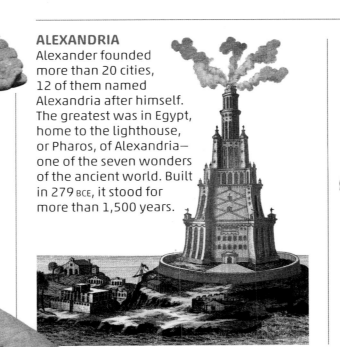

ALEXANDRIA
Alexander founded more than 20 cities, 12 of them named Alexandria after himself. The greatest was in Egypt, home to the lighthouse, or Pharos, of Alexandria—one of the seven wonders of the ancient world. Built in 279 BCE, it stood for more than 1,500 years.

MACEDONIAN PHARAOHS
After Alexander's death, Egypt had Macedonian rulers from 305 to 30 BCE. They dressed as Greeks in their daily life, but appeared on temple walls as traditional pharaohs. This relief shows Cleopatra VII—the last active ruler.

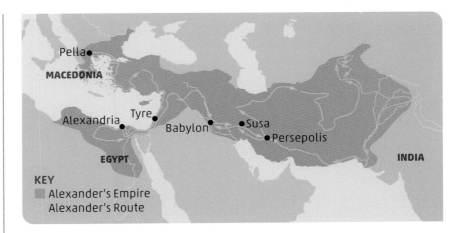

KEY
■ Alexander's Empire
Alexander's Route

A HELLENISTIC WORLD
From Macedonia, Alexander's empire stretched far and wide. Following his conquests, Greek became a common language spoken across western Asia. In the new Hellenistic cities, people dressed in Greek fashions, worshipped Greek gods, and watched Greek plays.

THE FIRST INDIAN EMPIRE

In 321 BCE, a warrior called Chandragupta Maurya founded the Mauryan Empire in ancient India. Under the Mauryans, whose empire lasted until 185 BCE, India was transformed from a series of small, rival kingdoms into an empire. In the early Mauryan period, Hinduism was the most widespread religion. A later ruler, Ashoka the Great, converted to Buddhism and helped spread his new religion across India and beyond.

EMPIRE FOUNDER
Chandragupta Maurya ruled from 321–296 BCE. As a young man, he is said to have met Alexander the Great, who inspired him to conquer India. He succeeded in conquering the north. His success in war was due in part to thousands of trained war elephants. These appear on the silver coins he issued.

▼ SACRED STUPAS
After converting to Buddhism, Ashoka did all he could to spread his religion. Across India, he built stupas—sacred mounds holding relics such as the ashes of the Buddha. He also sent missionaries to Southeast Asia. Four carved gateways were added to Ashoka's Great Stupa at Sanchi in the 1st century BCE. This is the western one.

Ashoka's original stupa is inside a larger, later mound.

Prayer walkway

The Buddha, shown as a wheel, preaches a sermon.

GREAT STUPA AT SANCHI
Ashoka's most famous monument is the Great Stupa at Sanchi, built as a pilgrimage site. Pilgrims would walk around the stupa in a clockwise direction, hoping to benefit from the power of the relics inside.

Toranas (ornamental gateways) face north, east, south, and west.

The four lions on this stamp, based on Ashoka's pillar at Sarnath, are India's national emblem.

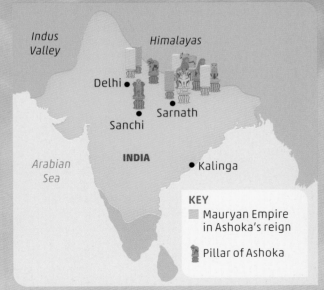

The crossbars are decorated with scenes from the Buddha's life.

ASHOKA'S EDICTS
Ashoka had a series of edicts engraved on pillars and rocks, instructing people how to live. One tells of his conquest of Kalinga. Instead of boasting of his victory, he expresses sorrow for the suffering caused. The edicts urge people to live good lives, according to Buddhist dharma (law), and encourage them to conserve forests and wildlife. Carved lions, bulls, and elephants top the pillars.

This panel shows the Buddha in a previous life as an elephant king.

EXTENT OF THE EMPIRE
The Mauryan Empire reached its height in Ashoka's reign (c. 268–232 BCE). By 260 BCE, Ashoka ruled all of India except for the southern tip. His pillars are mostly found in northern India, but his edicts were also inscribed on rocks around the empire.

Guardian spirits called yakshas support and protect the gateway.

Indus Valley

Himalayas

Delhi

Sarnath

Sanchi

Arabian Sea

INDIA

Kalinga

KEY

Mauryan Empire in Ashoka's reign

Pillar of Ashoka

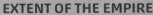

THE QIN DYNASTY
UNIFIES CHINA

In the 5th century BCE, China was made up of seven small, rival kingdoms. By 221 BCE, Qin Shi Huang, ruler of the western kingdom of Qin, had defeated his rivals and created China's first united state. Taking the title of First Emperor, he built new roads to link different parts of the state and established a common written language and currency. However, he was a harsh ruler, and the Qin dynasty collapsed in 206 BCE, four years after his death.

The generals were the tallest statues, standing 6 ft (2 m) high.

Mold for shaping the head

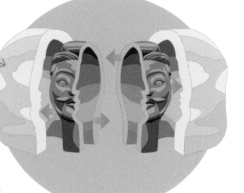

1 MOLDS
The potters used molds to make the warriors' heads, arms, hands, and armor. After molding the basic head shape, artists added the individual features by hand.

▶ TERRA-COTTA WARRIOR
Qin Shi Huang spent many years preparing for the afterlife. His burial tomb was guarded by an army of more than 8,000 life-size terra-cotta warriors. Each warrior had a different face, perhaps modeled on real soldiers in the Qin army. This statue is of a general, shown by his headdress and elaborate uniform.

Original statue

The details on the uniform were carved by hand.

2 BUILT IN SECTIONS
The bottoms of the gowns were built by hand from strips of clay. The different sections were created individually, then stuck together with wet clay. Each statue had a hollow body, while the legs were made from solid lumps of clay.

3 FINISHING TOUCHES
The finished statue was baked in a kiln, then coated with a lacquer varnish, and painted with bright colors. The paint on the original statue has long since crumbled away, but the replica on the right shows what it might once have looked like.

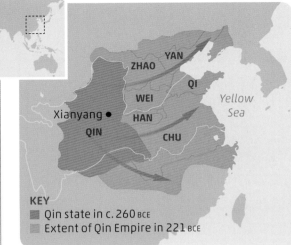

KEY
- Qin state in c. 260 BCE
- Extent of Qin Empire in 221 BCE

CONQUERING THE WARRING STATES
In 221 BCE, Qin armies conquered the last of their six rival kingdoms. The emperor pulled down the frontier walls that separated the kingdoms, uniting China as a single state.

GUARDING THE TOMB
The emperor's tomb, under a mountain built by forced laborers, took around 38 years to complete. Near the tomb were four pits that held the terra-cotta warriors, who carried real weapons made of bronze. Their role was to protect the emperor in the afterlife from the spirits of the men he had killed in battle. The terra-cotta army was discovered by chance in 1974 by farmers digging a well.

Modern painted replica

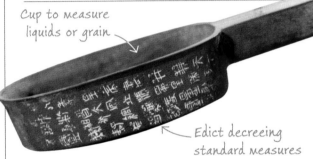

Cup to measure liquids or grain

Edict decreeing standard measures

UNITING THE EMPIRE
After uniting China, the emperor introduced standard measures, coins, and a system of writing. This bronze measuring cup carries an edict written by the emperor. His laws regulated every aspect of Chinese life.

HARSH RULE
The emperor maintained power using harsh punishments, including live burials. This painting shows the execution of scholars who disagreed with his ideas, and the burning of their books. His aim was to impose total control over his subjects.

SILK ROADS
LINK EAST AND WEST

More than 2,000 years ago, a network of overland trade routes linked Europe and Asia. Known as the Silk Roads, they connected the Roman Empire in the west with Han dynasty China in the east. People traveling the routes carried ideas and religions as well as luxury goods. Diseases also spread: there were deadly epidemics of smallpox, measles, and bubonic plague in both empires. The exchange continued until the late 15th century, when Europeans began a new age of trade by sea.

▶ CHINESE SILK-MAKING

The trade routes were named after Chinese silk. This was the product most valued in the west, where Romans became obsessed with the luxurious fabric. Chinese silk production was a closely guarded secret until 552 CE, when two Byzantine monks visiting China smuggled silkworm eggs out of the country.

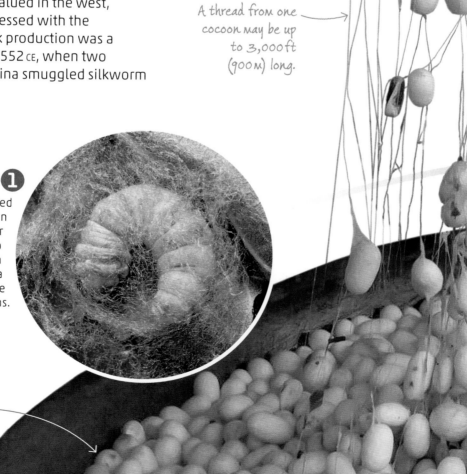

Cocoons are suspended from a stick for unwinding.

A thread from one cocoon may be up to 3,000 ft (900 M) long.

SILK WORMS ❶
Silk worms are the larvae of a domesticated moth called the *Bombyx mori*, and feed on mulberry tree leaves. After about a month, they start to wrap themselves in a cocoon of raw silk, made from a single thread they produce from their mouths.

Boiling makes it easier to unwind the threads.

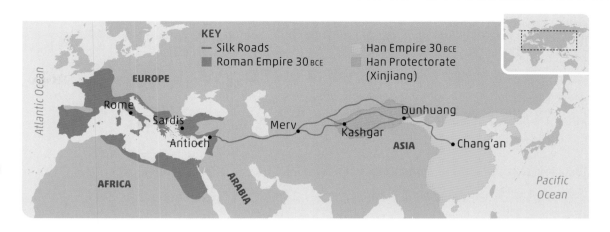

KEY
— Silk Roads
Roman Empire 30 BCE
Han Empire 30 BCE
Han Protectorate (Xinjiang)

THE SILK ROADS

The first overland trade routes were created by nomads moving with flocks across the treeless steppes of Asia. Later, merchants with camel caravans traveled the Silk Roads. Trade brought wealth to oasis towns in the desert and to the cities in Persia and Afghanistan.

HEAVENLY HORSES

In 125 BCE, Han Emperor Wudi learned that "heavenly horses," faster and stronger than any in China, could be found among the nomads to the northwest. To ensure a supply of horses, Wudi expanded the Han Empire into Central Asia. This helped establish the Silk Roads.

The Han dynasty bronze horse of Gansu

LUXURY GOODS

Many products were traded along the Silk Roads apart from silk: Roman glassware, gold, and silver; incense from Arabia; spices from southeast Asia and India; lapis lazuli from Afghanistan; and Chinese jade and porcelain. These luxury goods were carried thousands of miles by camels.

Central Asian lapis lazuli bird

Roman glassware

Indian silver coin

Chinese jade tiger

SPREADING IDEAS

Ideas and religions spread along the Silk Roads. This Chinese painting, on silk, shows a Buddhist monk traveling with a tame tiger. Astronomy, medicine, and philosophical ideas were also exchanged, and stops on the route, such as Dunhuang, became centers of learning.

2 SILK COCOONS
Inside the cocoons, the larvae change into pupae, before turning into adult moths. To stop the moths emerging, which would break the precious threads, the cocoons are boiled in water. They are then unwound to produce long strands of silk.

3 SILK SPINNING
A Uighur woman from the Xinjiang region of western China uses a traditional spinning wheel to wind the fine threads from many cocoons together to make a single long, thick thread. Silk has been spun like this, before being woven into cloth, for thousands of years.

4 COLORFUL SILK
Silk fabric is prized for its strength; lightness; and smooth, shiny appearance. It is cool in summer and warm in winter. These colorful silks are on sale in a market in Kashgar in Xinjiang, once an important stop on the routes.

BUDDHISM
SPREADS ACROSS ASIA

Buddhism first emerged in northern India in the 5th century BCE. By the 3rd century BCE, the religion had spread across India (see pages 68–69) and beyond. As it traveled across Asia, it absorbed local influences and took on different forms. Today, Buddhism is the world's fourth-largest religion, with more than 500 million followers.

Built in 652 CE, the multistory pagoda is 210 ft (64 M) high.

SACRED PAGODA
The northern form of Buddhism is known as Mahayana, meaning "greater vehicle." As it spread, other ideas were mixed in to the religion. In China, Buddhism merged with Confucianism and Daoism, systems of belief that also taught people how to live. It reached its peak in the 7th century, under the Tang dynasty. At this time, the Chinese built pagodas to house sacred Buddhist texts.

BRANCHES OF BUDDHISM
Buddhism is based on the teachings of a prince from Nepal called Siddhartha Gautama. He is known as the Buddha. Monks, missionaries, diplomats, and traders spread the teachings of the Buddha through India and across Asia. Over time, the religion split into two branches. Theravada Buddhism spread across South Asia from the 3rd century BCE, while Mahayana Buddhism spread along a northern route to East Asia, eventually reaching Japan in 552 CE.

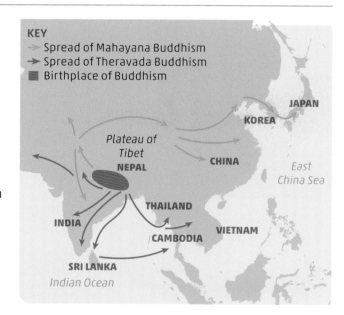

KEY
→ Spread of Mahayana Buddhism
→ Spread of Theravada Buddhism
■ Birthplace of Buddhism

Plateau of Tibet
NEPAL
JAPAN
KOREA
CHINA
East China Sea
INDIA
THAILAND
VIETNAM
CAMBODIA
SRI LANKA
Indian Ocean

The raised hand mudra (gesture) means "don't be afraid."

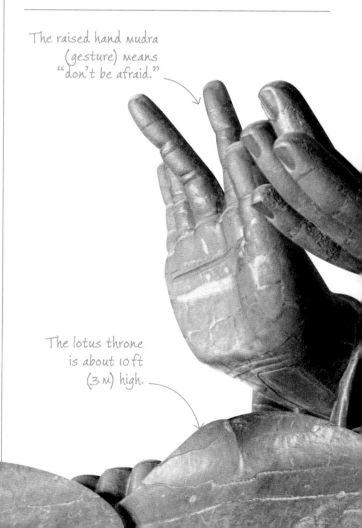

The lotus throne is about 10 ft (3 M) high.

FINDING ENLIGHTENMENT
The oldest form of Buddhism, Theravada means "teachings of the elders." Following the Buddha's teaching that the goal of life was to find true enlightenment, Theravadan Buddhists became monks or nuns and lived a simple life of prayer and meditation. Rulers in countries such as Thailand built monasteries for them. Here, young Thai monks study in the jungle with an elephant, an animal sacred to Buddhists.

▶ **GREAT BUDDHA**

Mahayana Buddhism reached Japan from China and Korea in the 6th century CE, later evolving into many different schools, with slightly different beliefs. The oldest are linked with Nara, where this massive Buddha statue sits in the Tōdai-ji Temple. It was built by Emperor Shomu (r. 724–749), who later became a Buddhist priest.

All the available bronze in Japan was used to make the statue, according to legend.

The current statue is a 17th-century replica of the original, which was destroyed in a fire in the 12th century.

THE GREAT BUDDHA statue is 49 ft (15 m) high

Once a year, monks, temple workers, and followers give the statue a ritual clean.

MESOAMERICAN
CIVILIZATIONS

More than 3,500 years ago, civilizations began to develop in what is today southern Mexico and Central America. These Mesoamerican cultures shared many features. People lived in cities ruled by kings, and worshipped similar gods at pyramid temples. Warfare was common as cities competed for resources, often taking prisoners of war. Across the region, people played the same ball game.

Spectators in elaborate headgear line the sides of the courts.

MEXICO

West Mexican cultures

Teotihuacán

Gulf of Mexico

Olmec

Maya Lowlands

Pacific Ocean

Zapotec

GUATEMALA

Maya Highlands

HONDURAS

EARLY MESOAMERICAN AND WEST MEXICAN CULTURES
c. 1600 BCE–500 CE

ANCIENT CULTURES
Mesoamerica means "middle America". It refers to the region stretching from southern Mexico in the west to Guatemala and Honduras in the east. It also describes the cultures that flourished there from around 1600 BCE. Other, distinct cultures developed in West Mexico.

THE OLMECS
The first Mesoamerican culture to emerge was that of the Olmecs, in the resource-rich coastal forests. From around 1200 BCE, they built monumental structures and carved huge stone heads, thought to be portraits of local rulers.

The Pyramid of the Sun towered over the city.

THE CITY OF TEOTIHUACÁN
The biggest Mesoamerican city was that of Teotihuacán, in the Valley of Mexico. At its peak from around 300 BCE to 600 CE, it was one of the largest cities in the world. It may have been the heart of an empire, and its influence was felt across Mesoamerica.

Every ball court had a playing alley, flanked by side walls.

▼ A BALL GAME MODEL

This clay model of a game on a ball court was made around 1,700 years ago by the Nayarit people of West Mexico, an area with a culture distinct from that of Mesoamerica – but where the ball game was also played. The rules and rituals of this team sport, which was central to later Maya culture, varied.

The ball could weigh as much as 9 lb (4 kg).

THE GAME IN ACTION

Players leaped through the air, using hips, shoulders, and buttocks to strike the ball. In some versions of the game, they aimed to hit the ball through a stone hoop. Made of rubber from native trees, the ball was solid and heavy, and so players wore thick padding for protection.

Two players in the center hope to block the ball.

Spectators lean forward, excited by the game.

This player challenges his opponents for possession of the ball.

Players bounced the ball off the ball-court walls.

DESERT DRAWINGS

Flying over Peru's Nazca Desert is the best way to see huge markings etched into the landscape below. Between 500 BCE and 500 CE, the Nazca people made hundreds of these patterns—known as geoglyphs—using soil, rocks, and even trees. The reason why remains a mystery. Some are simple shapes, while others are animals, including hummingbirds and monkeys. This spider is 154 ft (47 m) long. The Nazca people lived in the fertile river valleys to the north and south of the lines, where they also built complex crop irrigation systems and designed beautiful pottery.

THE
CELTS
DOMINATE EUROPE

Before the Romans expanded their empire, much of Europe was home to the Celts, whose civilization flourished between the 8th and 1st centuries BCE. The Celts lived in many different tribes and did not think of themselves as a single people. Yet they spoke related languages and shared similar customs, religious beliefs, and styles of art. The culture and languages of the Celts still survive in parts of Europe today.

HILL FORTS
In Britain, Celtic tribes built massive hill forts, such as Maiden Castle in southern England. It was topped with wooden ramparts and surrounded by a maze of ditches to confuse attackers. The fort was home to hundreds of people living in timber roundhouses.

WARRIOR QUEEN
Each Celtic tribe had its own king or queen. When the Romans conquered Britain, Boudicca, queen of the Iceni, led a huge revolt against the invaders. In 61 BCE, she sacked three Roman towns before being defeated.

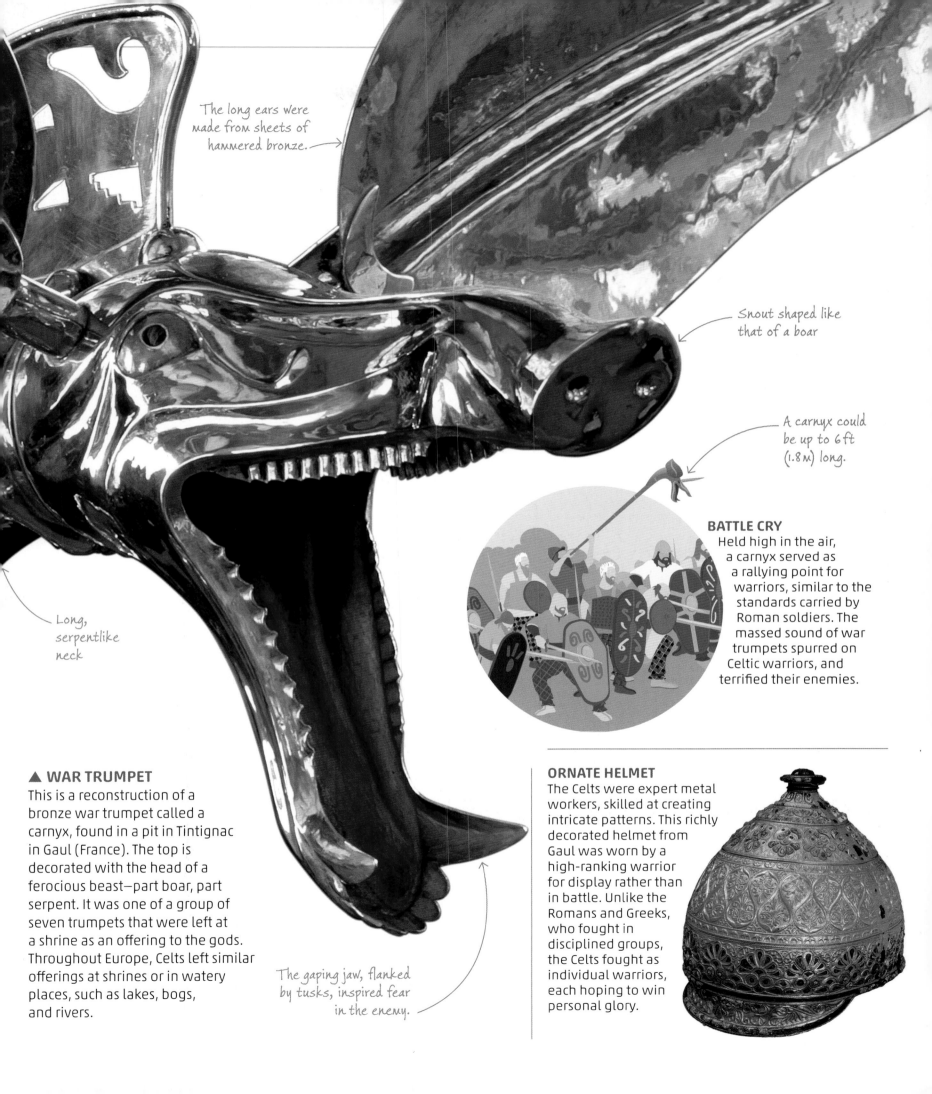

The long ears were made from sheets of hammered bronze.

Snout shaped like that of a boar

A carnyx could be up to 6 ft (1.8 m) long.

BATTLE CRY
Held high in the air, a carnyx served as a rallying point for warriors, similar to the standards carried by Roman soldiers. The massed sound of war trumpets spurred on Celtic warriors, and terrified their enemies.

Long, serpentlike neck

The gaping jaw, flanked by tusks, inspired fear in the enemy.

▲ WAR TRUMPET
This is a reconstruction of a bronze war trumpet called a carnyx, found in a pit in Tintignac in Gaul (France). The top is decorated with the head of a ferocious beast—part boar, part serpent. It was one of a group of seven trumpets that were left at a shrine as an offering to the gods. Throughout Europe, Celts left similar offerings at shrines or in watery places, such as lakes, bogs, and rivers.

ORNATE HELMET
The Celts were expert metal workers, skilled at creating intricate patterns. This richly decorated helmet from Gaul was worn by a high-ranking warrior for display rather than in battle. Unlike the Romans and Greeks, who fought in disciplined groups, the Celts fought as individual warriors, each hoping to win personal glory.

Short sword, also known as a gladius

THE ROMANS BUILD AN EMPIRE

Two thousand years ago, the Romans created one of the most successful empires in history. With the help of a disciplined army, the Romans were able to bring neighboring lands under their control. The sharing of a common culture led people from many places to see themselves as Roman. This empire's legacy is still seen today, from architecture to government.

Linking shields in this way, known as a "testudo"—or tortoise—formation, protected legionnaires from enemy attack.

▲ **FIGHTING FORCE**

The finest soldiers in the Roman army were heavily armed foot soldiers called legionnaires. They were full-time professionals, who fought in tight formation. Hobnailed sandals, called *caligae*, gave legionnaires a good grip and protected their feet, as they marched up to 19 miles (30 km) a day.

Raised shields protect soldiers from arrows.

CENTURION'S HELMET

A unit of 80 legionnaires, called a century, was commanded by an officer called a centurion. He wore a distinctive helmet with a sideways crest, which helped his men see him in battle.

The shield, called a scutum, has an image of an eagle and a thunderbolt—symbols of the god Jupiter, protector of the empire.

A bed roll and a cloak were rolled up and strapped on top of the pack.

LEGIONNAIRE PACK

On the march, a legionnaire carried everything he needed in a pack called a sarcina, which attached to a pole that rested on his shoulder. His equipment included a pickax for digging, a cooking pot, a water flask, and a bag holding food rations to last three days.

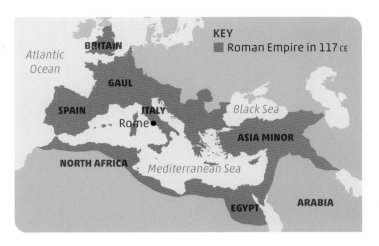

EMPIRE AT ITS HEIGHT

The empire reached its greatest extent in 117 CE, under Emperor Trajan. It stretched 2,485 miles (4,000 km) east to west, and included tens of millions of people. For the only time in history, all the lands around the Mediterranean Sea belonged to a single state, ruled from Rome.

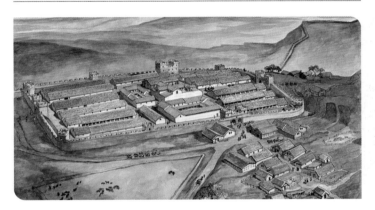

MAINTAINING CONTROL

Roman soldiers were builders, constructing roads, camps, and frontier defenses such as Hadrian's Wall across northern Britain. At regular points along the wall there were great forts, always built to a standard plan. Forts and roads helped the army control the empire's borders.

SPREADING ROMAN CULTURE

This is Timgad, a frontier city in southern Algeria, founded by Emperor Trajan. Originally settled by retired soldiers, it also attracted a population of Africans. Cities like Timgad, with bath houses and theaters, spread Roman culture far and wide. Most of the people who lived here had never seen Rome, yet they came to see themselves as Romans.

The wheel is attached to a strong lifting arm.

The person inside walks continually on the treads like a pet hamster in a wheel.

ANCIENT ROMAN ENGINEERING

The Romans were the greatest builders and engineers of the ancient world. They invented concrete, allowing them to build huge structures quickly and cheaply. Using arches, they built aqueducts to bring water to growing cities. Many Roman constructions are still standing today, and classical building styles continue to influence architecture.

STRONG STUFF

The Romans made concrete using lime mortar, rubble, and volcanic ash. The mortar held the concrete together, the rubble gave it strength, and the ash created a chemical reaction making it even stronger. This wall in Empúries, Spain, has a concrete core.

ENDURING DOMES

The Romans used concrete to build domes, such as the Pantheon, a temple in Rome built by Emperor Hadrian in around 120 CE, which still stands today. For the first time, a large interior space could be roofed over without needing columns to hold up the ceiling.

ROMAN ROADS

The Romans built a vast network of roads connecting the outposts of their empire to Rome. Built by soldiers, Roman roads had layered foundations and curved surfaces for drainage. Famously straight, the Appian Way stretches from Rome to the heel of Italy.

◀ TREADWHEEL CRANE

The treadwheel crane was a lifting machine invented by the Romans. The large wheel was turned by people inside walking on the wheel's treads. The turning wheel wound a rope, raising heavy loads into the air. The Romans enslaved people they captured in wars, putting them to work in quarries and on building sites. Enslaved people would have turned the treadwheel.

Weights anchor the crane.

A treadwheel crane lifts heavy stone.

Two men turn the treadwheel.

SEGOVIA AQUEDUCT

An aqueduct is an artificial channel carrying water to a city through a tunnel or along an arched bridge. One of the best preserved of all Roman aqueducts, in Segovia, Spain, has 167 arches.

BUILDING AN AQUEDUCT

It took great engineering skill and manpower to build aqueducts, which could be more than 62 miles (100 km) long. Built out of concrete and stone, they were designed so that water flowed downhill with gravity. Treadwheel cranes were used to raise blocks of stone. Wooden scaffolding enabled teams of builders to work at every level.

In the medieval period, many **trade routes** that were first established in ancient times **expanded** and got busier. **Goods**, new **technologies**, **religions**, and **ideas spread** around the world, transported over land and across the sea. Meanwhile, **powerful new empires** reshaped the world's borders.

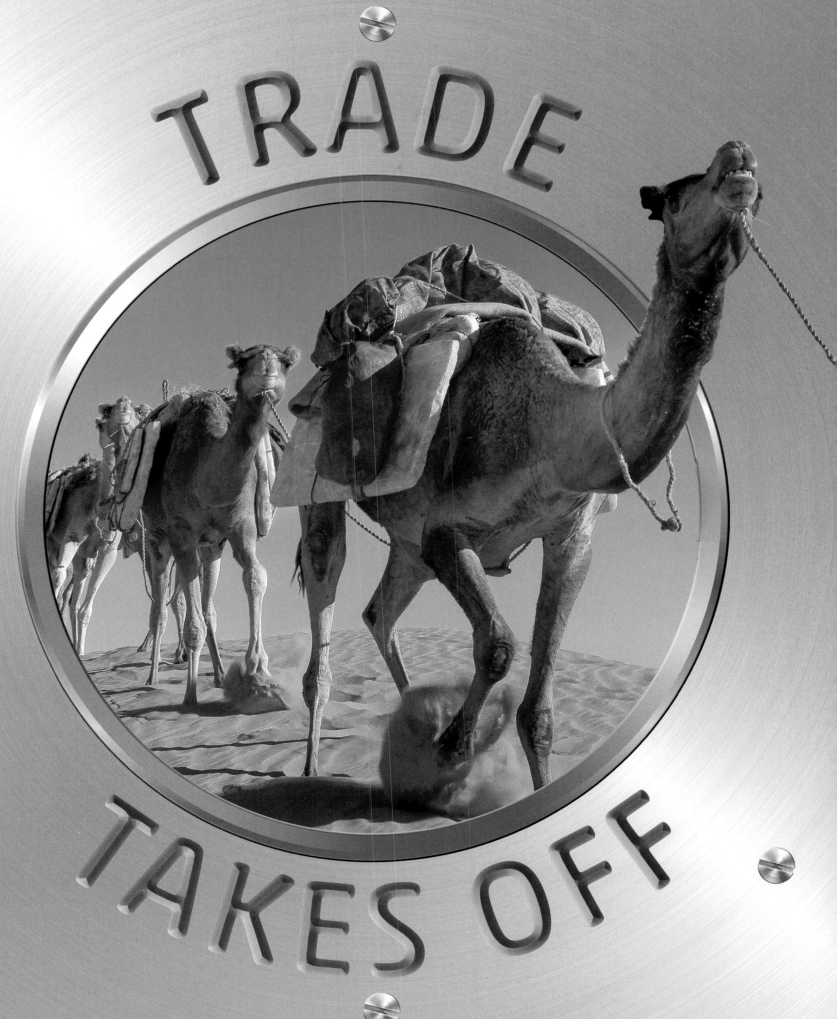

TRADE

TAKES OFF

TIMELINE OF THE
MEDIEVAL WORLD

In the thousand years after the collapse of the western Roman Empire, powerful new states were created in West Asia, Europe, and Africa. Great empires ruled in China and in parts of the Americas. Islam, a new religion, was born, and extraordinary feats of navigation took Vikings across the North Atlantic and Polynesians to remote Pacific islands.

450

476
End of Empire
The western part of the Roman Empire (split in two since 395 CE) comes to an end as General Odoacer overthrows the boy emperor Romulus Augustulus.

SELJUK JUG

1150
Mississippi mound cities
Peoples of the Mississippi river basin in North America build the first towns on the continent. Each one is based around large ceremonial mounds.

1095
Christian Crusades
Pope Urban II calls up an army of Christian knights to help the Byzantine emperor fight the Muslim Seljuks and establish control over the lands around Jerusalem, ruled by Muslims. Setting out in 1096, this is the first of many such Crusades.

c. 1041
Movable type
In Song-dynasty China, Bi Sheng invents a movable type made of ceramic characters. This new technology is used to mass-produce printed books.

1025
Chola Empire
Ruler Rajendra Chola builds an empire in the Indian Ocean after attacking the Indonesian state of Srivijaya.

1066
The Norman Conquest
Duke William of Normandy wins the English throne by defeating the Saxon king Harold II at the Battle of Hastings.

1040
The Seljuk Turks
The Seljuk Turks of central Asia conquer the Persian Ghaznavid emirate. They go on to drive the Byzantines out of Anatolia (in modern-day Turkey) in 1071.

SHOGUN MINAMOTO YORITOMO

INCA MODEL OF A LLAMA

GENGHIS KHAN

1206
Genghis Khan
The Mongol warrior Temüjin is proclaimed Genghis ("universal") Khan, uniting the rival Mongol tribes. By the time of his death in 1227, he had conquered an empire that covered most of China and central Asia.

1185
The Kamakura shogunate
The Heian era in Japan comes to an end following a war between rival clans. Minamoto No Yoritomo founds the Kamakura shogunate in Japan, beginning a period of military government that will last until 1868.

c. 1200
The Inca Empire
Manco Cápac founds the Inca state at Cuzco in what is now southern Peru. By the 1470s, it is the greatest empire in the Americas, with a vast road network, strict administrative system, and fine arts and crafts.

1235
The Mali Empire
After defeating his enemies in battle, Sundiata Keita is crowned Emperor of Mali. He gains control of the lucrative trans-Saharan trade routes.

500s
Maya city-states
The Maya people build an advanced civilization in southern Mexico and Guatemala, with complex city-states linked by a rich trading network.

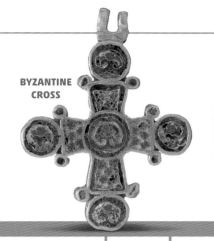

BYZANTINE CROSS

622
Islam is founded
The prophet Muhammad flees from Mecca to Medina in the *hijra* (flight), an event that marks the start of the Muslim era and the first year of the Islamic calendar.

711
Invasion of Spain
Muslim Arabs and Berbers from North Africa invade Spain. Naming it al-Andalus, they control parts of it until 1492, when they are expelled by the Spanish.

MINARET IN SAMARRA

527–565
Byzantine expansion
Emperor Justinian expands the eastern Roman Empire, later known as the Byzantine Empire, to its greatest extent. The empire, with Constantinople as its capital, lasts until 1453.

618
Tang China
The new Tang dynasty takes power in reunified China, and rules until 907.

750
The Abbasid Caliphate
The Abbasids overthrow the Umayyad caliphate and take power in West Asia. They last until 1258, founding capitals in Baghdad and Samarra.

936
Unification of Korea
Three rival kingdoms in Korea are united by Taejo of the Goryeo dynasty.

c. 802
Khmer Empire
Jayavarman II unites the Khmer people of Cambodia, creating a dominant civilization in southeast Asia, which lasts until the mid-1400s.

CHARLEMAGNE

793
Vikings on the move
Viking raids against western Europe begin with an assault on Lindisfarne Abbey in England. The Vikings also form trade networks along the coasts of Europe and through Russia to the Black Sea.

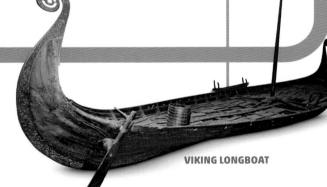

VIKING LONGBOAT

ANGKOR WAT, CAMBODIA

800
Emperor Charlemagne
On Christmas Day, Pope Leo III crowns the Frankish leader Charlemagne as Emperor of the Romans, re-creating the Roman Empire in western Europe.

1347
The Black Death
There is an outbreak of bubonic plague in Crimea. Carried by rats, it spreads west across Europe. By 1353, it has killed around 200 million people, approximately half the European population.

MING VASE

1325
Aztec capital
The Aztecs (Mexica) of central America build a new capital at Tenochtitlán, in what is now Mexico City. By 1500, their empire dominates the region.

1370

c. 1280
Polynesian navigators
Sailing large outrigger canoes and navigating by the stars and sea currents, Polynesian colonists reach New Zealand, the furthest point of their oceanic travels.

c. 1300
Ife thrives
The Yoruba Ife kingdom is powerful and wealthy. It has accomplished artists and strong trade networks with other West African kingdoms.

IFE BRONZE HEAD

1337
The Hundred Years' War
Edward III of England launches a war to try to claim the French throne. With breaks, the war lasts 116 years, ending in 1453.

1368
Ming China
Rebel leader Zhu Yuanzhang overthrows the Mongol Yuan dynasty and establishes the new Ming dynasty, which rules China until 1644.

BARBARIANS
INVADE EUROPE

For centuries, the Roman Empire had been threatened by Germanic tribes from northern Europe. These people, known to the Romans as barbarians, were not a united group, but belonged to many different tribes. As the Roman Empire declined, the barbarians migrated in huge numbers across its eastern and northern borders. After the empire fell, the invaders swept across Europe, creating new kingdoms for themselves in former Roman territories.

▶ **ANGLO-SAXON HELMET**
In the 5th century, tribes of Angles, Saxons, and Jutes came to Britain from Denmark and north Germany. These people, later known as the Anglo-Saxons, formed several small kingdoms, often at war with each other. Some Anglo-Saxon kings were buried in ships with their treasured possessions. This helmet was discovered in a ship grave of a 7th-century Anglo-Saxon king at Sutton Hoo in England.

FALL OF ROME
This carving shows a barbarian warrior attacking a Roman soldier. The western Roman Empire (see page 92) came to an end in 476 when a Germanic warrior called Odoacer overthrew the last emperor, Romulus Augustulus, and made himself king of Italy.

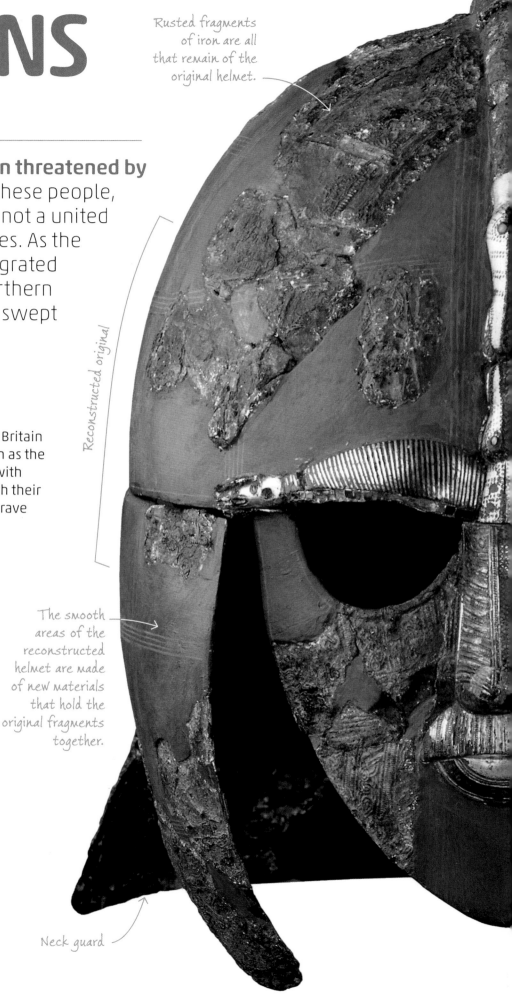

Rusted fragments of iron are all that remain of the original helmet.

Reconstructed original

The smooth areas of the reconstructed helmet are made of new materials that hold the original fragments together.

Neck guard

Dragon, with wings forming the helmet's eyebrows, and its tail representing the mustache

Two Germanic warriors with horned headgear

Modern replica

Flap protects cheek

GERMANIC KINGDOMS IN THE LATE 5TH CENTURY

KEY
- Ostrogoths
- Visigoths
- Franks
- Anglo-Saxons
- Other Germanic kingdoms
- Independent Germanic tribes

THE GREAT MIGRATIONS

During the great migrations, huge numbers of people poured across the frontiers of the Roman Empire in search of new lands to settle. By the late 5th century, the barbarian tribes had spread far and wide, forming kingdoms across Europe and northern Africa.

OSTROGOTHS AND VISIGOTHS

One of the most feared Germanic tribes, the Goths, was split into two groups—the Visigoths, who founded kingdoms in Spain and southern France, and the Ostrogoths, who invaded Italy. Many Goths were skilled metalworkers who made intricate objects, such as brooches, inlaid with precious stones.

Visigoth eagle brooch

THE FRANKS

By 511, the Franks, led by King Clovis I, had conquered most of the former Roman province of Gaul (modern France). A later Frankish king, Charlemagne, extended the empire to include much of western Europe, and brought Christianity to the lands he had conquered. In 800, he was crowned Holy Roman Emperor by the Pope.

Bronze statue of Charlemagne

BYZANTINE
EMPIRE

For hundreds of years, the Roman Empire ruled much of Europe and North Africa. But by 395 CE, it had split into two. The western half fell apart (see page 90), but the eastern half survived to become the Byzantine Empire, which lasted for 1,000 years despite coming under frequent attack. Its name comes from Byzantium, an earlier city on the same site as Constantinople (modern-day Istanbul), the empire's capital

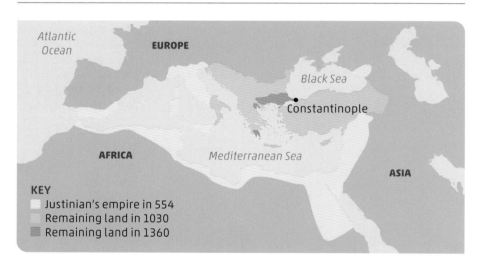

DWINDLING EMPIRE
The Byzantine Empire was at its greatest extent under Emperor Justinian in the 6th century. Over time, it lost ground to the Arabs who conquered West Asia and North Africa, and to the Turks who seized Anatolia (in modern-day Turkey). By the 1300s, the Byzantine Empire had been reduced to a small area of land around Constantinople.

DEFENDING THE EMPIRE
The Byzantine Empire was constantly fighting off invaders. In 717, an Arab fleet attacked Constantinople, but the Byzantine defenders used "Greek fire" to save the city. This mysterious substance ignited on contact with water, setting fire to the enemy ships.

▶ **JUSTINIAN THE GREAT**
Emperor Justinian I, who ruled 527–565, set out to restore the Roman Empire to its past glory by capturing parts of the western Roman empire lost to Germanic invaders. This glorious mosaic in a church in Ravenna, Italy, depicts him as a Roman emperor.

EMPRESS THEODORA
Justinian's wife Theodora ruled alongside her husband. Initially an actress, she was a powerful, intelligent woman. As one of Justinian's chief advisers, she influenced laws that improved the rights of women at the time.

Mosaics were made of tiny bits of colored stone.

Halo, a Christian
symbol of holiness.

Purple robe
of a Roman emperor

CAPITAL OF THE EAST

Defended by strong city walls, the capital
Constantinople was filled with beautiful
palaces and churches. Hagia Sophia (above)
was built as a church by Justinian in 537.

ORTHODOX CHRISTIANITY

Images of holy figures, such as Jesus and
his mother Mary, were revered in the
Orthodox Church—the branch of Christianity
of the Byzantine Empire. This gold-silver
medallion of Mary is from around 1100.

BEGINNING OF THE END

In 1204, a Crusader army attacked and
looted Constantinople. The empire
survived but was weakened. In 1453
the city was conquered by the Ottomans
(see pages 160–161) and the empire
came to an end.

ISLAM SPREADS

The religion of Islam began in Arabia in the 7th century when the Prophet Muhammad began preaching its message. The new religion spread rapidly as Arab armies swept out of Arabia to conquer a vast empire. As their culture mixed with those of conquered lands, vibrant civilizations emerged, leading to a golden age of art and science (see pages 106–107).

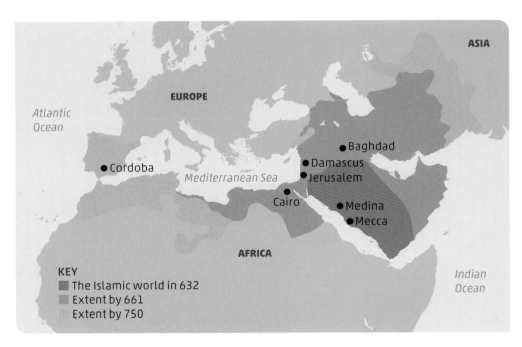

KEY
- The Islamic world in 632
- Extent by 661
- Extent by 750

A NEW RELIGION GAINS GROUND
Around 610, Muhammad began spreading his message from his hometown of Mecca, and then from Medina. By the time of his death in 632, most of Arabia had adopted the new religion. Islam expanded rapidly under the first four caliphs (rulers). Their successors, the Umayyad caliphs, ruled an area stretching from Central Asia to Spain.

▶ MOSQUE BUILDING
As Muslim rulers conquered new territory, they brought with them their religion and culture. Mosques, places of prayer for Muslims, were soon built in varying styles across the Islamic world. The first one was the courtyard of Muhammad's house in Medina. The Great Mosque at Cordoba, Spain (known to its Arab rulers as al-Andalus), was the largest mosque in the early Islamic world, famous for its red-and-white horseshoe arches.

FINDING MECCA

One of the most important duties for Muslims was, and still is, to pray five times a day, at set times. Prayers could be recited anywhere, but it was important to know the direction of Mecca, and its sacred Kaaba, in order to face toward it when praying. As the Islamic world expanded, methods were developed to help followers locate the direction of Mecca.

The Kaaba

THE KAABA
Muhammad taught his followers to direct their prayers toward the Kaaba, Islam's most sacred shrine, which stands inside the Great Mosque in Mecca, in Saudi Arabia.

Mihrab

THE MIHRAB
From early times mosques were built with a niche called the mihrab in the wall to indicate the qibla (sacred direction) of the Kaaba.

Qibla indicator, an astronomical instrument that includes a compass

HANDY TOOL
Using a qibla indicator like this one, Muslims could work out the location of Mecca from wherever they were in the world.

POLYNESIANS
SAIL THE PACIFIC

More than 3,000 years ago, the ancestors of people now known as Polynesians began migrating from islands northeast of New Guinea. No one knows exactly why they did so, but they sailed across open expanses of ocean, navigating by the stars and their knowledge of wave patterns and bird movements. They took plants and animals with them and, over time, settled on many of the scattered islands of the Pacific Ocean. Their descendants live today right across this vast region.

▶ TRADITIONAL BOATBUILDING SKILLS
This 26-ft (8-m) replica of a drua, a fast-sailing double-hulled canoe from Fiji, is part of a seafaring history going back thousands of years. Polynesian voyagers braved the Pacific on similar, but much larger, vessels which were sturdy but not as easy to maneuver. They passed on their boatbuilding skills by word of mouth from generation to generation, and on different islands, different models were developed.

Two sails catch lots of wind for a speedy journey.

A platform holds the two hulls together, and provides a seating area.

OCEAN VOYAGER
The first settlers to arrive in Hawaii would have sailed across 2,000 miles (3,200 km) of open ocean in twin-sailed canoes like the one above, an incredible feat of navigation.

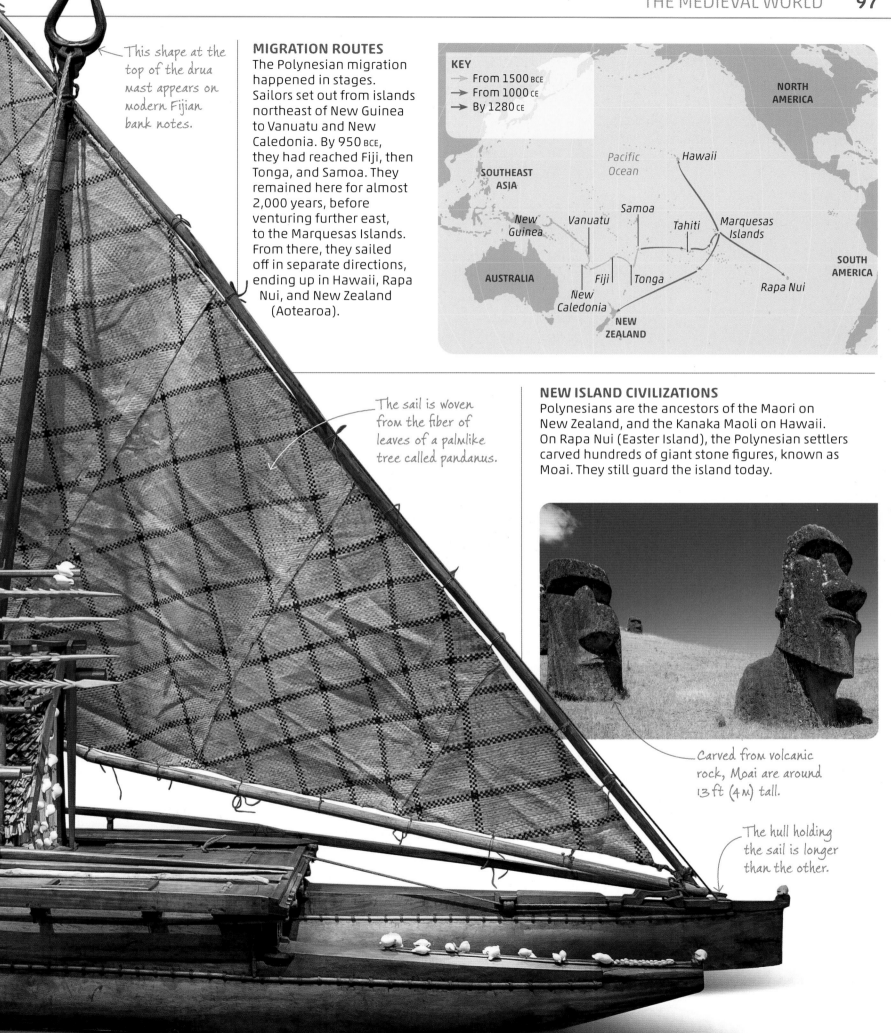

This shape at the top of the drua mast appears on modern Fijian bank notes.

MIGRATION ROUTES

The Polynesian migration happened in stages. Sailors set out from islands northeast of New Guinea to Vanuatu and New Caledonia. By 950 BCE, they had reached Fiji, then Tonga, and Samoa. They remained here for almost 2,000 years, before venturing further east, to the Marquesas Islands. From there, they sailed off in separate directions, ending up in Hawaii, Rapa Nui, and New Zealand (Aotearoa).

KEY
From 1500 BCE
From 1000 CE
By 1280 CE

NORTH AMERICA

Pacific Ocean

Hawaii

SOUTHEAST ASIA

New Guinea

Vanuatu

Samoa

Tahiti

Marquesas Islands

AUSTRALIA

Fiji   Tonga

New Caledonia

Rapa Nui

SOUTH AMERICA

NEW ZEALAND

The sail is woven from the fiber of leaves of a palmlike tree called pandanus.

NEW ISLAND CIVILIZATIONS

Polynesians are the ancestors of the Maori on New Zealand, and the Kanaka Maoli on Hawaii. On Rapa Nui (Easter Island), the Polynesian settlers carved hundreds of giant stone figures, known as Moai. They still guard the island today.

Carved from volcanic rock, Moai are around 13 ft (4 m) tall.

The hull holding the sail is longer than the other.

▼ MAKING CHOCOLATE

The Maya valued cacao (cocoa) beans so much that they used them as money and placed them in the tombs of their rulers. Chocolate was also made into a drink. To prepare it, the beans were fermented and roasted, then ground to a paste, to which water and cornmeal were added. This thick liquid was spiced and frothed, then served in special beakers.

A rolling pin made of stone crushes the beans.

The cacao beans are mashed against a stone grinding tablet called a metate.

Fermented and roasted beans

THE WORLD OF
THE MAYA

Around 2,000 years ago, a great civilization emerged in the Yucatán Peninsula in Central America. People known as the Maya built cities with huge stone pyramids and palaces, each with its own ruler. Maya culture was sophisticated, with advanced mathematics and astronomy. The Maya made chocolate from the beans of cacao trees that grew around their cities. Today, millions of Maya people still live in Central America.

ASTRONOMY AND CALENDARS

The Maya were excellent astronomers who accurately observed and recorded the movements of the stars, moon, and planets. They were able to track the passage of time and created complex calendars. This tower in the Maya city of Chichen Itza was an observatory for viewing the heavens.

CUP OF COCOA

Maya nobles drank chocolate from tall, elegant beakers decorated with designs that sometimes indicated the status of the owner. Chocolate was a highly prized drink, consumed at religious rituals and when rulers gathered.

The jaguar god is shown enjoying a cup of chocolate.

WRITING

The Maya writing system used glyphs—symbols that represented sounds (like "wa" and "ka") or objects. There were hundreds of glyphs that could be put together to make sentences. The Maya carved the glyphs in stone, painted them on drinking cups and other objects, or wrote them down in books made of bark or leather.

ka   ka

wa

GLYPH FOR "KAKAWA" (COCOA)   **"BAHLAM" (JAGUAR)**

FROTHY CHOCOLATE

The Maya liked their chocolate drink frothy. They poured the mixture over and over again between two containers to get air into the liquid and make it foamy. Honey was added to sweeten the drink.

MAYA GODS

The Maya worshipped many gods, and performed ceremonies such as ritual ball games to honor them. There were creator gods and gods responsible for specific things. One of the most important was the maize god, since maize was the staple food of the Maya.

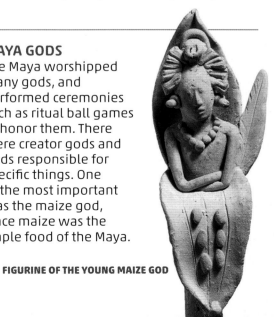

FIGURINE OF THE YOUNG MAIZE GOD

THE GOLDEN AGE OF IMPERIAL CHINA

After long periods of conflict and civil war, two powerful imperial dynasties ruled China: the Tang (618–907) and the Song (960–1279). Peace, stability, and emperors interested in the arts led to a golden age of culture and invention. Foreign trade grew, and China's influence reached across East Asia.

Hair tied up high on the head in a popular Tang-era hairstyle

All senior officials wore a black, winged cap.

EMPEROR XUANZONG
The longest ruling Tang emperor was Xuanzong (712–756). During the first part of his long, 44-year reign, China became powerful and prosperous. Xuanzong loved literature and music, opened music schools, and also introduced many reforms.

Long sleeves emphasize the flowing movements of the dancer who would sway in time to the music.

▶ MUSIC AND DANCE
These elegant clay figures of a dancer and three musicians were made during the Tang dynasty. They show the refinement of the imperial court, both through the craftsmanship that went into making them, and the art forms they portray. Encouraged by emperors, music and dance flourished, while delicate figurines like these were made to put in tombs to accompany the dead in the afterlife.

CHINESE HARP

The traditional Chinese harp, known as the *konghou*, was popular in the Tang era. The player plucked the strings with the thumbs and index fingers of both hands.

Strings made of animal tendons

A wind instrument known as a sheng

Pipa, a four-stringed lute

Originally bright, the colors have faded since the figurines were made.

Musicians are seated on their knees to play.

SONG DYNASTY TECHNOLOGY

During the Song era, China was far ahead of Europe in terms of innovation. Advances included new canal building technologies and gunpowder (see pages 102–103). In the 12th century, the magnetic compass was perfected to be used at sea, and looked very similar to this 19th-century model.

PRINTING

At this time, woodblock printing was used to make art, books, and the world's first paper money. Words and pictures were carved onto a wooden block, which was then covered in ink and pressed onto paper. Around 1050, China invented the first movable type.

The fuse is lit before launching the bird into the air.

Fuse inserted into gunpowder

EXPLOSIVE STUFF
A bamboo or paper tube was packed full of the explosive gunpowder mix. A fuse at the top was lit, burning slowly down its length to set fire to the gunpowder.

Casing made of bamboo or paper

Gunpowder packed into tube

Set of explosive tubes tied to the "body"

FIRE CRACKERS
When young bamboo burns, it makes a popping sound. People would throw bamboo onto fires to fend off evil spirits. Later they filled hollow bamboo stems with gunpowder to make even louder bangs. This is the origin of firecrackers, still used in Chinese New Year celebrations today.

◀ FIRE CROW
The Chinese used gunpowder to make rockets and "fire-arrows" that they launched from bows at the enemy. Rockets came in many shapes. This replica of a "fire crow" is based on a design in a 14th-century Chinese manual. When the fuse is lit, the bird is thrown in the air and glides toward the enemy. As the gunpowder tubes beneath its wings explode, it becomes a flaming projectile.

GUNPOWDER
CHANGES WARFARE

Gunpowder was invented in China, around 1,200 years ago. It is a mixture of three substances—charcoal, sulfur, and saltpeter—that when ignited burn quickly to create an explosion. Before long, Chinese soldiers were using gunpowder in warfare. As knowledge of gunpowder spread around the world, weapons that made use of it were developed to become ever more deadly and powerful.

FIRST CANNONS
Early Chinese weapons were made of bamboo tubes stuffed with small stones and gunpowder which could be fired at the enemy. Next, the Chinese started making cannons—metal tubes that were strong enough to withstand bigger explosions and could hurl large stones with destructive force.

GUNPOWDER SPREADS TO EUROPE
The Mongols, who invaded China in the 13th century, quickly learned about gunpowder and spread the new technology along the Silk Road. By the 14th century, gunpowder technology had reached Europe. This image shows cannons bombarding the walls of Orleans in 1428, during the Hundred Years War.

Aerodynamic wing shape makes the rocket fly farther.

Bird shape made of a bamboo frame covered in paper

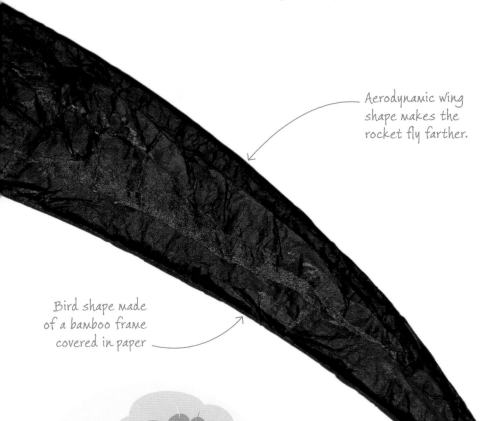

CHEMISTRY
An alchemist in 9th-century China discovered gunpowder by accident, while trying to create a potion that would grant eternal life. He experimented with a substance called saltpeter (potassium nitrate), which went off with a flash.

EARLY HANDGUNS
Early firearms used gunpowder to fire bullets that could pierce armor, but they were heavy and awkward. Soon lighter and more accurate guns replaced bows and pikes on the battlefield. From the 17th century, muskets like this were the standard weapon.

Support needed to aim and fire a musket

VIKING BERSERKER

Raised sword

Berserkers were fierce Viking warriors. They were said to bite their shields to work themselves into a frenzy before going into battle. This chess piece, carved from walrus ivory, was made in Norway some time after the Viking era was over, showing that their fearsome reputation lived on in people's minds.

LONG-DISTANCE TRADE

Swedish Vikings pioneered trade routes down the rivers of Russia as far as the Black Sea and Islamic lands. They exchanged amber, furs, and enslaved people for Arabic silver coins, silk, and spices. Viking traders carried small sets of scales to measure the weight of the coins to determine their worth.

Arabic script on silver coin found in Sweden

VIKINGS AT HOME

When the men went out to sea, women took charge of the household and farmwork. Their work also included weaving cloth for clothes and sails. Viking houses consisted of one big room, shared by people and their animals.

VIKINGS
RAID AND TRADE

Viking raiders, attacking suddenly from the sea, struck fear in 9th-century Europe. Sailing in their longboats from Denmark, Norway, and Sweden, they ransacked settlements along foreign coasts. Some stayed on, founding communities in England, Ireland, Scotland, and France. The Vikings were great traders and explorers, too. They traded with Arab merchants, and sailed west across the Atlantic to settle in Iceland and Greenland. They even reached Newfoundland, Canada, becoming the first Europeans to land in the Americas.

▶ **VIKING LONGSHIP**

This is a replica of a Viking longship—the long, narrow ships built for strength, speed, and ease of handling. They were fitted with a large, square sail made of cloth for long journeys at sea. Boats like this could ride big ocean waves, but also took Vikings far inland along Europe's rivers.

A dragon head was often fitted at the front of the ship—a terrifying sight for those spotting it approaching from the shore.

Overlapping wooden planks gave the boat's hull strength and flexibility.

When not in use, the sail was rolled up to the spar, which was lowered and stored on deck.

ROWING THE SHIP
When close to shore, or when there was no wind, the sail was taken down and oars were put out. The largest ships had crews of up to 80 men. When rowing, they sat on wooden chests used to stow their belongings. They kept their battle axes beside them, ready to grab.

Sails were made of wool cloth, often dyed red.

Holes along the sides of the ship held the long wooden oars used when rowing the boat.

ISLAMIC SCIENTISTS SPREAD KNOWLEDGE

The medieval period was a golden age for Islamic science. Scholars in the Islamic world preserved and built upon ideas of the ancient Greeks and Romans, which had fallen into neglect in Europe. They kept alive knowledge of medicine, astronomy, mathematics, and engineering, and made amazing discoveries of their own.

Back

The alidade (rule) is rotated to make observations.

USING AN ASTROLABE

Astrolabes can be used to find the altitude of a star, useful for calculating the location of places on Earth. The observer holds the astrolabe vertically, then rotates the *alidade* (rule) to line up with the star. The altitude can then be read from the degree scale on the rim.

▶ ASTROLABE

Islamic astronomers used the astrolabe—a complex instrument that was used for many purposes, from telling the time of day to finding the direction of Mecca (see page 95). This one was made in al-Andalus (Muslim Spain), in the 14th century.

The user looks through sights at both ends of the alidade.

Scientist working with an astrolabe

SCIENTISTS AT WORK

Astronomers are shown here hard at work in the observatory of Taqi al-Din, a great Islamic scientist from Turkey. He wrote more than 90 books on a range of subjects from medicine to astronomy and engineering, including how a steam turbine could be used to drive a mechanical device.

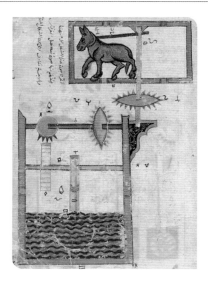

AMAZING INVENTIONS

A brilliant 12th-century engineer, Ismail al-Jazari created all kinds of ingenious machines, and published a book with detailed descriptions of each one. His machines, powered by water, wheels, and gears, ranged from floating musicians playing musical instruments to practical inventions such as this donkey-driven water pump.

Inner circle has the names of the zodiac in Arabic and Latin.

This astrolabe is made of bronze and silver.

The inner plate is removable. It can be changed for a plate whose marks relate to what the night sky looks like at the observer's location.

The top plate is called the rete. It is a map of stars and constellations and can be rotated. When using this side of the astrolabe, the observer holds it horizontally in their palm.

THE SCIENCE OF GLASSMAKING
Islamic glassmakers made great advances, too. They discovered new techniques for coloring glass with metals such as silver to give a shiny effect, and for cutting intricate designs onto the surface. Islamic glassware was exported far and wide, finding its way to Europe where it inspired craftsmen in Venice to create their famous glass.

This mosque lamp from Syria has Arabic inscriptions in colored glass paint.

Hand drum used to make the first sounds of creation

The cobra represents reincarnation, while the hand next to it is raised in a gesture to dispel fear.

◀ **BRONZE ART**
The Chola were a Hindu dynasty. They worshipped Shiva, one of most powerful Hindu gods. This sculpture portrays Shiva as Nataraja, the lord of dance. It shows him dancing within a ring of flames and symbolizes his powers of destruction and renewal. Chola artists were famous for these elegant bronze figurines. Shiva was the most popular, but they depicted other Hindu deities, too.

The demon of ignorance is trampled under Shiva's foot.

Ring of fire symbolizes the cycle of life

Flame of destruction

CHOLA KINGS
RULE AN INDIAN EMPIRE

Between the 9th and 13th centuries, the Chola kings built one of the greatest empires in Indian history. The Chola heartland lay in what is now the state of Tamil Nadu in southern India, but the empire controlled most of South India, Sri Lanka, and the Maldives, and Chola influence extended throughout Southeast Asia. The Chola kings were great patrons of art, architecture, literature, music, and dance.

TEMPLE BUILDERS
Built of massive granite blocks, the Brihadisvara temple in Thanjavur, Tamil Nadu, is one of the largest in South India. It is one of several Hindu temples built by the Chola kings. These places of worship were also centers of social and cultural life.

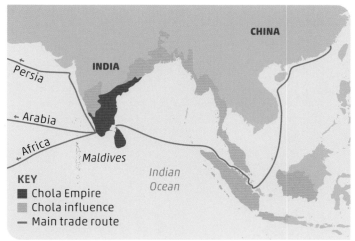

KEY
- Chola Empire
- Chola influence
- Main trade route

TRADING POWER
The Cholas used their strong navy to gain control over trade. They subdued neighboring coastal states and collected tributes. Chola traders and diplomats spread the influence of Chola art and culture, as well as goods. Trade routes led to and from China and the Islamic world.

PRECIOUS CARGO
Rubies and pearls were exported on ships from the Chola Empire. Other cargoes included spices and raw cotton.

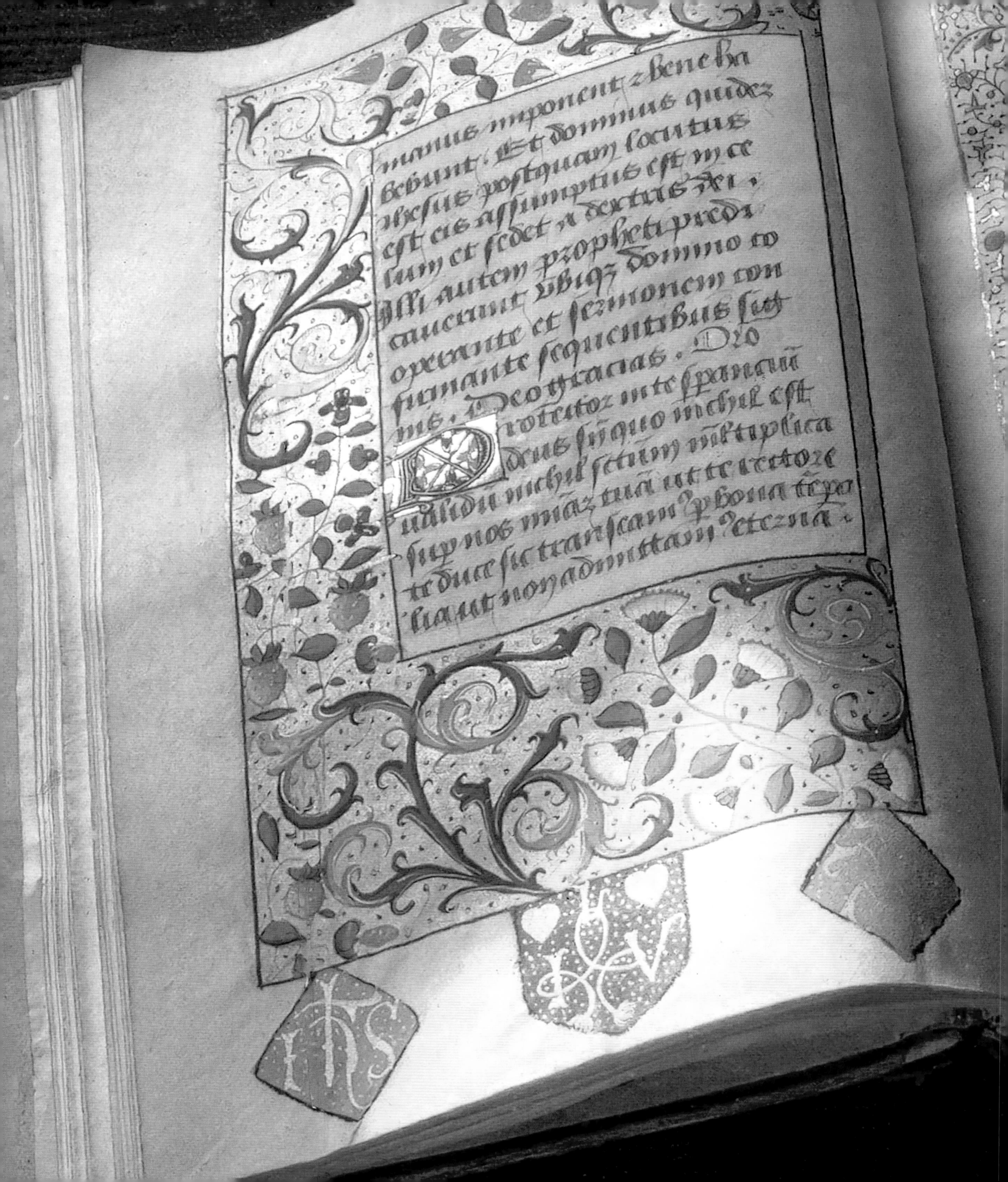

manus imponent· et bene ha
bebunt· Et dominus quidez
ihesus postquam locutus
est eis assumptus est in ce
lum et sedet a dextris dei·
Illi autem propheti predi
cauerunt vbiqz domino co
operante et sermonem con
firmante sequentibus sig
nis· Deo gracias· Deo
...rotector in te sperancium
...deus sine quo nichil est
...validum nichil sanctum multiplica
sup nos miam tuam ut te rectore
te duce sic transeam· p bona tempo
ralia ut no admittam? eterna·

WORK OF ART

In medieval Europe, before printing was invented, books were made by hand. In this prayer book from the 15th century, text has been written down in carefully shaped letters, with beautiful hand-painted illustrations and shiny gold-leaf details. Known as illuminated manuscripts, these books have pages made of specially prepared animal skin, called parchment. If more than one book was needed, the original had to be carefully copied. This laborious work was usually done by monks in monasteries, which were early centers of learning.

▶ LADY AT COURT

Noblewomen at the Heian court were stylish, educated, and had the right to own property. They took great care over their clothes, wearing between 10 and 40 silk robes layered on top of each other. Some of a lady's skill lay in matching colors and patterns according to seasons and moods. Men dressed fashionably, too. Beautifully dressed, all took part in elaborate ceremonies, played games, and followed the court intrigues and rivalries.

Top layer of patterned silk brocade

STATUS SYMBOL

Painted folding fans originated in Japan during the Heian era. At this time, only the upper classes were allowed to use them. The number of strips on the fan signified the owner's rank.

Women wore white makeup with tinted lips, and blackened their teeth—maybe to avoid them looking yellow against the white skin.

Many layers of silk are neatly arranged at the neck.

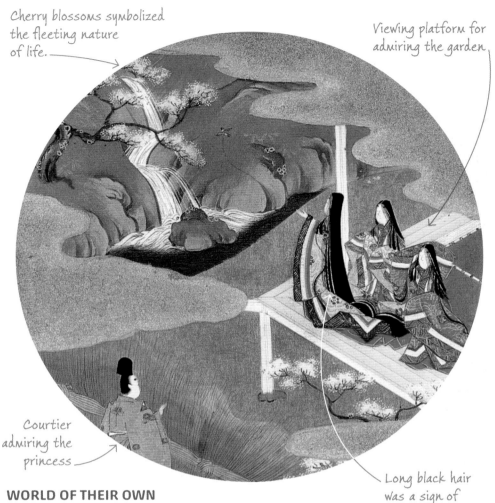

Cherry blossoms symbolized the fleeting nature of life.

Viewing platform for admiring the garden

Courtier admiring the princess

Long black hair was a sign of female beauty.

WORLD OF THEIR OWN

Life at the Heian court was very refined and far removed from the daily life of ordinary people outside the palace. Courtiers spent time contemplating the changing seasons and how this made them feel, often writing poetry about it. This painting shows a princess admiring cherry blossoms, accompanied by two ladies-in-waiting.

JAPAN
IN THE HEIAN ERA

A high point of Japanese culture began when the imperial court moved to Heian-kyo (Kyoto) in 794. Life at the Heian court was dominated by a small but powerful class of nobles who placed great value on elaborate rituals of dress and etiquette. They encouraged fine writing, painting, and a love of nature, while letting regional governors rule the provinces.

POETRY AND NOVELS

Many of the women at court wrote poetry and novels. One of the more famous was a lady-in-waiting called Murasaki Shikibu. Her novel about a dashing prince, *The Tale of Genji*, is considered one of Japan's classic masterpieces.

A NEW CAPITAL

Heian-kyo (modern Kyoto) had wide, straight streets lined with wooden buildings, busy markets, and fine gardens. The Byodo-in temple, pictured above, is one of very few Heian-period buildings to have survived.

END OF AN ERA

After 400 years, the Heian court began to lose control. Local landowners formed private armies of samurai—skilled warriors who vowed to defend their lord. War broke out as rival clans competed for power. In 1185, the Minamoto clan founded the first shogunate, ending Heian rule.

**THE WARLORD
MINAMOTO NO YORITOMO**

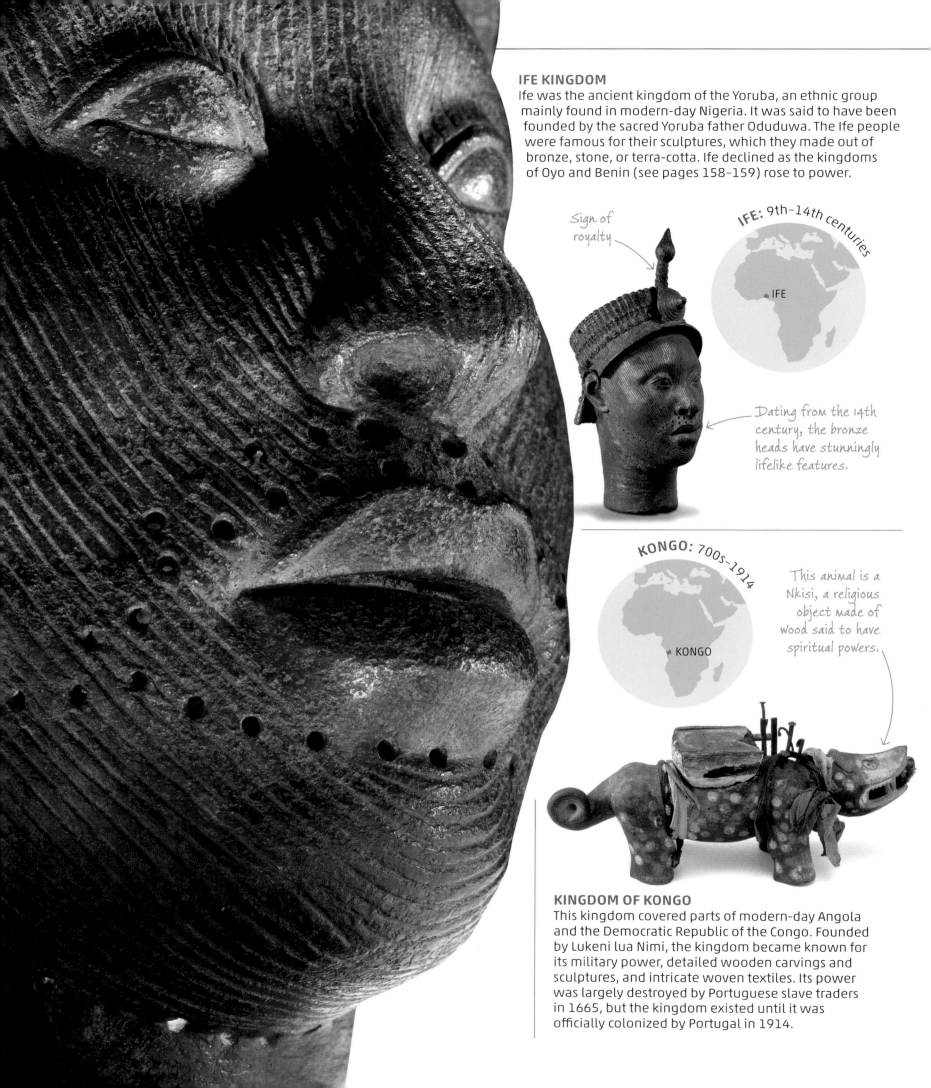

IFE KINGDOM

Ife was the ancient kingdom of the Yoruba, an ethnic group mainly found in modern-day Nigeria. It was said to have been founded by the sacred Yoruba father Oduduwa. The Ife people were famous for their sculptures, which they made out of bronze, stone, or terra-cotta. Ife declined as the kingdoms of Oyo and Benin (see pages 158–159) rose to power.

Sign of royalty

IFE: 9th–14th centuries

IFE

Dating from the 14th century, the bronze heads have stunningly lifelike features.

KONGO: 700s–1914

This animal is a Nkisi, a religious object made of wood said to have spiritual powers.

KONGO

KINGDOM OF KONGO

This kingdom covered parts of modern-day Angola and the Democratic Republic of the Congo. Founded by Lukeni lua Nimi, the kingdom became known for its military power, detailed wooden carvings and sculptures, and intricate woven textiles. Its power was largely destroyed by Portuguese slave traders in 1665, but the kingdom existed until it was officially colonized by Portugal in 1914.

KINGDOMS OF AFRICA

In medieval times, many different kingdoms emerged across the African continent. Among the earliest was the gold-rich Ancient Ghana, which existed from the 7th to 13th centuries, when Mali (see page 126) took over as the most powerful state in West Africa. Many others flourished, trading with countries in Asia, Arabia, and later, Europe. All were rich in art and culture, with religions ranging from local, multi-god faiths to Islam and Christianity.

Bird statues made from soapstone were placed inside the enclosure.

Like other Lalibela churches, St. George's was carved straight from the rock, in the shape of a cross.

ETHIOPIAN EMPIRE: 1200s–1974

ETHIOPIA

The **GREAT ENCLOSURE** in Great Zimbabwe

The Great Enclosure, probably a royal palace, was encircled by stone walls up to 32 ft (10 m) high.

THE ETHIOPIAN EMPIRE
The Ethiopian Empire had its roots in ancient Aksum (see page 51) and was an Orthodox Christian state. In Lalibela, one of its holiest places, several rock-hewn churches were created in the 13th century. The court moved around, following nomadic tradition, but in 1635 a great imperial capital was founded at Gondar. The empire lasted until 1974, when Ethiopia became a socialist republic.

KINGDOM OF ZIMBABWE: 1100s–1450

ZIMBABWE

KINGDOM OF ZIMBABWE
The rulers of the Kingdom of Zimbabwe got rich from controlling the gold trade between inland regions and the Swahili trading cities on the Indian Ocean coast. The ancient city of Great Zimbabwe is in ruins today but still reveals traces of a wealthy, well-organized state.

THE CHRISTIAN CHURCH GROWS IN POWER

By the 10th century, Christianity had spread through most of Europe. Its organization was known as the Church. At its head was the Pope, and under him were bishops, priests, and monks. The Church wielded huge power and influence over people's daily life. In medieval times, most people couldn't read, and relied on priests to and relied on priests to teach them the Bible.

TRAVELING PILGRIMS
Pilgrims would travel long distances to visit famous relics, hoping for a miraculous cure or to win God's forgiveness for their sins. Others would journey to Rome to pray in the city's many churches. Pilgrims were men and women from all ranks of society, kings as well as peasants. To stay safe on the roads, they often traveled in organized groups.

▶ **SACRED RELICS**
In the Christian faith, people who had led holy lives or died as martyrs defending the faith are known as saints. Relics (remains) of a saint, like a bone or a piece of clothing, were held to have miraculous powers. They were kept inside containers called reliquaries, which people would touch, or pray next to. This silver boot, made in Basel, Switzerland, in 1450, was said to contain the bones of a small boy killed at the time of Jesus.

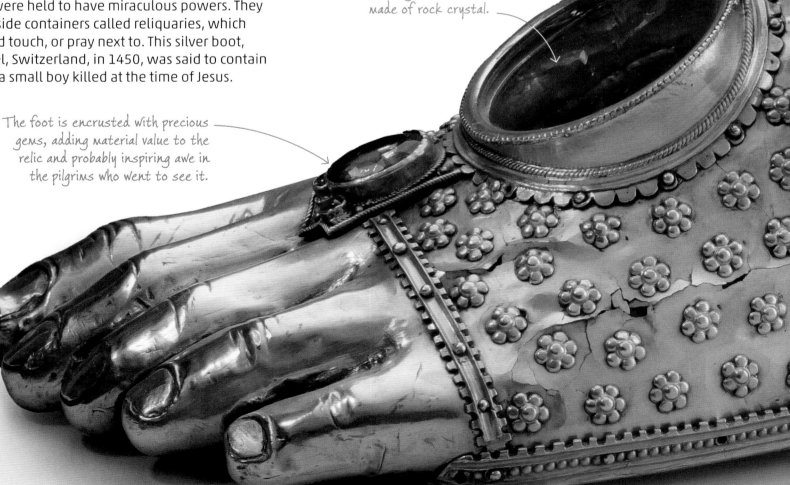

Pilgrims could view the bones through this window made of rock crystal.

The foot is encrusted with precious gems, adding material value to the relic and probably inspiring awe in the pilgrims who went to see it.

Tiny gold crosses symbolize Christian faith.

Measuring 9½ in (24 cm) from heel to toe, the reliquary is made of a base of wood covered in silver with gilded details.

POWERFUL POPES

The Pope, who lived in Rome, had religious authority over all people, including kings and emperors. Rulers who disobeyed him could be threatened with excommunication (being excluded from the Church), a fate nobody wanted to risk. The Pope wore a golden crown, called a tiara, such as the one seen here.

BUILDING CATHEDRALS

In the growing cities, great churches called cathedrals rose up, visible from far and wide. Many became centers of learning, housing the first universities. This cathedral, towering over the rooftops, is Notre Dame in Paris, France.

HEAVEN OR HELL AFTER DEATH?

People believed that unless they followed the Church's teachings, they would end up in hell rather than in heaven. In churches, wall paintings like this one gave a frightening vision of what the agonies of hell would be like.

MEDIEVAL KNIGHTS
SERVE THEIR LORDS

Elite soldiers in gleaming armor, knights fought on horseback in the army of a king or lord. These professional fighters had to provide their own armor and warhorses, and be prepared to fight when called. They formed a crucial part of the strict social order that defined medieval Europe, known as the feudal system.

The helmet is lined to cushion blows, while the eye slit is minimal.

A separate plate protects the chin and neck.

KNIGHT TO BE
A teenage squire was a knight in training. He took care of his knight's horse and armor in return for learning how to fight. As armor and horses were expensive, both knights and squires usually came from noble families.

The heavy plates were fitted and tied together one by one.

The mace head is fluted to create a sharp, piercing edge.

▶ **KNIGHT IN SHINING ARMOR**
A knight's armor completely covered his body from head to toe. It was made of many steel plates held together with leather straps. Although it weighed about 55 lb (25 kg), a knight could move around in it quite easily. Underneath it, he would wear a padded shirt, called a doublet, for comfort and protection.

Dagger for close combat

AROUND THE CASTLE

Kings and lords lived in castles that dominated the surrounding countryside. Peasants farmed the land around the castle, giving part of the annual harvest to the lord as rent. He gave them protection inside his castle walls in times of war and sorted out disputes between neighbors.

INSIDE THE CASTLE

Castles were home to the lord, his family, knights, and servants. The more important the lord, the bigger his castle. As well as private rooms, a chapel, kitchen, and gardens, every castle had a great hall for entertaining guests. Here a king presides over a splendid banquet in his great hall.

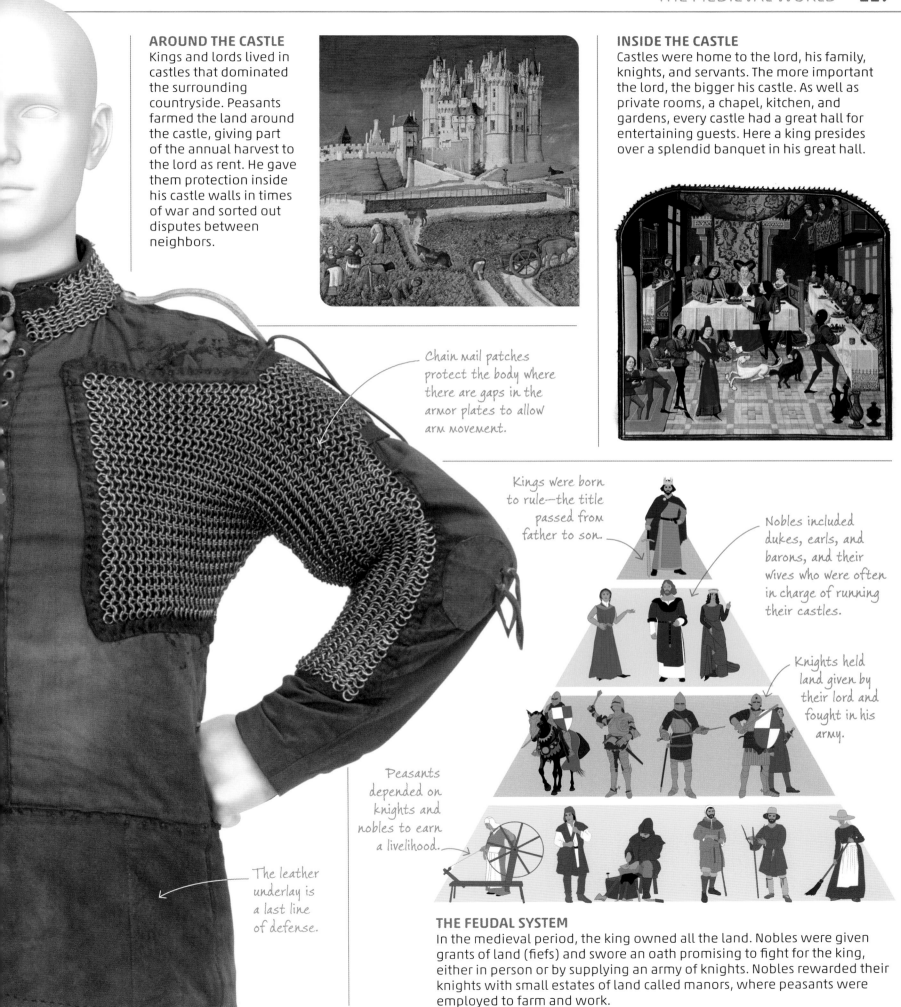

Chain mail patches protect the body where there are gaps in the armor plates to allow arm movement.

Kings were born to rule—the title passed from father to son.

Nobles included dukes, earls, and barons, and their wives who were often in charge of running their castles.

Knights held land given by their lord and fought in his army.

Peasants depended on knights and nobles to earn a livelihood.

The leather underlay is a last line of defense.

THE FEUDAL SYSTEM

In the medieval period, the king owned all the land. Nobles were given grants of land (fiefs) and swore an oath promising to fight for the king, either in person or by supplying an army of knights. Nobles rewarded their knights with small estates of land called manors, where peasants were employed to farm and work.

THE CRUSADES

In the 11th–13th centuries, wars were fought between Muslims and Christians in West Asia. Known in Europe as Crusades, they began in 1096 when an army of knights from various European countries, backed by the Christian Church, set out to conquer Jerusalem—a holy city for both Islam and Christianity that had been under Muslim rule for nearly 500 years.

Upper part of castle contained hall, chapel, and stables.

DEFENSIVE WALLS
Two circular walls studded with towers defended Krak des Chevaliers. The inner wall was much higher than the outer, so the defenders could fire arrows down on any attackers who managed to penetrate the outer defenses.

Dry moat

OCCUPIED LANDS

Between 1098 and 1109, the Crusaders created four states in the lands they occupied. Edessa was recaptured by the Muslims in 1144, and the others came under mounting pressure as Muslim power revived, despite fresh Crusaders arriving. In 1291, the Kingdom of Jerusalem became the last one to fall.

Arrow-slit windows for firing on attackers

▶ CRUSADER CASTLE

After capturing Jerusalem in 1198, some Crusaders stayed on in West Asia. Vastly outnumbered, they built huge castles to defend the territories they had seized. During the conflicts that followed, many castles changed hands at least once. Built on solid rock, Krak des Chevaliers (Qal'at al-Hisn) survived three sieges before falling to a Muslim army in 1271.

CRUSADER STATES IN WEST ASIA

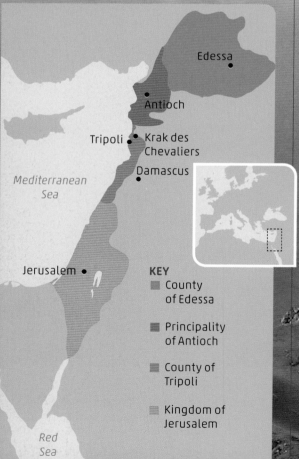

Edessa

Antioch

Tripoli • Krak des Chevaliers

Damascus

Mediterranean Sea

Jerusalem •

KEY

- ■ County of Edessa
- ■ Principality of Antioch
- ■ County of Tripoli
- ■ Kingdom of Jerusalem

Red Sea

SIEGE WEAPONS
Muslims and Crusaders attacked each other's castles with siege weapons like this trebuchet—a huge catapult that hurled heavy stones at castle walls. A team of around 5 to 20 men was needed to fire a trebuchet.

FIGHT BACK
The Muslim fight against the Crusader kingdoms in West Asia was led by Salah al-Din (Saladin). In 1187, he defeated a large Crusader army at the Battle of Hattin before recapturing the city of Jerusalem after a short siege.

CULTURAL EXCHANGE
Muslims and Christians didn't just meet in battle. Crusaders learned a lot from Islamic culture and took new ideas back with them to Europe. They discovered a taste for new foods, including sugar, which was unknown in Europe at the time, and trade between east and west increased.

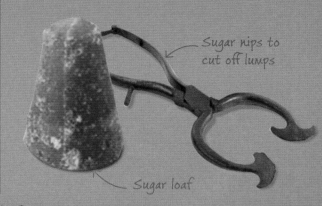

Sugar nips to cut off lumps

Sugar loaf

Round projecting towers were difficult to attack.

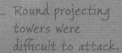

THE
MONGOLS
CONQUER ASIA

In the 13th century, Mongol warriors swept with terrifying force out of their homeland in Central Asia to conquer lands stretching from China in the east to Russia in the west. At their head was Genghis Khan, a war leader of genius who was proclaimed ruler in 1206. He united the warring Mongol tribes and turned them into one of the most fearsome mounted armies ever seen.

▶ MONGOL WARRIOR

Highly skilled horsemen, Mongol warriors were trained from birth to spend long hours in the saddle. Each warrior had one or two small, speedy horses. They wore light armor of hardened leather, which allowed them to move and turn quickly in battle. A favorite tactic was for a group of warriors to pretend to retreat, then turn suddenly and ambush their pursuing enemies.

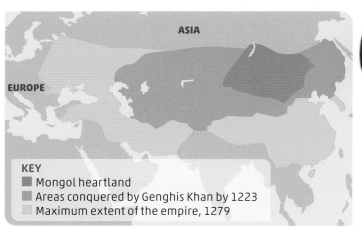

KEY
- Mongol heartland
- Areas conquered by Genghis Khan by 1223
- Maximum extent of the empire, 1279

THE MONGOL EMPIRE

It took the Mongols just 50 years to build the largest land empire in history. It included the whole of China, Central Asia, Iran, and West Asia, and posed a threat to kingdoms and people in eastern Europe. It was hard to rule such a large area, and the empire broke up into smaller states.

LIFE ON THE MOVE

The Mongols were nomadic herders who moved with their horses, camels, sheep, and goats across the grasslands of Mongolia. On arriving at a new pasture, they quickly erected their portable, round felt houses called *gers* (yurts).

Studded leather plates

Sturdy iron helmet

BOW AND ARROW
Mongolian children learned archery skills from an early age, both for hunting and fighting. Riding at speed, mounted warriors would turn in the saddle to fire a storm of deadly arrows at the enemy.

Quiver holds arrows, ready for use

The bow is strong but lightweight.

Undercoat of silk

KUBLAI KHAN
Genghis Khan's grandson Kublai Khan conquered southern China and, in 1276, put an end to the Song dynasty who ruled there. He made himself emperor, founding the Yuan dynasty, and moved the Chinese capital to Dadu (Beijing). During his reign, trade along the Silk Road (see pages 72–73) reached new heights.

Shield made of wicker, covered in leather, and studded with iron

Leather armor protecting the horse

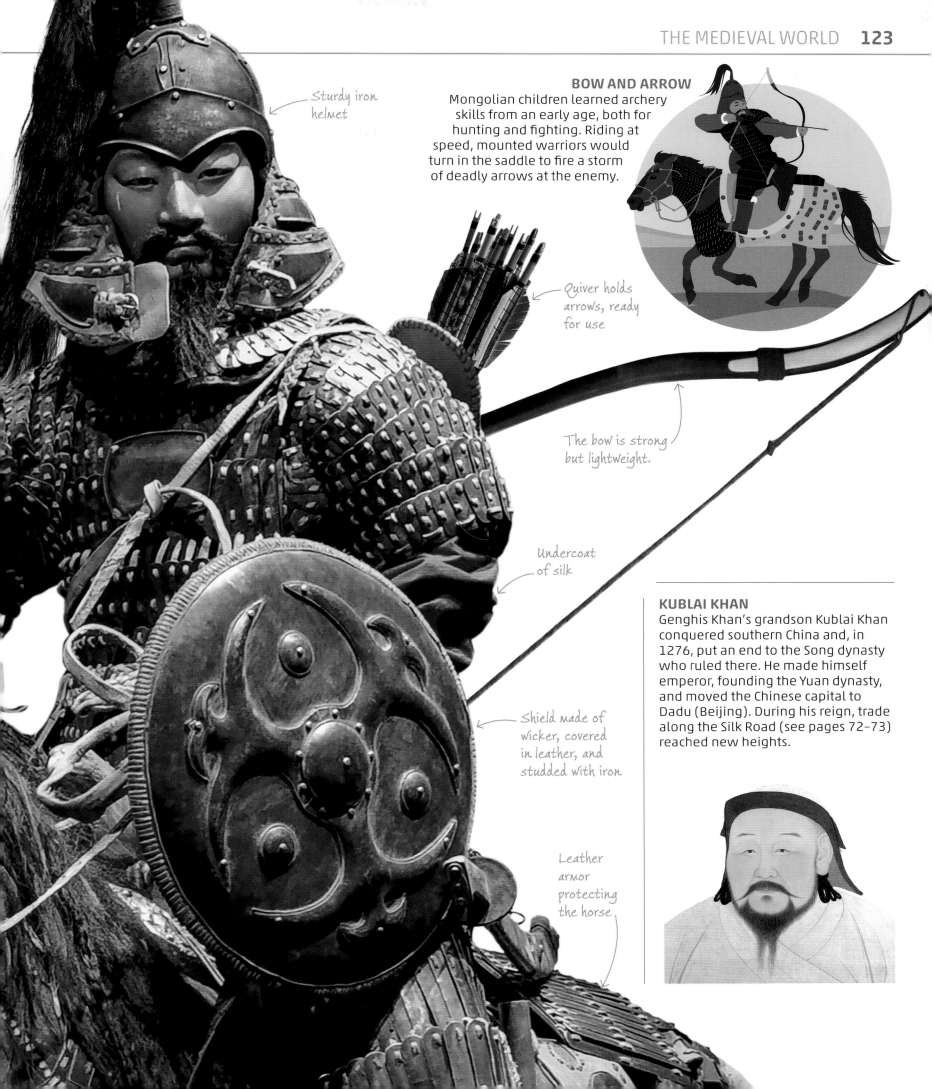

THE PEOPLES OF NORTH AMERICA

Over thousands of years, people spread over every part of North America, from the frozen tundra of the Subarctic to the baking deserts of the Southwest. There were hundreds of different tribes, each with unique traditions and ways of life influenced by the natural environments in which they lived.

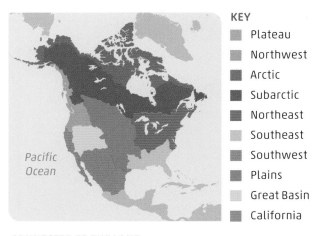

KEY
- Plateau
- Northwest
- Arctic
- Subarctic
- Northeast
- Southeast
- Southwest
- Plains
- Great Basin
- California

Pacific Ocean

CONNECTED TO THE LAND
North America is divided into 10 major bioregions, each with its own climate and physical features such as mountains, plains, rivers, coasts, or deserts and each home to many different peoples. Each tribe or nation was strongly connected to the land they called home. The objects below come from a specific tribal homeland, marked in black on that object's map.

FARMERS AND TRADERS
This ceremonial pot shaped like a man was made by people living in the Mississippi valley between 1000 and 1400 CE. The Mississippians were settled farmers, growing maize, squash, and beans. They built houses and temples on top of earthen mounds and traded as far as the Rocky Mountains and Great Lakes.

SEAFARING FISHERPEOPLE
This carved wooden figure, half-jaguar and half-human, was made by the Calusa people who inhabited the sandy coasts and inlets of the Everglades region of southwest Florida. They were seafarers whose main diet was shellfish and fish, which they caught with nets. Some Calusa may even have sailed to Cuba and traded with the people there.

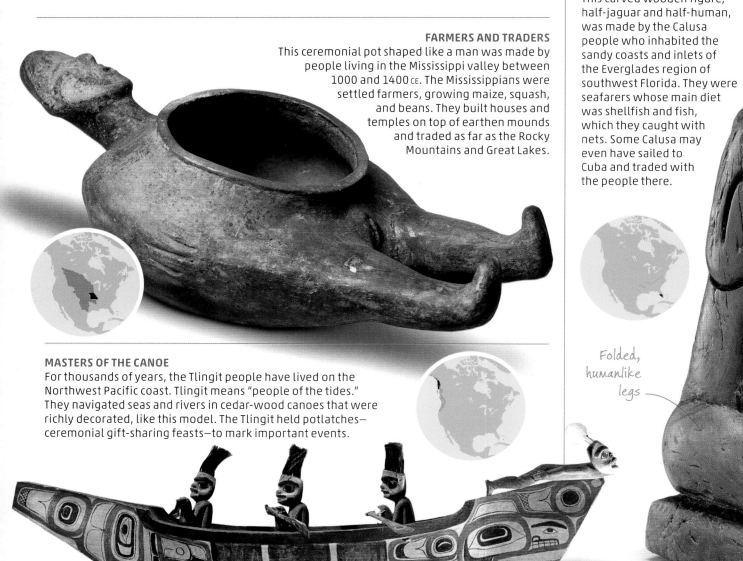

MASTERS OF THE CANOE
For thousands of years, the Tlingit people have lived on the Northwest Pacific coast. Tlingit means "people of the tides." They navigated seas and rivers in cedar-wood canoes that were richly decorated, like this model. The Tlingit held potlatches—ceremonial gift-sharing feasts—to mark important events.

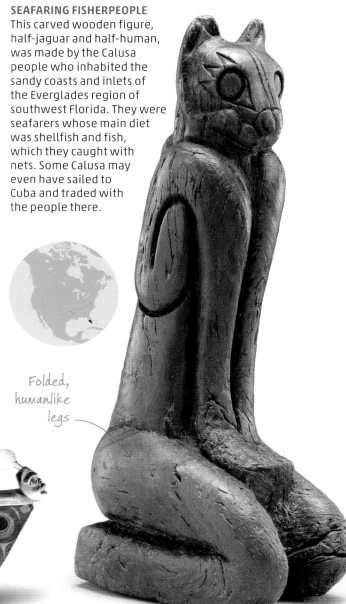

Folded, humanlike legs

EXPERT WEAVERS
The Navajo, or Dine, people migrated into the deserts of the Southwest from the north about 600 years ago. They combined their traditional hunting and gathering way of life with farming, which they may have learned from the Pueblo people, and became skilled at making pottery and weaving textiles.

SKILLED CRAFTSPEOPLE
People living in what is now southern Ohio made fine crafted objects like this carved tobacco pipe in the shape of a beaver around 2,000 years ago. They also made ornaments of copper and traded with people from the Atlantic coast and Rocky Mountains.

Smoke was inhaled through the hole.

Eyes made of turquoise stone

CLIFF DWELLERS
The Ancestral Pueblo people of the Southwest were farmers who lived in villages built into the steep sides of canyons more than 1,000 years ago. Some of their buildings were several stories high, accessible by rope or wooden ladders. Pueblo artisans carved this frog from decayed wood.

SOUTHEASTERN PEOPLES
The Southeast is a diverse region of mountains, marshes, and coastal plains. People living in parts of Florida and Alabama around 1,000 years ago were hunters and fishers, who cultivated crops such as sunflowers and gourds in small gardens. They made elaborate pottery in the shape of animals and humans.

This urn may have contained the ashes of an important person.

Face painted black to represent a mask

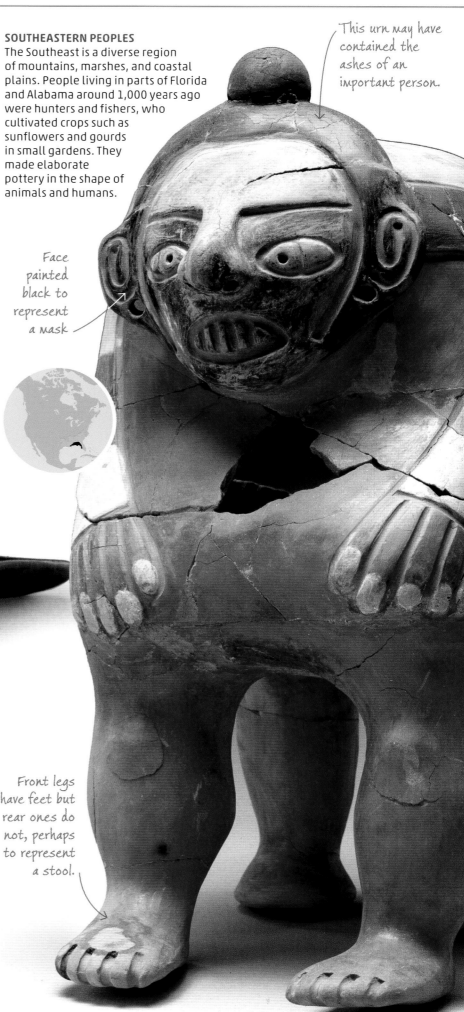

Front legs have feet but rear ones do not, perhaps to represent a stool.

CENTER OF TRADE

Mali was positioned between the salt mines of the desert in the north and the gold mines in the south. Caravans entering Mali were taxed, too, adding to the empire's riches and allowing for strict control over all trade routes.

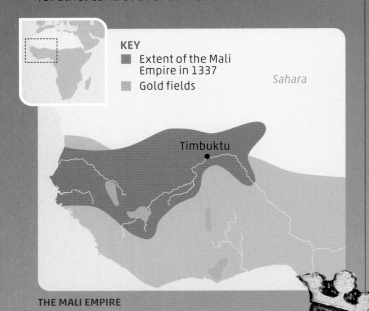

KEY
- ■ Extent of the Mali Empire in 1337
- ■ Gold fields

Sahara

Timbuktu

THE MALI EMPIRE

RICHEST RULER

Mansa Musa came to the throne in 1312. He used his large army to double the empire's size and increased control over the salt and gold trade. He went on a pilgrimage to Mecca in 1324, during which he gave away a lot of gold. Word of his riches spread far and wide.

MANSA MUSA

TIMBUKTU

The trading hub of Timbuktu soon became a world-renowned center of learning. After his pilgrimage to Mecca, Mansa Musa built the great Djinguereber mosque (below). It held treasured manuscripts and attracted many scholars.

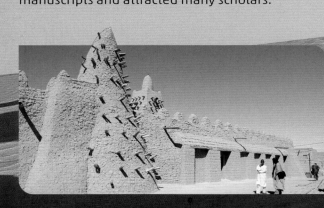

AN EMPIRE BUILT ON SALT AND GOLD

African kingdoms played an important role in global trade in medieval times. One of the mightiest was the Mali Empire in West Africa. From the 1230s, Mali controlled access to the gold and salt trade routes in the region. The kingdom expanded, and its rulers grew rich. The most famous ruler, Mansa Musa, was the world's wealthiest man. Mali began to decline in the 15th century, as its neighbor states rose to power.

▶ SALT TRADE CARAVAN

Camel caravans were the most effective way to transport salt; they are still doing the same job today. Salt slabs were dug up in the mines of Taghaza in the Sahara Desert to the north of Mali. The large slabs were carried by camels into Mali's trading towns. Trade complete, the caravans returned north, loaded with gold and other goods. Several hundred or even several thousand camels could make up a caravan.

Mansa Musa was depicted in the Catalan Atlas. Made in Spain in 1375, this was a map of the known world and showed important people, too.

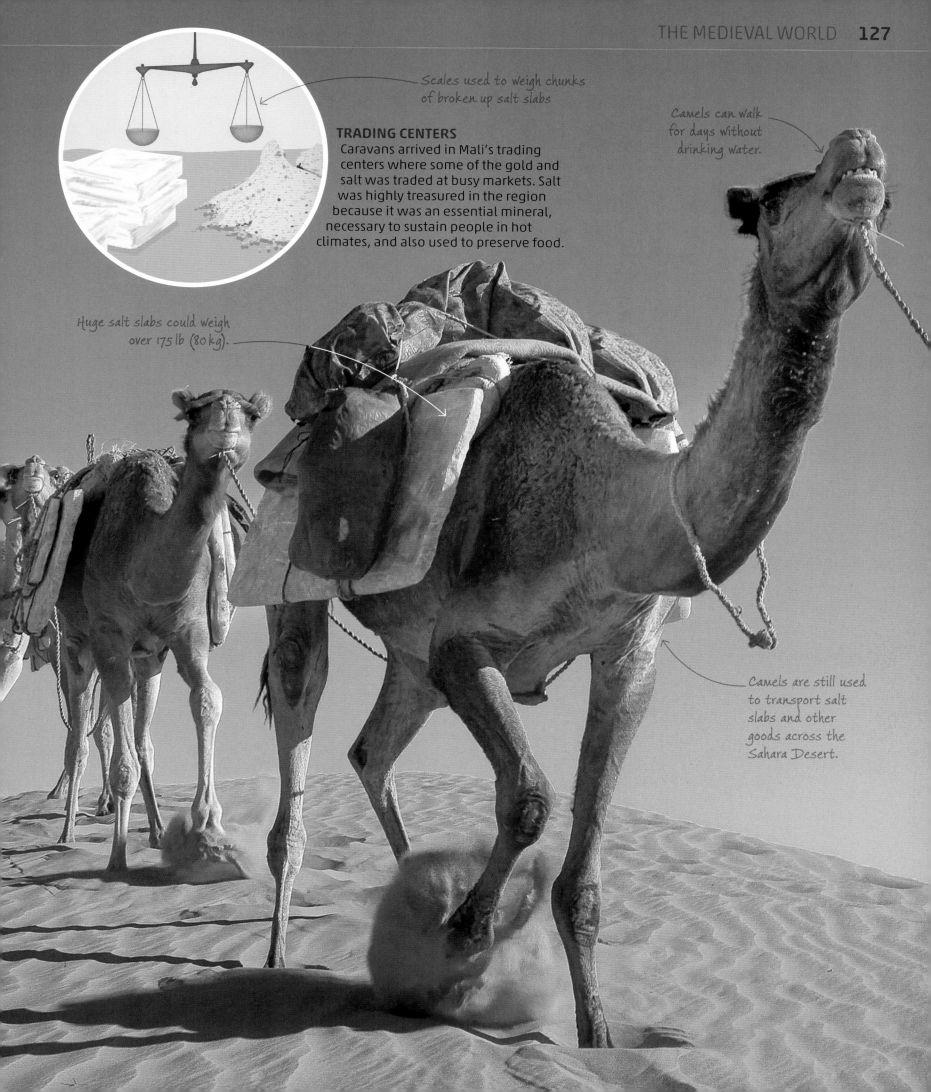

Scales used to weigh chunks
of broken up salt slabs

Camels can walk
for days without
drinking water.

TRADING CENTERS
Caravans arrived in Mali's trading
centers where some of the gold and
salt was traded at busy markets. Salt
was highly treasured in the region
because it was an essential mineral,
necessary to sustain people in hot
climates, and also used to preserve food.

Huge salt slabs could weigh
over 175 lb (80 kg).

Camels are still used
to transport salt
slabs and other
goods across the
Sahara Desert.

LOST KINGDOM

The Khmer Kingdom was one of the most powerful nations in Southeast Asia. Founded in 802, it increased in size and wealth as it gained control over the fertile, rice-growing areas in what is today Thailand, Cambodia, Laos, and Vietnam. In 1120, King Suryavarman II began building temples in his capital, Angkor—including the gigantic Angkor Wat, still the largest religious complex in the world. But wars with rival kingdoms and loss of trade led to decline. In 1440, the city of Angkor was abandoned, and many of its temples were ruined and overgrown.

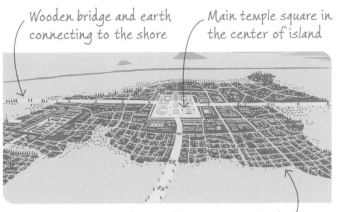

Wooden bridge and earth connecting to the shore

Main temple square in the center of island

Man-made islands for growing food

THE EMPIRE OF THE AZTECS

The Aztec people settled in the Valley of Mexico around 1300. Within a century, they had conquered or allied with all the neighboring city-states to build a highly organized empire that extended into other parts of Central America. The ruler lived in the capital Tenochtitlán. Subject regions had to pay tribute, in the form of food, cloth, and luxury goods. The Aztecs, more properly known as the Mexica, ruled much of Mexico until it fell to Spanish invaders in 1521 (see pages 156–157).

THE AZTEC CAPITAL
The Aztecs built their capital city of Tenochtitlán on an island in a lake. It was said that an eagle revealed this site to them by landing on a cactus. The city was one of the largest in the world. Food for the huge population of 200,000 was grown on small artificial islands of rich soil, known as *chinampas*.

TRAVELING MERCHANTS
Merchants called *pochteca* traveled throughout the empire and beyond to obtain desired and rare items, such as feathers, precious stones, textiles, and cocoa beans. They also acted as spies, sending back vital information to the capital. Their role was highly valued, and they lived in their own area of the city.

▶ MOSAIC SKULL MASK
This mask is thought to represent Tezcatlipoca, one of the Aztecs' most powerful gods. It is made from a human skull, and was probably worn by an Aztec priest in religious ceremonies. The skull is decorated with tiny tiles arranged into an intricate mosaic. The materials used came from different parts of the empire, including vibrant turquoise, a gemstone that was highly prized by the Aztecs.

EAGLE WARRIORS
All Aztec boys had to have military training, but only the best became eagle or jaguar warriors, the elite soldiers of the Aztec army. They gained this rank through showing courage in war and capturing prisoners. This clay figurine shows an eagle warrior in battle outfit. Featuring an eagle head and wings, these outfits were made of thick cloth covered in feathers.

GOD OF MANY THINGS
Tezcatlipoca was the god of rulers and sorcerers, as well as patron deity of the schools where warriors were trained. All Aztec boys and girls went to school and were educated in their history and culture. They had close families, where they learned everyday skills, crafts, and morals.

Tezcatlipoca's name translates as "Smoking Mirror."

The black tiles are made from lignite, a type of coal.

Turquoise, a precious blue-green mineral

Conch shells line the eyes made of pyrite, a shiny mineral.

Coral lines the nasal cavity.

Lining made of animal skin covers the inside of the skull.

Straps made of deerskin leather were originally painted red.

Most of the teeth are still attached to the skull.

THE INCA
RULE A MOUNTAIN EMPIRE

In the 15th century, the Inca people ruled one of the largest empires in the world. It stretched some 2,500 miles (4,000 km) from Ecuador to Chile, along the Pacific coast, with its capital at Cuzco, high in the Andean mountains. The Inca ruled their empire using a network of roads, keeping food supplies in storehouses along the way, and maintaining a well-organized army.

MOUNTAIN CITY
The spectacular Inca city of Machu Picchu was built in the 15th century. Perched high in the mountains of the Andes, it has around 200 stone structures linked by hundreds of stone steps.

This ruler is wearing a tunic of high value.

FINE FABRICS
The Inca were skilled weavers, producing cloth from soft llama, alpaca, or vicuña wool, with intricate geometric designs. The finest were reserved for people of high status. More valuable than gold, they were often presented as gifts and used as offerings to the gods and ancestors.

USEFUL LLAMAS
Llamas, and smaller alpacas, were a vital part of Inca life. Able to live at high altitudes, they were used as pack animals. They also provided wool and meat, and their manure was burned as fuel.

Canopy of bird feathers gave shade and shelter

The Sapa Inca

TRAVELING RULERS
The ruler of the empire, the Sapa Inca, was believed to be descended from the sun god, Inti. He traveled everywhere on a litter, or ceremonial chair. This was carried by four bearers, who had to tread carefully on the steep, narrow roads.

Sheer drop to valley below

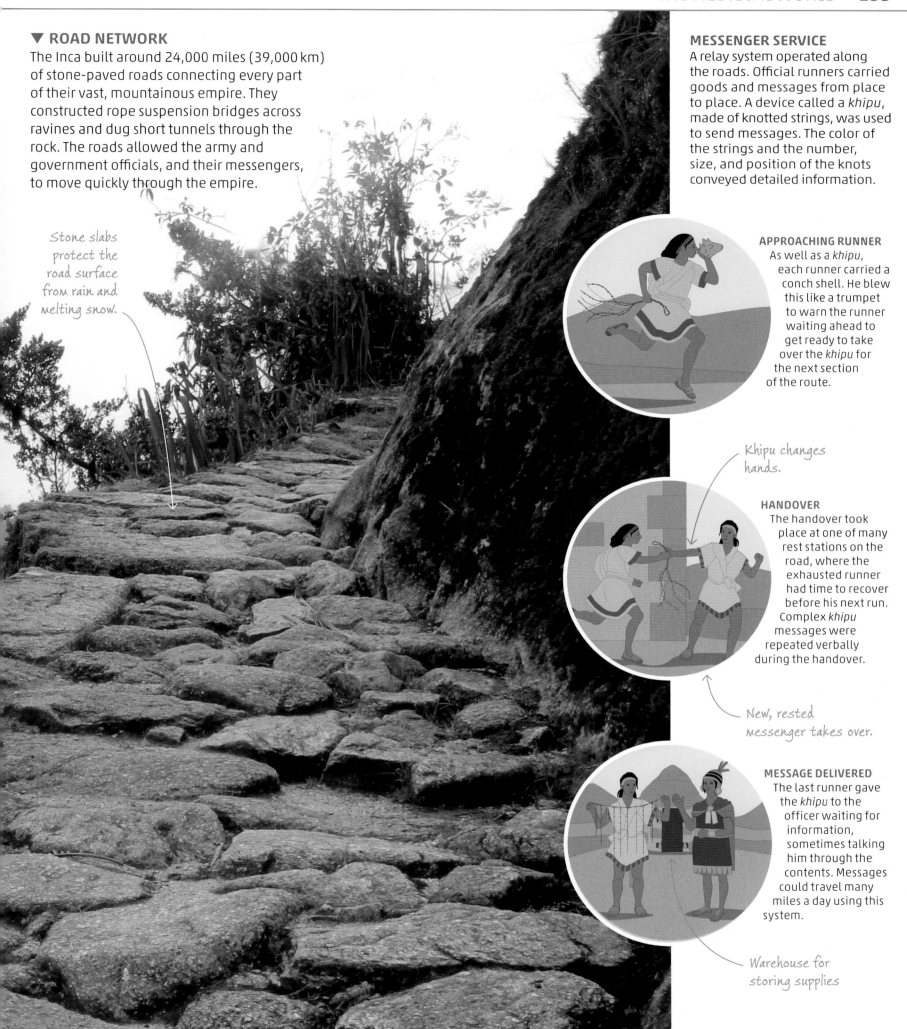

▼ ROAD NETWORK

The Inca built around 24,000 miles (39,000 km) of stone-paved roads connecting every part of their vast, mountainous empire. They constructed rope suspension bridges across ravines and dug short tunnels through the rock. The roads allowed the army and government officials, and their messengers, to move quickly through the empire.

Stone slabs protect the road surface from rain and melting snow.

MESSENGER SERVICE

A relay system operated along the roads. Official runners carried goods and messages from place to place. A device called a *khipu*, made of knotted strings, was used to send messages. The color of the strings and the number, size, and position of the knots conveyed detailed information.

APPROACHING RUNNER

As well as a *khipu*, each runner carried a conch shell. He blew this like a trumpet to warn the runner waiting ahead to get ready to take over the *khipu* for the next section of the route.

Khipu changes hands.

HANDOVER

The handover took place at one of many rest stations on the road, where the exhausted runner had time to recover before his next run. Complex *khipu* messages were repeated verbally during the handover.

New, rested messenger takes over.

MESSAGE DELIVERED

The last runner gave the *khipu* to the officer waiting for information, sometimes talking him through the contents. Messages could travel many miles a day using this system.

Warehouse for storing supplies

TRADE GROWS
IN EUROPE

Life became much easier for people in Europe after 1100.
Harvests were good, the population grew, and towns sprang
up—all of this led to a boom in trade, helped by expanding
trade networks. People became wealthier, fueling a demand
for luxury goods from further away. Long-distance trade routes
connected people and goods across Europe and beyond.

▶ MARKET STALL

Weekly markets took place in many towns. Stalls could sell
anything from farm produce to imported wares, such as Spanish
leather; English wool; furs from northern Europe; and fine cloth,
silks, and spices from Italy. These goods were sourced at large
fairs that drew in merchants from all over Europe. This
is a model of a leather merchant's stall, displaying
prepared skins as well as the latest shoe models.

*Frame could
be folded up and
stored, making it easy
to transport from
market to market.*

BUSTLING TRADE
Markets were busy affairs,
providing goods as well as
entertainment and opportunities
for socializing. They usually took
place in the town centers. Farmers
from the surrounding areas sold
or bartered surplus vegetables,
cheese, or eggs for items like
leather shoes or flasks.

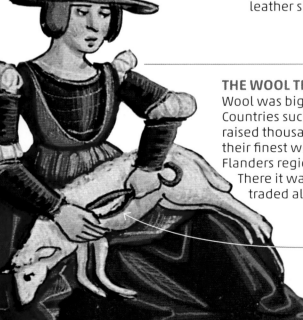

THE WOOL TRADE
Wool was big business in medieval Europe.
Countries such as England and Spain, which
raised thousands of sheep each year, exported
their finest wool to cloth-making towns in the
Flanders region of Belgium and northern Italy.
There it was made into cloth, which was
traded all over Europe.

*Sharp scissors made of
iron were important tools
for shearing sheep.*

Leather
tankard
for drinking

NORTHERN TRADERS
The Hanseatic League was an association of mainly German coastal cities that controlled sea trade in northern Europe, and stamped out piracy in the Baltic Sea. Its influence ran from Novgorod in Russia to London, England.

TRADE WITH ASIA
The Italian city of Venice grew rich on trade with Asia. Venetian ships sailed to ports at the western end of the overland routes from China and India. Once there, they would pick up valuable cargoes of silks and spices.

EARLY BANKS
Banks developed to handle the money involved in trade, and to provide loans for kings and merchants. Banking first emerged in Italy in the 14th century—the word "bank" comes from the Italian "banca," which was the bench where money was exchanged.

PLAGUE
HITS EUROPE

In the mid-14th century, a deadly outbreak of bubonic plague, known as the Black Death, spread along trade routes. In Europe, it is estimated that up to 60 percent of the population died in four years. This wasn't the first, nor the last, big outbreak—waves of plagues continued to hit and affect society for centuries to come.

▶ **PLAGUE DOCTOR**
Bubonic plague broke out many times in Europe between 1350 and 1700. In the 17th century, doctors sent out to treat patients sometimes wore beaked masks to protect themselves from infection. They believed, wrongly, that the disease spread in foul air given off by rotting material.

The hood covered the entire head to prevent air coming into contact with the body.

SPREAD OF THE BLACK DEATH

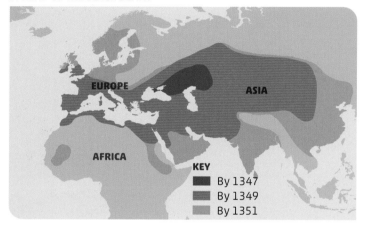

EUROPE

ASIA

AFRICA

KEY
By 1347
By 1349
By 1351

THE BLACK DEATH
The plague known as the Black Death killed up to 200 million people worldwide between 1346 and 1358. It began in Central Asia and soon spread to China, Iran, and West Asia. From Constantinople (today Istanbul, in Turkey) it traveled around the Mediterranean Sea into Africa and Europe via trade caravans and merchant ships arriving in ports and towns.

PLAGUE SPREADERS
A strain of bacteria called *Yersinia pestis* caused bubonic plague. The bacteria lived on rats, and blood-sucking fleas passed bacteria from rats to humans. Ships were full of rats, helping the plague spread from port to port along busy trade routes. At the time, people didn't fully understand this, or how to prevent or cure it.

PLAGUE BACTERIA

BLACK RAT

FLEA

A CHANGED SOCIETY

Around half the population of Europe died in the Black Death, which struck priests and nobility as well as peasants. This painting of Death taking a wealthy young lady showed that neither youth nor riches could protect. Huge areas of land were deserted as survivors fled to the towns to become paid workers. The feudal system (see page 119) and its strict social rules became hard to maintain.

STUFFED BEAK

The birdlike beak contained dried flowers, medicinal herbs, and spices. Two tiny holes near the nostrils allowed the doctor to breathe.

Fragrant things placed inside the beak were thought to ward off "bad air."

PERSONAL PROTECTION

People in crowded city streets took to carrying pomanders—small boxes filled with perfumes or herbs—to protect themselves from the bad air they believed caused the plague.

17TH-CENTURY POMANDER

THE MING DYNASTY
RULES CHINA

In 1368, a peasant warlord called Zhu Yuanzhang seized power in China. Toppling the Mongol Yuan dynasty, he became the first Ming emperor. Determined to keep out future invaders, the Ming repaired and strengthened the Great Wall of China. During nearly 300 years of Ming rule, cities grew and foreign trade expanded.

▼ **GREAT WALL OF CHINA**
The Great Wall extends west from the capital, Beijing, for a total of 13,000 miles (21,000 km) along China's northern border. Parts of it date back 2,000 years. The Ming added brickwork to existing earth walls and built tall towers and passes to keep their empire safe.

STRONG DEFENSES
Around 25,000 watchtowers lined the wall, but there were also several passes like the one seen here. A pass was a large fortified gate and command post, protected by massive ramparts of brick and stone. Soldiers were stationed on the three-storied tower over the gate to keep watch for invaders from the north.

The distance between watchtowers can be as little as 1½ miles (2.5 km).

FORBIDDEN CITY
The Ming emperors built a huge palace complex in Beijing. Surrounded by a moat and high defensive walls, it was called the Forbidden City because nobody could enter it without the emperor's permission.

THE FLEET OF ZHENG HE
To display the power of the Ming dynasty, admiral Zheng He made seven long sea voyages in 1405–1433. His fleet of huge ships loaded with gifts visited as many as 30 kingdoms around the Indian Ocean.

MING PORCELAIN
The Ming period is famous for its blue-and-white porcelain, a type of fine, hard pottery. At that time, only Chinese potters knew the secret of making it. The imperial factories turned out porcelain on an industrial scale. By 1600, porcelain was being exported in huge quantities to Europe to meet the demand.

Chinese dragon, a popular motif on Ming vases

SIGNALING SYSTEM
When the soldiers in a watchtower spotted a raiding party north of the wall, they raised the alarm by sending smoke signals by day, or burning a fire at night. As neighboring towers spotted the smoke, they would light their own, until everyone was on alert.

A path along the top of the wall is wide enough for 10 soldiers to march shoulder to shoulder.

KEEPING TIME

People have tracked time for thousands of years, but the earliest methods were far less accurate than those of today. From the 13th century, when the first mechanical clocks appeared, it slowly became possible for people to keep time more accurately. Clocks evolved, becoming more complex and able to account for smaller units of time. As time-telling became more precise, people's lives evolved to match.

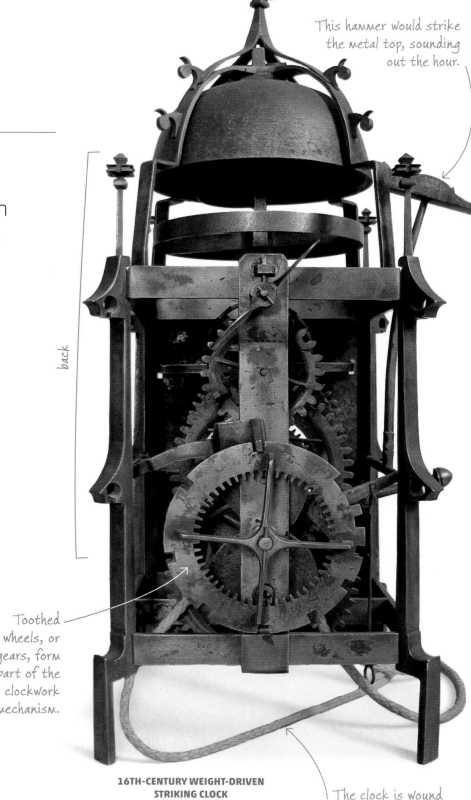

This hammer would strike the metal top, sounding out the hour.

back

Toothed wheels, or gears, form part of the clockwork mechanism.

16TH-CENTURY WEIGHT-DRIVEN STRIKING CLOCK

The clock is wound to lift the weights attached to these ropes. As the weights fall, they drive the clock. To allow them to fall freely, the clock was wall-mounted.

ANCIENT TIMEKEEPING

In ancient times, people's lives were dictated by the daylight hours between sunrise and sunset. Observing the sun allowed them to work out roughly what point in the day they had reached, and early tools, such as this Greek sundial, were used to track the passing of hours.

A stick called the gnomon casts a shadow on the dial.

Markings for hours

PUBLIC CLOCKS

The first European mechanical clocks were built in the 13th century. They were mounted on church towers or in public squares, and chimed to let people know that it was time to stop what they were doing and attend church service. Some doubled as astronomical clocks, showing the position of the moon, sun, and stars in the sky.

▲ CLOCKS AT HOME

The first clocks made to be used in the home appeared in the 15th century. They showed only hours, not minutes. The earliest form of mechanical clock, they were weight-driven like the one shown here, and had to be wound up very often to tell time correctly.

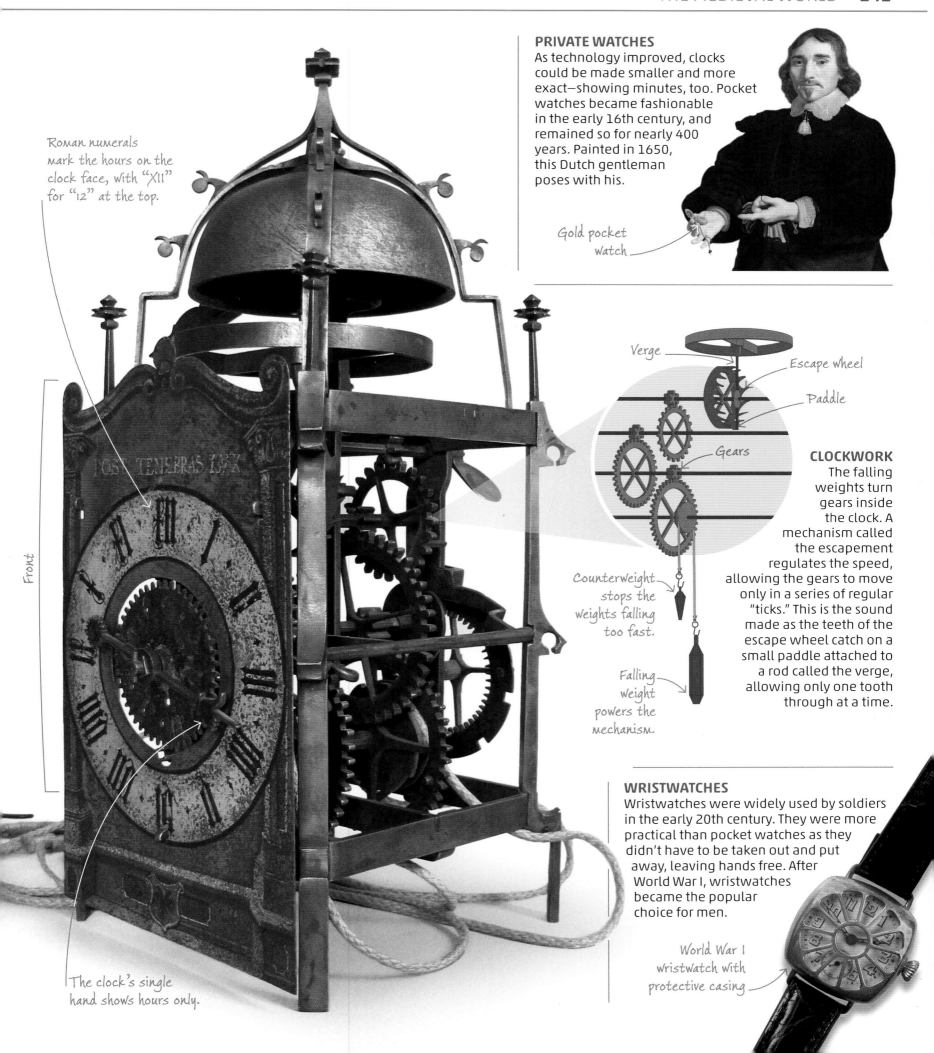

Roman numerals mark the hours on the clock face, with "XII" for "12" at the top.

Front

The clock's single hand shows hours only.

PRIVATE WATCHES

As technology improved, clocks could be made smaller and more exact—showing minutes, too. Pocket watches became fashionable in the early 16th century, and remained so for nearly 400 years. Painted in 1650, this Dutch gentleman poses with his.

Gold pocket watch

Verge

Escape wheel

Paddle

Gears

Counterweight stops the weights falling too fast.

Falling weight powers the mechanism.

CLOCKWORK

The falling weights turn gears inside the clock. A mechanism called the escapement regulates the speed, allowing the gears to move only in a series of regular "ticks." This is the sound made as the teeth of the escape wheel catch on a small paddle attached to a rod called the verge, allowing only one tooth through at a time.

WRISTWATCHES

Wristwatches were widely used by soldiers in the early 20th century. They were more practical than pocket watches as they didn't have to be taken out and put away, leaving hands free. After World War I, wristwatches became the popular choice for men.

World War I wristwatch with protective casing

In Europe, Africa, the Americas, and across Asia, several countries carved out **vast empires** that sometimes even stretched across **continents**. However, the **wealth** of empire was rarely shared fairly, and many people **suffered** at the hands of the **imperial powers**. In some parts of the world, people rose up against their rulers, sparking **revolutions** that led to the creation of new **democracies**.

EMPIRES

EXPAND

TIMELINE OF THE EARLY MODERN WORLD

Many of the characteristics that define today's society took shape in the early modern world. People from different continents encountered each other for the first time and goods and ideas began to flow around the globe. All over the world inventive thinkers experimented with new ways of organizing governments and societies.

1435

1438
The Inca Empire
Emperor Pachacutec begins a rapid expansion of the Inca empire, dominating the mountainous Andes region of South America.

THE SIEGE OF BUSANJIN FORTRESS

1568
The Dutch Republic
Led by William of Orange, the Protestant-dominated Netherlands rises in revolt against its Catholic Spanish rulers. An independent republic is established in 1579 and Dutch independence is internationally recognized in 1648.

SHACKLES

1526
First transatlantic slave ship
A Portuguese ship takes enslaved Africans across the Atlantic to Brazil. This is the first voyage in what becomes a 344-year trade in human lives.

1519
First circumnavigation of the world
Sponsored by the Spanish crown, Portuguese-born Ferdinand Magellan begins a journey around the world with three ships. Only one ship completes the voyage, in 1522.

1592
Japan invades Korea
Hideyoshi, ruler of central Japan, launches the first of two unsuccessful invasions of Korea. His armies are finally defeated in 1598.

1526
The Mughal Empire
Led by Babur I, a direct descendant of the Mongol Genghis Khan, the Muslim Mughals invade India from Afghanistan. They establish an empire that lasts until 1857.

1519
Invasion of America
Spaniard Hernan Cortes begins the subjugation of the Aztec Empire of Mexico. This is followed by the conquest of the Inca Empire of Peru by Francisco Pizarro in 1531–1535.

JAMESTOWN

1600
The East India Company
A new English trading company is formed to trade in the Indian Ocean. Between 1757 and 1858 it carves out a huge commercial and territorial empire.

1618
The Thirty Years' War
A major conflict between Catholics and Protestants breaks out in the Holy Roman Empire in Europe. The war lasts for 30 years, involving all the major European powers except England.

EMPEROR SHUNZHI

1607
Jamestown
The first permanent English settlement in America is established at Jamestown on the James River in what is now Virginia.

1643
Louis XIV becomes king
The young Louis XIV becomes king of France, ruling until 1715. He fights to increase French power and prestige in Europe throughout his long reign.

1644
A new Chinese dynasty
Manchu people from an area north of China seize control of the country, ushering in a new, non-Chinese dynasty that will rule until it is overthrown by revolution in 1911.

c. 1439
Printed books
German printer Johannes Gutenberg is the first person in Europe to use movable type in a printing press, allowing him to print books.

BENIN WARRIOR STATUE

1453
The Ottoman Empire
The Ottoman Turks capture Constantinople and bring the Byzantine Empire to an end, creating their own vast empire in West Asia, North Africa, and Europe.

1464
The Songhai Empire
Sunni Ali becomes king of Songhai in the western Sahel. He conquers the trading cities Timbuktu and Djenné and creates a vast new empire in West Africa.

c. 1440
Rise of Benin
Ewuare the Great becomes oba, or king, of the city-state of Benin in West Africa. He greatly expands Benin's territory while also fostering religion and the arts.

1480
Muscovy throws off Tatar rule
Ivan III ceases to pay tribute to the Mongol Golden Horde. Muscovy begins to expand across Russia as an independent principality.

SAFAVID TILE

1501
The Safavid Empire
Under the leadership of Ismail I, the Safavids seize control of Iran. They are the first native dynasty to rule the country since the Sasanian Empire fell in 651.

1492
Columbus reaches the Americas
The Italian navigator Christopher Columbus makes his first voyage across the Atlantic, sponsored by the Spanish crown. He discovers a continent unknown to Europeans.

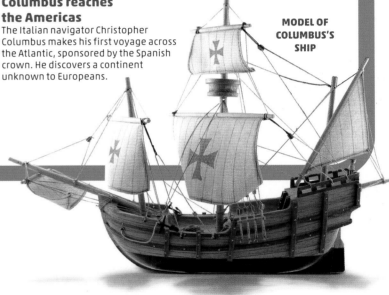

MODEL OF COLUMBUS'S SHIP

1517
The Reformation
German priest Martin Luther protests against the Catholic Church in Germany, prompting a Protestant Revolution that spreads across Europe.

1492
The Reconquista
Spanish Catholic monarchs Isabella and Ferdinand conquer Granada, defeating the Muslim Moors who had occupied areas of Spain and Portugal since the 8th century.

1682
Peter the Great
Peter becomes Czar of Russia. He rules until 1725, founding the new capital of St. Petersburg in 1703 and creating the Russian Empire in 1721.

1768
The voyages of Captain Cook
British Captain James Cook sets out on the first of three voyages to explore the Pacific. His crew includes botanists, artists, and astronomers; he visits Tahiti, New Zealand, Australia, and Hawaii.

1776
American independence
Conflict between Britain and its 13 North American colonies descends into open warfare in 1775. A year later, the colonies declare their independence, which they win in 1783 after the British surrender in 1781.

GUILLOTINE

1790

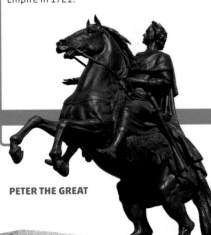

PETER THE GREAT

1757
The British in India
Robert Clive leads British East India Company forces to victory over the Bengali ruler Siraj ud-Daulah. He secures the company's dominance in Bengal, leading to the first British territorial acquisition on the subcontinent.

1789
The French Revolution
Revolution breaks out in France as Parisians storm the Bastille Prison. A republic is formed in 1792 and King Louis XVI is tried and executed the following year.

ARCHITECTURE AND ENGINEERING
The dome of Florence Cathedral in Italy, completed in 1436, was the largest dome built in Europe since the days of ancient Rome. Its architect, Filippo Brunelleschi, studied Roman monuments before beginning his design.

POLITICAL IDEAS
One of the most influential books of the Renaissance was *The Prince* by Italian diplomat Niccolò Machiavelli. His book advises rulers on how to win and keep power. His suggestion that political cunning was more important than doing good shocked many people but had a lasting impact.

NEW KINDS OF ART
Inspired by the discovery of lifelike Greek sculptures, Renaissance artists moved away from the stiffness of medieval art to portray people and nature in a much more realistic way. Carved by the artist Michelangelo from a single block of marble, this 17-ft- (5.17-m-) high statue of the Biblical hero David is an icon of Renaissance art.

▶ LEONARDO'S MECHANICAL LION
The multi-talented Italian artist, scientist, and engineer Leonardo da Vinci is one of the most famous figures of the Renaissance. He designed a mechanical lion as a gift for the King of France. At an official ceremony it walked toward the king and offered him flowers. This life-size reconstruction is based on Leonardo's original drawings.

The tongue was made from a separate piece of wood than the rest of the head.

THE RENAISSANCE REVOLUTIONIZES IDEAS

The period known as the Renaissance (meaning "rebirth") marked a new era in the history of thought. It began in the 1400s when European artists and scholars rediscovered the art, architecture, and writings of the ancient Greeks and Romans. What they found inspired new ideas about painting, sculpture, and engineering, and brought significant changes to politics and science.

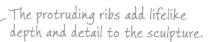

The protruding ribs add lifelike depth and detail to the sculpture.

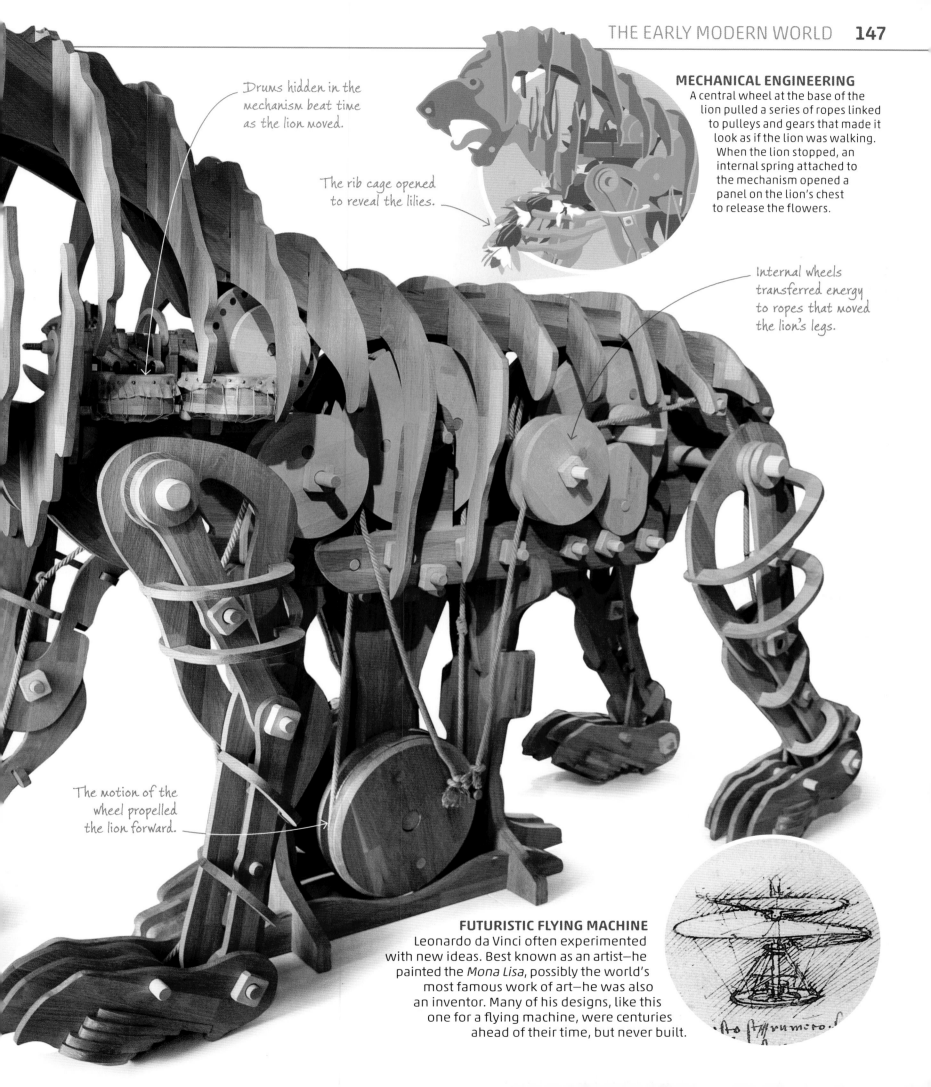

Drums hidden in the mechanism beat time as the lion moved.

The rib cage opened to reveal the lilies.

MECHANICAL ENGINEERING
A central wheel at the base of the lion pulled a series of ropes linked to pulleys and gears that made it look as if the lion was walking. When the lion stopped, an internal spring attached to the mechanism opened a panel on the lion's chest to release the flowers.

Internal wheels transferred energy to ropes that moved the lion's legs.

The motion of the wheel propelled the lion forward.

FUTURISTIC FLYING MACHINE
Leonardo da Vinci often experimented with new ideas. Best known as an artist—he painted the *Mona Lisa*, possibly the world's most famous work of art—he was also an inventor. Many of his designs, like this one for a flying machine, were centuries ahead of their time, but never built.

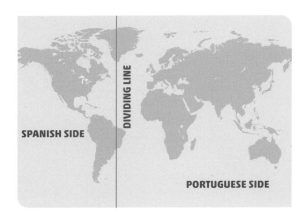

CLAIMING TERRITORY

Both Spain and Portugal claimed the lands they had visited. The two nations agreed that land to the west of an imaginary line in the Atlantic would belong to Spain, and land to the east to Portugal. The people who lived in these lands were not consulted.

The mapmaker has made these Caribbean islands too large.

Newfoundland (Canada) is pictured but North America is missing.

SAILING TECHNOLOGY

Portuguese mariners adapted methods of sail and ship construction they observed from skilled Arab sailors to create sturdy ships called caravels. These vessels could withstand the buffeting winds and strong currents of the Atlantic Ocean and made long-range voyages possible.

EXPLORERS
MAP THE GLOBE

From the mid-1400s, Portuguese and Spanish sailors began exploring down the coast of Africa and across the Atlantic in search of a sea route to Asia. The returning voyagers brought news of lands and peoples previously unknown in Europe, inspiring waves of European explorers, traders, and settlers to sail overseas.

THE AMERICAS

The features of the ostrich-egg globe are superimposed in red on an actual globe. The mapmaker has made South America too big and missed North America entirely.

▶ **THE FIRST GLOBE**

This is the first known globe showing the whole world, made in Italy around 1510. Although the map, carved onto two ostrich-egg halves that were then glued together, is not accurate, it does show recent European discoveries in Asia and the Americas.

TWO-WAY EXCHANGE

The connection between Europe and America linked two separate worlds. Before the first voyages, people in Europe had never tasted a tomato, and people in the Americas did not have horses. The two-way transfer of plants, animals, and diseases across the Atlantic Ocean is called the Columbian Exchange.

Diseases
Europeans brought many diseases to the Americas, such as smallpox. These spread rapidly among local people, killing millions.

The mapmaker had to imagine most of the Asian interior.

THE SPICE ISLANDS
The goal of the early European explorers was to find a sea route to the Spice Islands (in modern-day Indonesia) so they could control the trade in expensive spices like pepper and nutmeg.

The globe's two halves were glued together along the Equator.

THE INDIAN OCEAN
On this part of the globe the mapmaker has imagined several large islands in the Indian Ocean and missed out most of Southeast Asia.

FLOATING FORTRESSES
Loaded with cannons, the turtle ships were used to fire on and destroy attacking ships before they could get close enough to inflict any damage. Slow and clumsy at sea, they were most effective in shallow coastal waters.

Iron spikes on the roof stopped enemies from boarding the ship and engaging in hand-to-hand combat.

Each oar was powered by four people, increasing the ship's pace and also improving maneuverability.

Cannons were fired through portholes on both sides of the ship.

THE
JOSEON KINGS
RULE KOREA

The Joseon kings came to power in 1392, ruling Korea for more than 500 years. In this time, Korea developed a unique cultural identity, influenced by the ancient Chinese philosophy of Confucianism. The country was also strong, using their mighty fleet of Geobukseon—or "turtle ships"—to save Korea from Japanese invasion during the Imjin War (1592–1598).

The large sail increased the ship's speed, but was taken down during battles.

Forward-facing cannons

▲ TURTLE SHIP

This is a modern replica of a Korean turtle ship. These ships, which were used by the Royal Korean Army from the early 15th century, owed their name to their protective shell-like covering. Each vessel was armed with up to 26 cannons. A fearsome dragon-shape head at the front held one cannon, and also a burner that gave off smoke to hide the ship from their enemies in short-distance combat.

This wooden crest with a gargoyle-like face was used for ramming into enemy ships.

Large anchor

WINNING STRATEGY

The turtle ships were the idea of Admiral Yi Sun-sin, who used them many times during the Imjin War. This painting shows Koreans firing on Japanese warships at the Battle of Myeongnyang, his most famous victory.

KOREAN ALPHABET

Hangul, the Korean phonetic alphabet of 28 letters, was introduced in 1446 at the court of Sejong the Great. Before this time, Korean was written in Chinese characters, which most people couldn't read. Pictured is a replica of *Hunminjeongeum Haerye*, the book which explains the creation of Hangul.

A CLASSICAL EDUCATION

During his 32 years in power, Sejong the Great improved the lives of ordinary people. He placed great importance on education, establishing grants to support learning in subjects from science to linguistics. Some children studied in places such as Byeongsanseowon Confucian Academy in Yandong, South Korea.

PRINTING
SPREADS IDEAS

In 1455 a German inventor, Johannes Gutenberg, used a new device called a printing press to print the first book in Europe. Before the printing press, books had to be copied out by hand, which was an expensive and time-consuming process. Only the rich could afford them, and few people could read or write. By making books and the knowledge they contained widely available, printing transformed the world of learning and ideas.

The letter stands clear of the metal block.

▶ MOVABLE TYPE
The key to Gutenberg's invention was movable type— pieces of metal bearing a single raised letter. The printer arranged the letters into words in a wooden frame that was then printed as a page. Because multiple copies could be made quickly before the letters were reordered to form different words, printing with movable type was cheaper and easier than copying by hand.

INKING THE LETTERS
Printers used two leather balls stuffed with horsehair to coat the type with ink made from a sticky mixture of soot and oil. They pressed the balls over the type to spread the ink over the letters as evenly as possible.

THE GUTENBERG BIBLE
The first book Gutenberg printed was the Bible. It was in Latin, the language of the Church, which few people could read. This helped spark the Reformation (see pages 154–155) when Bible translations were made and printed in most European languages. Many people wanted to own a Bible and read it for themselves, which helped increase literacy.

A slot on each letter held it in place in the wooden frame.

USING THE PRINTING PRESS

To print a page, a sheet of paper held in a frame was placed over the inked type. The printer lowered a heavy weight on top of the type and paper until the two pressed together, leaving the raised letters indelibly stamped on the sheet.

Paper held in wooden frame ready to be placed on the type.

Inked type

The "Gothic" lettering was based on the written script of the time.

Pulling the handle lowers the weight onto the paper.

THE POWER OF THE PRESS

The printing press had a huge and lasting impact. By 1500, fewer than 50 years after its invention, at least 9 million books had been printed in more than 280 European cities. As the numbers of books and pamphlets kept rising, new ideas circulated rapidly.

READING FOR ALL
Printing spread literacy as there was now so much more to read. Libraries and reading societies sprang up in towns where people (mostly men) could read newspapers and catch up with the latest ideas.

SHARING SCIENTIFIC KNOWLEDGE
Printing allowed thinkers to publish and share their work, changing the way people viewed the world. This illustration of a two-humped camel is from an early printed book about natural history.

SPREADING REVOLUTIONARY IDEAS
Pamphlets and books spread new political ideas. For example, books calling for equal rights and a fairer society helped to inspire the American and French Revolutions (see pages 186–189).

THE WESTERN CHURCH SPLITS

For hundreds of years, the Catholic Church was the only major form of Christianity in Western Europe. By the early 1500s, it had become very powerful. People accused the Church's bishops and priests of corruption, and a great movement demanding change, called the Reformation, swept through Europe. It left the Church divided into two opposing groups, with Catholics on one side and Protestants, as the many different groups of reformers came to be known, on the other.

▶ **DIFFERENT PLACES OF WORSHIP**
Reformed Protestant churches look very different from Catholic ones. The Catholic church on the left is covered in gold. Statues of saints surround the ornate altar, which is the center of worship. The Protestant church on the right is much plainer, and a simple white cloth covers the altar, or communion table.

Incense is burned as part of the ritual.

CATHOLIC SERVICES
For Catholics, the priest acts as a bridge between God and the people. When he offers bread and wine at the altar, they believe it becomes the body and blood of Jesus Christ. At the time of the Reformation, and up until the 1960s, Catholic services were held in Latin.

THE REFORMATION BEGINS

In 1517, Martin Luther, a German priest, nailed a list of complaints known as the 95 Theses to a church door. Among other things, Luther was angry with the Church for allowing the sale of indulgences. These were religious promises to shorten the time a deceased person's soul spent in torment before going to heaven. Catholic leaders resisted change, so Luther's supporters decided to break away from the Church and worship in their own way.

RELIGIOUS WARS

The Reformation plunged Europe into a series of conflicts lasting 150 years as Catholics and Protestants fought bitterly. Many acts of atrocity were carried out in the name of religion. In 1572, a Catholic mob slaughtered French Protestants in the streets of Paris during what became known as the St. Bartholomew's Day Massacre. The wars ended in 1648.

PROTESTANT SERVICES

In Protestant churches, the minister leads the service from the pulpit or reading desk, where he preaches and explains the Bible to the congregation. Unlike Catholics, from the time of the Reformation Protestants held services in people's native languages instead of Latin. For many Protestants, the communion bread and wine are symbols of Christ's body and blood, and do not change into them.

THE SPANISH
INVADE
THE AMERICAS

Explorers first landed in the Americas in the 1490s. Spanish soldiers soon followed, seeking their fortune in the land reputed to be full of gold. Known as "conquistadors," they overthrew the great civilizations of Central and South America, claiming their lands for the Spanish crown. Millions of Indigenous people died and their cities were looted and destroyed.

Gold and silver from artifacts made by the Inca or Aztecs were often melted down and used for coins.

▶ SPANISH COINS
The Spanish conquistadors found huge deposits of silver in Mexico and South America. They began minting large quantities of silver coins, including the "pieces of eight" (*pesos de a ocho*), which were worth 8 Spanish *reales*. Circulating throughout Europe and as far as China, and highly treasured by pirates, these silver coins made Spain a global power.

SILVER MOUNTAIN
The richest silver mine of all was in the side of a mountain at Potosí, Bolivia. As well as using Indigenous forced labor, the Spanish transported thousands of enslaved Africans to work there. The silver attracted business, and a thriving town sprang up here. In 1572, a Royal Mint opened in the city.

This "piece of eight" was minted in Potosí itself, as indicated by the inscription and the "P" and the "8."

The Aztecs were armed with spears, bows, and sharp-edged clubs.

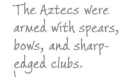

Tlaxcalan warrior

VIOLENT ENCOUNTER

Many Indigenous peoples resisted. The invaders had the advantage of guns and horses, which were unknown in the Americas at this time, but resistance continued for hundreds of years. The Spanish victory was secured by making alliances with some Indigenous peoples. This painting shows the defeat of the Aztecs (see pages 130–131). Warriors from Tlaxcala, who had long been enemies of the Aztecs, are pictured fighting alongside the Spanish.

Many coins minted in Potosí were melted down and reminted in Spain, often in Seville.

Aztec people suffering from the horrors of smallpox

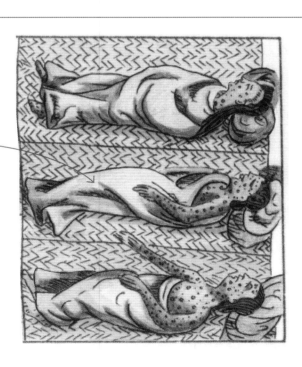

DEADLY DISEASES

Around 80 percent of the Indigenous population was wiped out by the Spanish invasion. They died in huge numbers because they didn't have immunity to infectious diseases brought over with the Europeans.

SETTLEMENTS AND MISSIONS

The Spanish invaders believed they had a religious duty to convert the Indigenous peoples to Christianity. They founded Christian churches and missions (organizations intended to spread the Christian faith), and tried to ban worship of the gods that local people believed in.

▶ BENIN BRONZES

Benin metalworkers were experts at making detailed plaques from brass and bronze. This plaque is part of a group of artifacts, known as the Benin Bronzes, that once decorated the palace of the oba of Benin. Metalworkers in Benin belonged to a group of craftworkers, known as a guild, who worked only for the king.

THE ROYAL PALACE

The pillars of the oba's palace, which was built in the 13th century, were adorned with thousands of brass plaques. They showed important events in Benin's history, and celebrated the ancestry of the oba. The palace was rebuilt in the early 20th century after the original was destroyed by the British in 1897.

THE OBAS

This picture shows an 18th-century oba riding on horseback. The obas were powerful leaders who were worshipped by their subjects as gods. The most famous oba was Ewuare the Great (ruled c. 1440–1480), who rebuilt much of Benin city and fortified the capital with huge moats and walls.

Warrior chief holding a ceremonial sword

Holes are left from the fixings that attached the plaque to the pillar.

Attendants are smaller, indicating their lower rank

THE KINGDOM OF BENIN

The kingdom of Benin was founded in the 11th century in the forests of West Africa. Its people, the Edo, were ruled by a king known as an oba, who lived in a vast palace at the heart of the walled city. By the 15th century, Benin had become a wealthy trading nation, famed for its ivory carvings and bronze statues. However, during the 18th century, the power of the obas waned, and the kingdom was eventually invaded by the British in 1897.

Portuguese soldier holding a gun

TRADE WITH PORTUGAL
The first European travelers to reach Benin were Portuguese explorers in 1485. A strong trading relationship developed, with Benin trading pepper, ivory, and palm oil for European goods such as brass and copper. This brass statue shows a 17th-century Portuguese soldier. The Portuguese brought guns to west Africa, and their soldiers often fought alongside the Benin armies against rival kingdoms.

THE FALL OF BENIN
In the 19th century, trade disputes led to tension between Benin and Britain. In 1897, British officials tried to visit Benin against the wishes of the oba. As the British men approached Benin, their party was attacked and killed. Britain retaliated by sending a huge military force to invade Benin. The city was burned to the ground, treasures were looted from the palace (above), and Benin became part of the British Empire.

THE OTTOMANS
BUILD AN EMPIRE

Over a period of more than 600 years, the Ottoman Empire extended from Turkey across Europe and West Asia. Although the empire's rulers (called sultans) and many of its citizens were Muslim, it was also home to Christian and Jewish people. By the 16th century, the empire was the greatest military power in Europe and it endured until the early 1900s.

▶ THE SIEGE OF VIENNA

In 1529, Sultan Suleiman I laid siege to Vienna in Austria. However, he failed to capture the city and the siege marked the western limit of Ottoman expansion. This image shows him encamped below the city with his guns trained on its walls. Suleiman's subjects called him "Suleiman the Lawgiver" because he brought the empire's many laws together into a single legal code.

RAPID EXPANSION

In 1453, the Ottomans captured the ancient Roman city of Constantinople. It became known as Istanbul and was at the center of the growing empire. The Ottomans recruited enslaved soldiers called janissaries from the people they conquered. The janissaries proved an effective military force that helped spread Ottoman power across the Eastern Mediterranean.

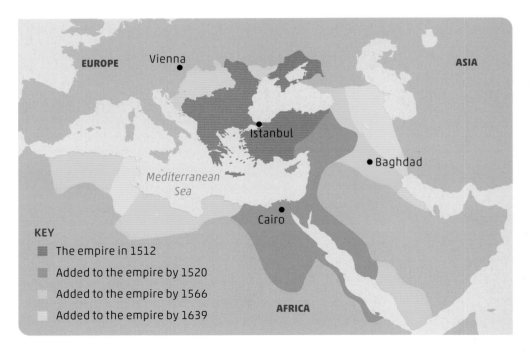

EUROPE   Vienna

ASIA

Istanbul

Baghdad

Mediterranean Sea

Cairo

AFRICA

KEY
- The empire in 1512
- Added to the empire by 1520
- Added to the empire by 1566
- Added to the empire by 1639

THE BATHHOUSE
Public bathhouses, or hammams, were built across the Empire as places where people could socialize and relax. It was also very important for the empire's Muslim citizens to be able to bathe before prayer.

WHIRLING DERVISHES
A mystic branch of Islam called Sufism was popular in the Ottoman Empire. Its followers, called dervishes, practice whirling, a dancelike form of religious meditation. Some dervishes helped convert conquered peoples to Islam.

A MULTILINGUAL CALENDAR
This calendar from the very end of the period of Ottoman rule features the date April 20, 1911, written in Arabic, Greek, French, Turkish, and several other languages. It shows how the Ottomans accommodated the various ethnic groups within their empire.

SIGNING THE COMPACT
Before landing, the male passengers signed the Mayflower Compact, agreeing to make and follow "just and equal laws" for the good of all. The women on board were excluded from taking part. The Compact is sometimes called the first written governmental document in North America.

▶ **PILGRIM PASSENGERS**
In September 1620, 102 people set sail from England to North America on a ship called the *Mayflower*. Many of the passengers belonged to a group of Protestant Christians known as the Pilgrims, who believed that the Church of England was corrupt and who wanted to create a purer version of the Church in America where they could worship freely.

This modern replica of the Pilgrims' ship is called *Mayflower II*.

Passengers were crammed into windowless "tween" decks.

EUROPEAN COLONISTS
COME TO NORTH AMERICA

Colonists from Europe began arriving in North America in the 1500s. Some were sponsored by aristocrats or merchants hoping to find wealth, first in the form of gold but later from valuable crops such as tobacco. Others sought freedom to worship how they chose. By the late 18th century, Europeans had laid claims to large parts of the continent. These lands were home to Indigenous peoples (see pages 124–125) whose communities were uprooted and even destroyed by the waves of European settlement.

THE FIRST PEOPLE
People had lived in North America for thousands of years before the coming of the Europeans. This large, decorated deer hide belonged to Powhatan, the leader of one such group. English colonists formed Jamestown, Virginia, near the Powhatan people. Relations between settlers and Indigenous peoples involved both trade and conflict.

A STRUGGLE TO SURVIVE
The first settlements were small and relied on trade with Indigenous peoples. This replica shows Plymouth, the town built at Cape Cod, Massachusetts, by the Pilgrims who sailed on the *Mayflower*. Although half the Pilgrims died in the first winter, their population had risen to 7,000 by 1690.

NORTH AMERICA IN 1754

Hudson Bay

Plymouth

Jamestown

Britain set up 13 colonies on the east coast.

Atlantic Ocean

Gulf of Mexico

KEY
- Britain
- France
- Spain
- Indigenous peoples

THE SPREAD OF SETTLEMENT
Over 250 years, European colonists spread across the east and south of America. British colonies dominated the Eastern Seaboard, while French people settled in Canada. Although Indigenous peoples already inhabited the land, both countries also claimed large areas in the north and west, though very few Europeans had traveled there. Some land was officially designated as belonging to the Indigenous peoples, but this was often ignored.

THE CANADIAN FUR TRADE
Beaver fur was used to make felt hats that were popular in Europe in this period. The desire to control the fur trade drove French colonization in what is now Canada. Colonists used canoes to travel down the St. Lawrence River and into the Great Lakes to trade guns and tools for furs from Indigenous trappers.

WHITE BEAVER FUR TOP HAT

SAFAVID SPLENDOR

The grand entrance to the Imam Mosque in Iran is covered with hundreds of intricately patterned tiles. In total, more than 475,000 cover the exterior of the building, glittering symbols of the power of the mosque's builder, Shah Abbas I. The Shah was the ruler of the Safavid Empire, an Islamic state that endured for more than two centuries between 1501 and 1736 and stretched from western Turkey across Persia to the mountains of Afghanistan. Abbas ordered the building of the mosque in 1611 as the centerpiece of Isfahan, his new capital city in the heart of the empire.

THE
QING DYNASTY
TAKES CONTROL OF CHINA

In 1644, the Qing swept across China from their homeland in Manchuria in the far north, toppling the ruling Ming dynasty. The Qing were Manchu people, while the majority of the Chinese population were Han. In their position as China's new rulers, the Qing combined elements from both Manchu and Han Chinese cultures.

▶ THE EIGHT BANNERS

Before the Manchus conquered China they had developed a way of organizing their society called the banner system. Every Manchu person was separated into one of eight groups, each marked by a different color banner and uniform. People lived, worked, and fought with other members of their banner. The Qing eventually absorbed other ethnic groups such as the Han into the banner system.

The banners were distinguished by the color of their armor.

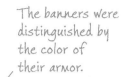

Long surcoats protected the legs.

MANCHU ARCHER

The Qing dynasty had a large and mobile army, which helped them conquer vast swathes of China rapidly. Many of their soldiers were horseback archers, who wielded bows made out of wood and raw bark.

Flag bears the dragon of the Qing dynasty.

IMPERIAL TOUR

The Kangxi Emperor reigned from 1661 to 1722. He was the third emperor of the Qing dynasty and was renowned for his interest in literature, the arts, and mathematics. He regularly toured China to assert his authority, inspect the empire, oversee his subjects, and maintain order.

A LEGAL HAIRSTYLE

Manchu men wore their hair in a style called the "queue" in which the front of the head was shaved and the remaining hair was braided. When the Qing conquered China, all males were required to wear the queue. Armed barbers traveled the country to ensure people had the cut.

QING CULTURE

The fifth Qing emperor, the Qianlong emperor was said to have published thousands of poems. His rule saw the development of what is today called Peking Opera, an elaborate form of theater that features music, acrobatics, and lavish costumes such as these.

SHOGUNS
SHAPE JAPAN

From the late 12th century, Japan was ruled by military leaders called shoguns. In 1603, a shogun named Tokugawa Ieyasu came to power. He was the first of the Tokugawa shoguns, who ruled Japan for more than 250 years—a time that came to be known as the Edo period. The shoguns brought peace and stability to Japan. However, they forced people to live in strict social classes, and in the 17th century, they banned foreign travel and closed Japan's borders to the outside world.

A peasant giving a back massage

FIRST TOKUGAWA SHOGUN
Tokugawa Ieyasu was the first of a long line of Tokugawa shoguns to rule Japan. The son of a daimyo (regional leader), he fought more than 90 battles on his way to power. He confiscated his rivals' lands and was appointed shogun by the emperor in 1603. Once in power, he made the other daimyos live in the capital Edo for several months a year in order to keep them under control.

The daimyo travelled in a private wooden box carried by peasants.

The samurai were trained warriors who kept law and order.

SOCIAL HIERARCHY
Japanese society during the Edo period was divided into strict social classes. The emperor, who was the ceremonial head of state, appointed the shogun, who ruled on his behalf. Next came the daimyo, or lords, and the samurai (aristocratic warriors). This scroll shows a procession of daimyo and samurai. They are accompanied by peasants, who were at the bottom of the social scale.

This wooden netsuke shows a samurai scholar reading a scroll.

FLOATING WORLD
Popular entertainment and culture flourished in Edo under the shoguns. Woodblock prints depicting scenes from everyday life were known as *ukiyo-e*, meaning "pictures of the floating world."

▲ JAPANESE NETSUKE

The production of netsuke—tiny figures of people, plants, and animals—was at its height during the Edo period. Carved from ivory or wood, netsuke were worn on men's sashes as a kind of toggle or button. The exquisitely carved netsuke shown here depict different aspects of Japanese life and culture.

CLOSED COUNTRY
The shoguns wanted to keep Japanese society free of foreign influences. They closed all Japan's ports, except for Dejima, a tiny artificial island in Nagasaki harbor, where Portuguese, and later Dutch, ships were allowed to trade.

Figure of a merchant carrying goods on his back

Ivory netsuke showing a samurai in combat with a hermit

Netsuke tucks over the sash from the back.

HOW NETSUKE WERE WORN
Many Japanese men wore traditional Japanese garments called kimonos. As kimonos had no pockets, items such as purses and pens were hung from their sashes on silk cords. A netsuke was affixed to the end of the cord to stop the objects from slipping off.

DEFENDING THE PORTS
Cargo ships in the Caribbean were especially vulnerable to pirate attacks. Strong fortifications were built to protect ports from pirate fleets that swooped out of island hideaways to raid defenseless ships.

FEARSOME FLAG
No one knows why the black flag bearing a grinning skull and crossbones was called the Jolly Roger, but it sent a terrifying message to anyone who saw it. Pirates flew the flag from the mast when they were about to attack.

Body displayed in a cage to deter other pirates

A PIRATE'S FATE
One of the most famous pirates in history was English sailor Captain William Kidd. In 1701, he was hanged in London for piracy after stealing a ship loaded with gold and silks in the Indian Ocean.

Kidd's body was left to swing over the Thames River for three years.

▶ HANGING CAGE
The British government sent special forces to clear the seas of pirates. Any pirate captain taken alive would face a grisly punishment. The pirate would be hanged, then his body left to rot inside an iron cage as a warning to others.

Iron bands held the victims' arms in place.

PIRATES
PLAGUE THE SEAS

Throughout history, pirates have prowled the world's seas and oceans in search of plunder. In the late 1600s, the Caribbean was one of the richest hunting grounds for pirates. Ruthless pirate captains lurked in the sea's warm waters, waiting to prey on Spanish treasure ships loaded with gold and other valuable cargo. As trade between Asia, the Americas, and Europe flourished, pirates attacked and robbed ships on every ocean of the world.

Clasps prevent the cage from opening.

This cage was never used—the pirate it was made for received a pardon.

PRIVATEERS

Piracy was not always considered a crime. European monarchs licensed sea captains, known as privateers, to attack enemy ships in return for a share of the profits. Sir Francis Drake was an English privateer who led many raids against Spanish ships in the late 1500s. This is a replica of his ship, the *Golden Hind*.

BARBARY PIRATES

For centuries, pirates operated out of ports on the North African coast, then known as the Barbary Coast, raiding coastal towns around the Mediterranean Sea and preying on Atlantic shipping routes. The US navy played a major role in defeating the pirates. This battle took place in Tripoli harbor, Libya, in 1804.

PIRATE QUEEN

Ching Shih was a Chinese pirate leader, who controlled the Red Flag Fleet that terrorized the South China Sea. To try to stop piracy in the region, the Chinese government issued an amnesty (pardon). Ching Shih surrendered her fleet and retired from pirate life in 1810.

THE
MUGHALS
UNIFY INDIA

The Mughals conquered and ruled over a large part of the Indian subcontinent from 1526 to 1857. Descended from the Mongols (see pages 122–123), these Muslim rulers unified the region and its people, many of whom were of different religious and cultural backgrounds. Many Mughal emperors took wives from Hindu Rajput families to forge alliances and extend control. Throughout this period, literature and arts flourished, while trade made the empire prosperous.

EMPEROR AKBAR
Babur founded the Mughal Empire in 1526, but it was his grandson Akbar (reigned 1556–1605) who expanded its territory and sought to bring together the large empire's diverse population. He introduced economic, religious, and social reforms, such as ending taxes that non-Muslims had previously been forced to pay. Akbar is portrayed on his throne in this miniature painting, an art form that was very popular with the Mughals.

▼ **WAR ELEPHANT**
A key reason why the Mughals were to able to reign for so long was their military might. They had a strong and technologically advanced army and used gunpowder, rockets, and grenades. Early on, they used traditional Indian war elephants, which made a fearsome sight and could trample enemies and batter fortifications. However, elephants were difficult to control in battle and were later used as a display of power rather than as war machines.

Spearman

Padded armor

An armored mahout (rider) controlled the animal, whose height provided a good overview of the battle.

Floral design in gold leaf on a Mughal cotton gown from the mid-18th century

TRADE AND TEXTILES

The Mughals gained a lot of wealth through international trade. They exported rice, indigo, raw cotton, and textiles. The luxurious cotton and silk fabrics used for Mughal gowns, and the elegant, thin cotton known as muslin, were the fabrics of choice for fashionable women in 18th-century Europe.

MUGHAL MARVEL

The Taj Mahal (above) was built by Emperor Shah Jahan to house the tomb of his second wife, Mumtaz Mahal. Completed in 1653, it took more than 20 years of hard work from thousands of laborers and elephants to build. It is a stunning example of Mughal architecture, inspired by Persian, Ottoman, Islamic, and Hindu traditions.

MODERN SCIENCE BEGINS

From about 1550, thinkers and scientists in Europe began making important discoveries in astronomy, medicine, and mathematics. Instead of relying on the teaching of the past, they tested new ideas by carrying out experiments and making their own observations. Their pioneering work laid the foundations of modern science.

PIONEERING ASTRONOMER
For centuries people believed that the Earth was at the center of the universe. In 1543, astronomer Nicolaus Copernicus published a book showing that the Earth and other planets orbit the sun.

THE SCIENTIFIC REVOLUTION
The 16th and 17th centuries saw a flood of exciting developments in science. The invention of instruments such as the telescope and the microscope led to new discoveries about the universe and the natural world. Scientists backed up their theories with precise calculations made possible by advances in mathematics.

GALILEO'S TELESCOPE
In 1609, Italian mathematician Galileo Galilei built a telescope to observe the heavens. He discovered the moons of Jupiter and supported the theory that the planets orbited the sun. His ideas got him into trouble with the Church.

NEWTON'S THEORIES
English scientist Isaac Newton's studies of light and motion form the basis of modern physics. He discovered that white light is made up of all colors, and that it is the force of gravity that keeps the planets moving around the sun.

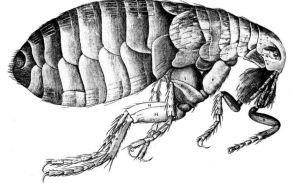

MINIATURE WORLD
Microscopes, invented around 1590, allowed scientists to observe objects too small to be seen with the naked eye. This detailed drawing of a flea comes from English scientist Robert Hooke's book *Micrographia*, published in 1665.

This 18th-century orrery shows only six planets—Uranus and Neptune had yet to be discovered.

▼ MODEL SOLAR SYSTEM
This mechanical model of the solar system, called an orrery, was used to demonstrate the movements of the planets and their moons. When a handle was turned, each planet moved on a separate path around the sun.

Framework of circles represents the heavens

Sun at the center, orbited by the planets

Saturn, with its rings and moons

Jupiter

Earth

OBSERVING NATURE

As travel between continents became easier, European artists and naturalists undertook journeys to record the plant and animal life of different places. Maria Sibylla Merian traveled with her daughter from her home in Amsterdam to Suriname in South America in 1699. Her paintings, such as this one of a spectacled caiman protecting its egg from a false coral snake, helped spread knowledge of the natural world. The image was included in the work of Carl Linnaeus, the Swedish scientist who invented the modern system of naming living things.

ABSOLUTE MONARCHS

Absolute monarchs rule with total power. They have complete control over their subjects, deciding the laws and when to go to war. In the 17th and 18th centuries, the rulers of European countries including Russia, France, Spain, and Denmark, reigned this way. These monarchs believed their power came directly from God—that it was their divine right to rule.

ROYAL SPLENDOR

Perhaps the best known of the absolute monarchs was the French king Louis XIV (r. 1643–1715). He was rightly known as the "Sun King"—everything in France orbited around him. He forced his nobles to live in the glittering palace he built for himself at Versailles, outside Paris, so that he could keep a close eye on them. The luxuries at court, as well as his costly wars, were paid for by collecting taxes from the French people. He ruled for 72 years, and made France the greatest power in Europe.

LOUIS XIV IN CORONATION ROBES

▼ **SYMBOL OF ROYAL POWER**
Crowns are a symbol of royal power dating back to ancient times. This golden crown, adorned with diamonds and four large precious stones, was made in 1671 for the coronation of King Christian V of Denmark. It was similar to that of Louis XIV, whom Christian admired – he also planned a Danish palace to rival the French Versailles.

The lily symbol of French royalty, known as the fleur-de-lis

Gold band decorated with diamonds, red garnets, and blue sapphires

STANDING ARMY

In medieval times, nobles provided kings with the soldiers they needed. But absolute monarchs took away the right of nobles to keep an army (and collect taxes and decide laws). Instead, rulers now kept their own armies of professional soldiers, always at the ready and with standardized uniforms and weapons. People had to pay high taxes to meet the enormous costs, which they bitterly resented, especially in times of hardship and famine.

Coronation crown

Orb symbolizing royalty

A cross positioned above the orb shows that only God is above the king.

ABSOLUTE MONARCH
Christian V ruled over Denmark and Norway from 1670 to 1699. He succeeded his father, Frederick III, who wrote absolute monarchy into Danish law. To further strengthen his royal power, Christian weakened the position of the Danish aristocracy by appointing German outsiders to offices of state.

END OF A KING
Britain's King Charles I (1625–1649) thought he could rule without Parliament, and upset many of his subjects by trying to impose his unpopular religious views on them. Civil war followed. Charles was captured, put on trial, and executed, and Britain temporarily became a republic under Oliver Cromwell.

PETER THE GREAT
TRANSFORMS RUSSIA

When Peter the Great became czar of Russia in 1682, his country was vast but old-fashioned and economically weak. Peter was determined to turn Russia into a modern, powerful state. He introduced new technologies from Europe and built a splendid new capital, St. Petersburg.

▶ **OUT WITH THE OLD**

The boyars, Russia's highest-ranking class of nobles, were fiercely traditional and slow to adapt to change. Peter ordered everyone at court to shave off their long beards and wear western clothes as a sign of modernity. Anyone who refused had to pay a tax. This caricature from 1698 shows Peter cutting off a reluctant boyar's beard.

Boyars, the nobles of medieval Moscow, traditionally had long beards.

THE YOUNG CZAR

Peter was only nine when he became joint czar with his half-brother Ivan. Warfare and ships fascinated Peter. On becoming sole ruler in 1696, he toured Europe to learn about the latest military and naval technologies, practicing shipbuilding in the process. He reigned until his death in 1725.

Peter, wielding scissors, is shown wearing European clothes and a barber's apron.

GROWING EMPIRE

When Peter became czar, Russia's territory was already huge, but it was landlocked in the west. Peter fought a war with Sweden to win access to the Baltic Sea. Under Catherine the Great (1762–1796), Russia expanded further, and even claimed territories in Alaska, North America.

KEY
- Russia by 1682
- Added to Russia by 1725
- Added to Russia by 1796

BUILDING A NAVY

Russia had no navy at all until Peter began building one from scratch. By the end of his reign, the Baltic fleet based at St. Petersburg boasted 49 warships and hundreds of smaller vessels. It was crucial in fighting Sweden, who dominated the Baltic region at this time. This is a replica of his first flagship, the *Shtandart*.

CHANGING CAPITALS

Though he was born in Moscow, the medieval capital of Russia, Peter always hated the city. In 1712, he moved the capital to St. Petersburg, the northern city he had founded by the Baltic Sea. The city boasted fine classical buildings designed by Italian architects.

PROGRESS UNDER CATHERINE

Catherine the Great, by birth a German princess, took the throne when her husband, Czar Peter III, died in 1762. Russia became an influential European power during her long reign. She brought scientists and philosophers to her court, and built an extensive fine art collection. She also led several successful military campaigns that increased the empire.

THE AGE OF ENLIGHTENMENT

In 18th-century Europe, exciting new ideas took hold. Writers and thinkers began to challenge existing beliefs about government, religion, and science, encouraging people instead to think for themselves. The ideas that sprang from this period, which came to be known as the Enlightenment, helped shape the modern world.

LIBERAL THINKER
French philosopher Voltaire played a leading role in the Enlightenment. Famous for his satirical writings in support of free speech and the freedom of religion, he was imprisoned twice by the French government.

The serving maid was usually the only woman to be seen inside a coffee house.

▲ EXCHANGE OF IDEAS
Drinking coffee was all the rage in the late 17th and 18th centuries, and the coffee houses that sprang up in major European cities were perfect places for exchanging views and ideas. These traditionally male-only establishments enabled thinkers, writers, and philosophers to sit together at long, communal tables and discuss news from the world of politics or hear about the latest scientific discoveries.

A server fetches coffee and a handful of clay pipes.

FEMALE RIGHTS

Women rarely had a voice during the Enlightenment. An exception was English writer Mary Wollstonecraft. In her book *A Vindication of the Rights of Woman*, she argued that education should be available to girls as well as boys, and that women deserved equal rights with men.

COLLECTING KNOWLEDGE

The *Encyclopédie* was one of the key works of the Enlightenment. Compiled by French philosopher Denis Diderot, this mammoth work of 28 volumes contained thousands of articles by leading Enlightenment thinkers.

Daily newspapers helped spread radical new ideas.

THE TRANSATLANTIC
SLAVE TRADE

Between the 16th and 19th centuries, European nations enslaved more than 12 million Africans. Taken from their homelands, people were shipped across the Atlantic and sold in the Americas where European colonies relied on enslaved labor. Among the enslaved, resistance began immediately, but it took more than 300 years before slavery was abolished (see pages 198–199).

▼ **SLAVE SHIP**
Enslaved Africans were taken across the Atlantic in ships, squashed together below deck with little room to move. The crossing could take up to 10 weeks. Attempted revolts were common, but rarely successful. This drawing shows the *Marie-Séraphique*, a French ship, packed with 307 enslaved men, women, and children.

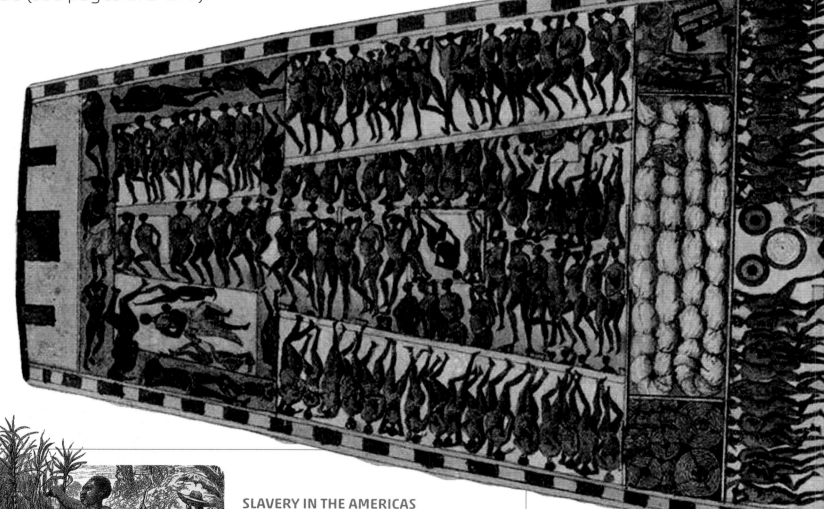

OVERHEAD PLAN OF THE 18TH-CENTURY SLAVE SHIP MARIE-SÉRAPHIQUE

SLAVERY IN THE AMERICAS
Enslaved people were forced to work on sugar, cotton, and tobacco plantations in the European colonies in the Caribbean, North America, and South America. From 1776, the newly formed United States relied heavily on slavery to build their nation. Conditions were hard and brutal. Many were beaten and abused, and those who tried to escape were severely punished if found.

THE MIDDLE PASSAGE

The forced Atlantic crossing was known as the "middle passage." It formed part of a system known as the "triangular trade." Set in place by European nations, this trade was based on ruthless profit. Ships never sailed empty, carrying goods from Europe to Africa; enslaved people from Africa to the Americas (the majority to Brazil); and products such as sugar, tobacco, and cotton back to Europe.

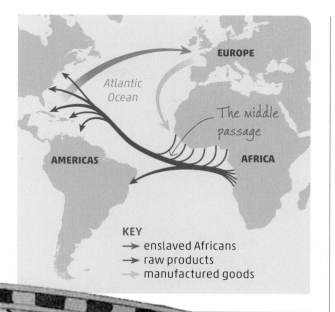

Atlantic Ocean

EUROPE

The middle passage

AMERICAS

AFRICA

KEY
→ enslaved Africans
→ raw products
→ manufactured goods

SLAVE FORTS

Slave forts were established by European trading companies along the West African coastline. They were designed to hold enslaved people, taken from further inland, until a ship came to collect them. This fort is Elmina Castle in current-day Ghana, which often kept up to 1,000 people in its dungeon.

Small storage areas held basic provisions for the journey.

CROSS SECTION of slave ship

Iron chains locked people together and to the wooden planks, stopping anyone from moving.

APPALLING CONDITIONS

Enslaved Africans were chained and placed in cramped conditions with no standing room. Forced to lie in their own filth, many became sick. Those who got sick were often thrown overboard. It is estimated that around two million Africans died on the crossing.

THE REDCOATS
British soldiers fighting in North America were known as Redcoats because of the color of their uniforms, as seen on the reenactors below. The British forces also included some German troops, called Hessians, and colonial soldiers who were still loyal to the British.

THE US FIGHTS FOR
INDEPENDENCE

In the 1760s, people living in the 13 colonies on the east coast of North America were ruled by Britain. The British government had just fought an expensive war against France, and it decided to raise money by taxing the colonists. Furious because they did not have a voice in the British Parliament, many colonists refused to pay. Angry protests and riots turned to revolution. The struggle for independence ended with British defeat in 1781, and the birth of a new nation—the United States of America.

PROTESTING THE STAMP ACT
The Stamp Act of 1765 was one of the first of the hated new taxes imposed by the British Parliament thousands of miles away. Outraged colonists took to the streets declaring "No taxation without representation." The protests were the first sign of the colonists' discontent with British rule.

▲ **AMERICAN REVOLUTION**
The first skirmishes in the war took place at Lexington and Concord, Massachusetts, in April 1775. The British Redcoats were successful at first, but in 1777 the Continental Army began to gain ground. The British finally surrendered at Yorktown, Virginia, in October 1781.

THE CONTINENTAL ARMY
George Washington was the commander-in-chief of the Continental Army, which he assembled to fight the British. They were made up of ill-equipped and barely trained soldiers, local militias, and volunteer troops. The mismatched uniforms on the reenactors below show that Washington's army was less well equipped than the British soldiers.

SEPARATION OF POWERS
The American Constitution of 1787 set out in writing how the new nation should be governed. Beginning with the words "We the People," it guaranteed the basic rights of American citizens. It also divided the government into three separate but equal branches—legislative, executive, and judicial—to prevent any branch of government from having power over another.

DECLARATION OF INDEPENDENCE
On July 4, 1776, representatives from all 13 colonies met in Philadelphia to sign the Declaration of Independence, a defiant statement that they were no longer under British rule. The former colonies were now a self-declared union of free and independent states responsible for governing themselves.

FIRST PRESIDENT
George Washington, who led the Continental Army to victory over the British, was unanimously elected as the first president of the United States in 1789. At that time, the government was based in New York City because Washington, D.C., hadn't yet been built. Washington's portrait still appears on every US one-dollar bill.

First Estate
(priests)

Second
Estate
(nobles)

Third Estate
(commoners)

AN UNFAIR SOCIETY
Glaring inequality and injustice fueled the Revolution. This cartoon shows an aristocrat and a priest—members of France's two wealthiest, but smallest, classes—riding on the back of a starving commoner who belongs to the largest class, the Third Estate.

REVOLUTION
SWEEPS FRANCE

On July 14, 1789, an angry mob, protesting against the King of France, attacked the Bastille, a royal fortress in Paris. Their actions started a revolution. Radical ideas spread quickly as the revolutionaries called for a fairer society under the slogan of "liberty, equality, and fellowship." The king and queen were placed under arrest and, later, executed. The monarchy was abolished and France became a republic.

WOMEN OF PARIS PROTEST
The Revolution inspired people from the poorer sections of society to take action. In October 1789, thousands of women from Paris, many armed with weapons, marched to the palace of Versailles to demand bread. Their resolve showed the new strength of the people.

The king's head was displayed to the crowd to prove he was dead.

Some accounts say the guillotine missed the king's neck and cut through the back of his jaw.

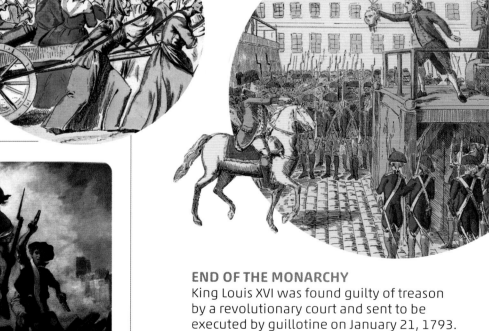

END OF THE MONARCHY
King Louis XVI was found guilty of treason by a revolutionary court and sent to be executed by guillotine on January 21, 1793. Huge crowds came to watch his execution. His unpopular wife, Queen Marie Antoinette, met the same fate 9 months later.

ENDURING IDEAS
The Revolution ended in violence and infighting but its ideas lived on, symbolized in this painting, "Liberty leading the People." Belief in equal rights and individual liberty influenced revolutionary uprisings in Europe and Latin America during the 19th century, and helped shape today's democratic governments.

The blade was angled for a cleaner cut.

The blade was raised by pulling a rope. Letting go of the rope sent the blade swiftly down onto the victim's neck.

▲ A SWIFT DEATH

The guillotine was designed to execute people as swiftly as possible. It was used to decapitate King Louis XVI as well as thousands of royal supporters. Later, as the leaders of the Revolution became more extreme, they guillotined former revolutionaries, who they now considered political enemies. In total almost 17,000 people were executed in what became known as the Reign of Terror.

The invention of **steam-powered machines** changed the way people around the world **worked**, **traveled**, and spent their **leisure time**. Many new technologies made life easier or more convenient for a **privileged few**, but not everyone was able to benefit. People began to campaign for **greater rights**, but the battles for **equality and justice** would be long and hard.

INDUSTRY

RISES

TIMELINE OF THE
AGE OF INDUSTRY

THE NEW FRENCH FLAG

No area of life was left unaltered by technological change during the industrial era. At the start of the period, horses were the fastest means of transportation, and people rarely traveled far from where they were born. By its end, cars and planes whisked people from place to place and new means of communication connected people on opposite sides of the globe.

1790

1792–1815
Revolutionary and Napoleonic Wars
Austria declares war on Revolutionary France in support of the deposed Louis XVI of France, who is executed in 1793. The fighting continues until Napoleon Bonaparte is defeated at the Battle of Waterloo.

A NEW JAPANESE RAILROAD

1869
Suez Canal opens
Built by the French diplomat and developer Ferdinand de Lesseps, the Suez Canal opens in Egypt. It connects the Mediterranean with the Red Sea and Indian Ocean.

1861–1865
US Civil War
Civil war breaks out in the United States as 11 Confederate states leave the Union. The Confederates are eventually defeated, and slavery is abolished in 1865.

GATLING GUN

1868
The Meiji Restoration
The shogun or military governor of Japan is overthrown and replaced by the emperor, as Japan begins a process of rapid modernization.

1867
The Dominion of Canada
The British provinces of Ontario, Quebec, Nova Scotia, and New Brunswick unite as the independent Dominion of Canada. They are later joined by British Columbia and Prince Edward Island.

1861
Unification of Italy
The northern Italian state of Piedmont, helped by French forces, evicts the Austrians from Italy. It then unites Italy under the rule of King Victor Emmanuel II.

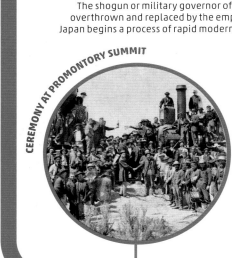

CEREMONY AT PROMONTORY SUMMIT

1876
The Indian Empire
After the demise of the British East Company in 1858 and the assumption of direct British rule, Queen Victoria becomes empress of India; her successors keep the title until 1947.

1884–1885
The Berlin Conference
Rival European powers meet in Berlin and settle their rival claims in Africa, dividing the continent between them. Only Liberia and Ethiopia remain independent.

BENZ PATENT-MOTORWAGEN

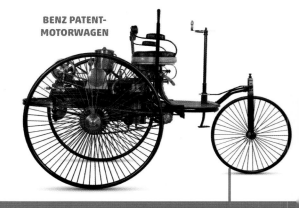

1869
Coast to coast rail
The Union Pacific and Central Pacific railroads meet at Promontory Point in Utah, completing the first transcontinental railroad in the US.

1871
German unification
The 27 German states are united, with Wilhelm I of Prussia as kaiser (emperor).

1876
The telephone
Scottish-born inventor and scientist Alexander Graham Bell patents the telephone. He first transmits a simple sentence and then a longer call.

BELL'S TELEPHONE

1886
First motor car
Designed and built by German engineer Carl Benz, the Benz Patent-Motorwagen is the world's first self-powered car. It has an internal combustion engine.

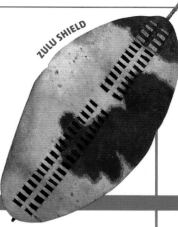

ZULU SHIELD

1796
World's first vaccine
English doctor Edward Jenner creates the first-ever vaccine. He injects an eight-year-old boy with cowpox as a remedy against smallpox, which is much more dangerous.

1803
Circumnavigating Australia
British sailor Matthew Flinders completes a voyage around Australia, proving that it is a single landmass.

1810–1821
Mexican independence
Mexico rebels against Spanish rule, eventually winning its independence. Colombia, Venezuela, and other South American nations do the same, winning independence by 1828.

JENNER ADMINISTERS A VACCINE

1807
Partial abolition of the slave trade
The British parliament outlaws the slave trade in the British Empire, although the practice of slavery remains legal until 1833.

DAGUERREOTYPE CAMERA

1816
Zulu Empire
Shaka becomes Inkosi, or king, of the Zulus, and uses advanced military tactics to expand his empire.

1842
China is opened up
After its defeat in the Opium Wars, China grants Britain trading rights. Later treaties give the same rights to other western nations.

1839
The first photographs
In France, Louis Daguerre invents the daguerreotype, the first publicly available photographic process.

1825
Public rail
The world's first public railroad to use steam locomotives opens in northeast England. It connects coal mines near Darlington to the port of Stockton.

1848
Year of Revolutions
Violent revolutions break out across Europe. Republics are proclaimed in Italy and a parliament is formed in Germany before most of the revolutions fail.

BESSEMER STEEL FURNACE

1855
Bessemer furnace
English inventor Henry Bessemer discovers a new and inexpensive industrial process to mass produce steel from molten pig iron. The process is used to make long-lasting steel rails for railroads.

THE WRIGHT FLYER

1895
The first movies
The public screening of movies, or motion pictures, begins in Paris with 10 short films shot by the Lumière brothers.

1903
First aircraft flight
On December 17, Orville Wright makes the first-ever powered flight, taking the *Wright Flyer* 120 ft (37 m) in 12 seconds. Orville and his brother Wilbur make three further flights on the same day.

1910

1890
Wounded Knee
The wars between the US and Indigenous nations end with a massacre of around 300 Lakota people at Wounded Knee, South Dakota.

1893
Women get the vote
New Zealand is the first country in the world to give women the national vote.

1904–1905
The Russo-Japanese War
Concerned by growing Russian influence in Korea, Japan declares war on Russia, destroying its fleet in Tsushima Strait and defeating its army at Mukden.

NAPOLEON
WAGES WAR IN EUROPE

Napoleon Bonaparte was a brilliant soldier who rose to become emperor of France. He made his name in the wars that followed the French Revolution, but then put an end to the new French Republic by declaring himself sole ruler. During his reign, he fought a series of wars to bring most of Europe under French rule. But after 20 years of almost continual warfare, his career ended in defeat and exile.

▶ NAPOLEON'S GRAND ARMY
These models represent soldiers and officers in Napoleon's Grand Army, which he formed in 1804 to fight his enemies across Europe. It was made up of recruits from many nations, and at its height numbered 685,000 men. Soldiers who showed skill and bravery in battle could be promoted to the top ranks, regardless of their background. There were many different roles, with uniforms to match—some of which are shown here. Model soldiers like these could be used for planning battles, but also became popular toys.

Heavy cavalrymen wore steel breastplates and rode sturdy war horses.

Hussars (light cavalrymen) were used for scouting.

Drummers gave a steady beat during battle.

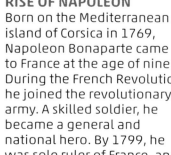

RISE OF NAPOLEON
Born on the Mediterranean island of Corsica in 1769, Napoleon Bonaparte came to France at the age of nine. During the French Revolution, he joined the revolutionary army. A skilled soldier, he became a general and national hero. By 1799, he was sole ruler of France, and in 1804 he crowned himself Emperor Napoleon I.

ON THE BATTLEFIELD
The Grand Army's victory at the Battle of Austerlitz (1805) gave Napoleon control of most of Germany. Here, he is seen on the battlefield on his white horse, just about to receive the message of victory.

Mamluk cavalryman recruited in Middle East

General in a bicorne (two-cornered) hat

Member of the elite Imperial Guard

KEY
- French Empire (1812)
- Conquered states and allies
- Nations against Napoleon (1813)

Atlantic Ocean

EUROPE

ASIA

Mediterranean Sea

AFRICA

NAPOLEON'S EUROPE
The French Empire in 1812 was much larger than France today. Napoleon's armies occupied most of Germany, Italy, Poland, and Spain while some countries were his allies. From early 1813, Britain, Russia, Prussia, Austria, Sweden, Portugal, and Sardinia joined forces to finally defeat him—it took until 1815, at the Battle of Waterloo.

THE BONAPARTE FAMILY
Napoleon Bonaparte was part of a large family. He placed his siblings on the royal thrones of Europe, including his brother Joseph (king of Spain) and Louis (king of Holland). His sister Caroline became queen of Naples, while others were made duchesses.

DEFEAT AND EXILE
In 1812, Napoleon invaded Russia. It was a terrible mistake. He reached Moscow but was forced to retreat just as winter was setting in. Most of his army died on the brutal journey home. It was the beginning of the end, and in 1815 the defeated Napoleon was exiled to the small island of St. Helena, far out in the Atlantic.

THE COLONIZATION OF AUSTRALIA

First Nations peoples have lived in Australia for thousands of years. Europeans began exploring the Pacific Ocean from the 15th century, looking for places to trade and set up colonies. However, it was not until the 18th century that Britain started building settlements on the Australian coast. Colonists forced First Nations peoples off their lands, destroying their lives, families, and culture in the process. The pattern of injustice and discrimination continues, and is only slowly being addressed today.

The **BULLET** traveled straight through the wooden shield

Handle made of red mangrove

▼ THE MOMENT OF CONTACT

This shield was carried by Cooman, a warrior of the Gweagal people, who lived in the area around Kamay (Botany Bay). In 1770, he was shot by British troops under the command of James Cook, who had landed in Kamay without permission. Cooman's shield was stolen and taken to Britain. It is now housed in the British Museum but there is a campaign to return it to the Gweagal people.

A CONNECTION TO COUNTRY

First Nations peoples have a close, interconnected relationship with their lands, waterways, and seas. This is called Country. Some sites have particular significance, including caves, springs, and mountains. Europeans dismissed First Nations people's ownership and claimed the land belonged to no one and could be taken.

HMS *ENDEAVOUR*

Although Europeans had been exploring the Pacific for many years, the first European to map the east coast of Australia was the Briton James Cook in the ship *Endeavour*. Cook and his crew had already traveled to the Pacific Islands and New Zealand when they arrived at Australia.

A THRIVING COLONY

In 1788, Britain declared that Australia was its colony. The first settlers were British convicts, sent to Australia against their will. They were forced to farm and build roads. After finishing their sentences, they could marry and buy land. From 1793, free settlers also arrived and the population grew rapidly. One of the main exports was wool, which was gathered on large sheep farms.

IMPACT OF COLONIZATION ON FIRST NATIONS PEOPLES

This is the flag of First Nations Australians. Although progress is being made toward justice, colonization inflicted great pain on the First Nations peoples. Many people died from diseases brought by the Europeans or were killed in the Frontier Wars with settlers, and land that had been theirs for generations was stolen.

Toussaint
Louverture

SLAVE REBELLIONS

Slave rebellions were frequent, and drew public attention to slavery. One of the largest took place in the French Caribbean colony of St-Domingue in 1791–1804. Led by Toussaint Louverture, the uprising was successful and led to the founding of the republic of Haiti.

THE UNDERGROUND RAILROAD

The Underground Railroad was not an actual railroad, but a secret network used by enslaved Americans to escape to places such as Canada, where they could be free. Harriet Tubman, who herself had escaped from slavery, worked within this network, helping to free at least 70 others.

Harriet Tubman

▶ THE ABOLITIONIST MOVEMENT

It took several centuries of protest from Black and white abolitionists for Western nations to abolish slavery. This happened at different times in different countries. Conditions for those who gained freedom remained awful in many circumstances, and the injustices of slavery had long-lasting impacts.

SUPPORT GROWS

From the late 1700s, many within Britain, particularly those of the Quaker religion, campaigned for abolition, often by starting petitions. This is an illustration from an 1826 children's book against slavery, called *The Black Man's Lament*.

A petition against slavery with many signatures

BRITAIN ABOLISHES SLAVE TRADE

In 1807, Britain abolished the slave trade due to pressure from many abolitionists, including Olaudah Equiano. A formerly enslaved man of Igbo descent, he wrote an autobiography which shined a light on the many horrors of slavery. Britain abolished slavery throughout its empire in 1833.

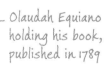

Olaudah Equiano holding his book, published in 1789

ABOLITIONISTS
FIGHT TO END SLAVERY

The transatlantic slave trade went on for more than 300 years. Throughout this long period, many enslaved Black people rebelled. Some who escaped wrote books exposing the truth about slavery and spoke out against it. But it was only in the 19th century, and as more white abolitionists joined their cause, that the slave trade, and later slavery itself, became outlawed in Europe and the Americas.

FREDERICK DOUGLASS

Frederick Douglass
continued to campaign for
civil rights until his death
at the age of 77, in 1895.

THE AMERICAN MOVEMENT
In the US, the struggle to end slavery
intensified from the 1830s. One of the most
active abolitionists was Frederick Douglass,
a man who had escaped slavery and then
traveled the world campaigning. Above, he
is depicted giving a speech at an abolitionist
meeting in Tremont Temple, Boston, in 1860,
which was broken up by the police and a
mob of anti-abolitionist citizens.

LAW CHANGES IN THE US
Sojourner Truth was a formerly
enslaved woman who became a
prominent abolitionist, seen
here meeting US President
Abraham Lincoln in 1864. By
1865, Congress passed the 13th
amendment of the US Constitution
which banned slavery except as
punishment for a crime.

LATIN AMERICA
WINS INDEPENDENCE

For around 300 years, huge stretches of South and Central America were ruled as colonies by Spain and Portugal. In the late 18th century, Spain introduced new laws that allowed only people born in Spain to hold important jobs in the colonies. This angered South American-born people, and they began to resent Spanish control. In the early 19th century, while Europe was distracted by the Napoleonic Wars, leaders across Latin America started to fight for independence.

▶ WINNING VICTORY

Small, local struggles broke out across Latin America, eventually becoming two major independence movements with separate leaders. In the north was Simón Bolívar, a soldier. In the south was another military officer, José de San Martín. They fought a series of battles against troops loyal to Spain, liberating Latin America one region at a time. This painting shows the final victory at the Battle of Carabobo, in 1821, when the Spanish surrendered by handing their flag to Simón Bolívar.

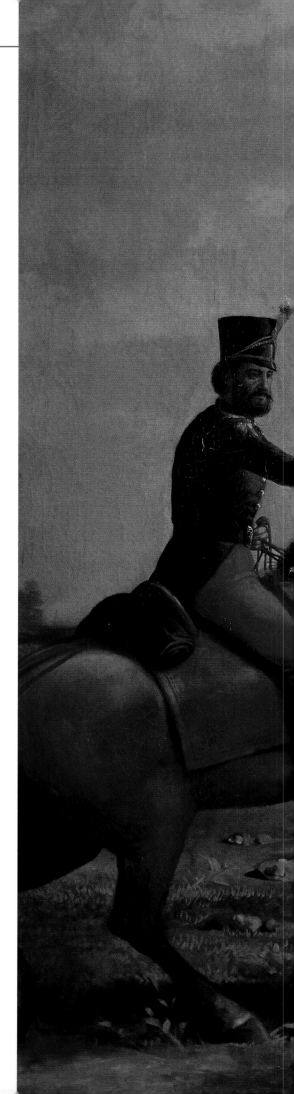

NEW NATIONS

Between 1808 and 1828 almost all of South and Central America broke free from European control. This map shows the year when each area became independent, and from which colonial power. The huge areas that had been controlled by Spain broke up into smaller independent states, each with their own governments.

MEXICO 1821

BRITISH GUIANA 1831

SURINAM 1815

GRAN COLOMBIA 1819

FRENCH GUIANA 1815

FEDERAL REPUBLIC OF CENTRAL AMERICA 1821

PERU 1821

BRAZIL 1822

BOLIVIA 1825

In 1840 this country split into several smaller states.

PARAGUAY 1811

Atlantic Ocean

UNITED PROVINCES OF LA PLATA 1816

URUGUAY 1828

Pacific Ocean

CHILE 1817

This state later broke up and became the new nation of Argentina.

Patagonia was never colonized.

KEY
- Spain
- Portugal
- Britain
- France
- The Netherlands

SOUTH AMERICA 1808-1826

GRAN COLOMBIA

Bolívar dreamed of uniting Spanish-speaking parts of the Americas into a single country. In 1819, he became President of Gran Colombia, a state that covered much of northern South America. Its flag is pictured here. However, his republic quickly fell apart, and split into smaller countries called Venezuela, Colombia, Panama, and Ecuador.

THE CRY OF FREEDOM

In Mexico, the fight for liberty began with a speech by a priest, Father Miguel Hidalgo y Costilla, in 1810. He called for the end of Spanish rule, for equality, and for land to be shared fairly. He was executed, but rebellion carried on until independence was declared in 1821.

SAME RULER, NEW EMPIRE

In 1807, the Portuguese royal family escaped Napoleon by relocating to their Brazilian colony. Later, the king returned to Portugal, leaving his son Pedro to rule Brazil. In 1822 Pedro (pictured) declared Brazil independent from Portugal, with him as its emperor.

THE INDUSTRIAL REVOLUTION

Rapid technological advances in late 18th-century Britain made it quicker and easier to manufacture goods. This led to a revolution in how people worked. Water- and later steam-powered machines could swiftly do jobs that people had previously done slowly and painstakingly by hand. Many workers moved from farms in the countryside to new industrial towns.

Looms weave cotton threads into cloth.

COTTAGE INDUSTRIES
Before the Industrial Revolution, goods such as textiles were made by hand in people's homes, or cottages. Spinning wheels like this one turned woollen or cotton fibers into thread to make clothes. They were often operated by women.

Water-powered spinning frames spin cotton fibers into thread.

WORKING CONDITIONS
Early factories employed men, women, and children. Factory workers no longer owned what they made—instead they gave the products of their work to their employers in return for a wage. Hours were long, pay was low, and conditions were grim and dangerous. From the 1830s, laws began to restrict working hours and the use of child labor.

HARNESSING STEAM POWER
Originally developed to pump water out of mines, from the 1780s the steam engine was used to power industrial machinery. The engine was driven by the steam produced from burning coal to boil water. Factories powered by steam could be built anywhere with a regular coal supply, so industrial towns and cities grew up around coal mines.

▲ TEXTILE MILL
Cotton production was the first industry to be mechanized. Early cotton mills relied on fast-flowing rivers to turn their giant water wheels. As the wheels turned, they transferred power to huge machines such as spinning frames that could spin 96 threads at once, far more than had been possible before. These water-powered machines made the mass production of cheap fabric possible.

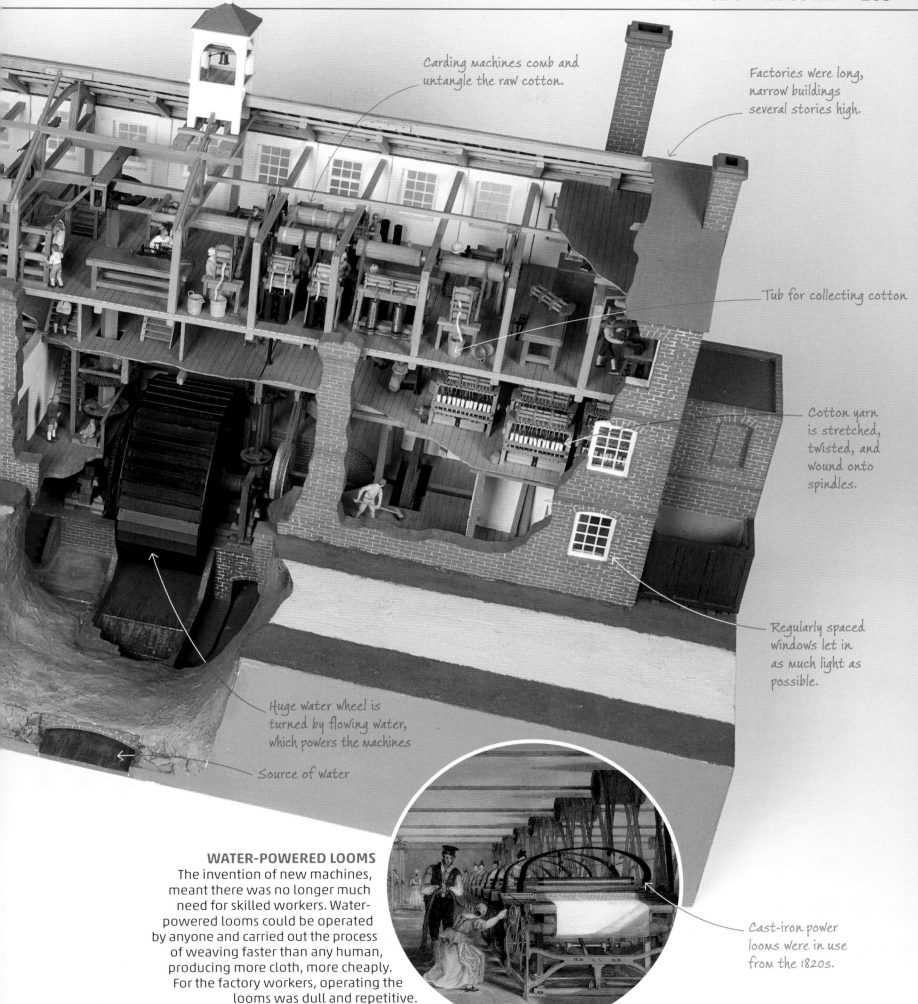

Carding machines comb and untangle the raw cotton.

Factories were long, narrow buildings several stories high.

Tub for collecting cotton

Cotton yarn is stretched, twisted, and wound onto spindles.

Regularly spaced windows let in as much light as possible.

Huge water wheel is turned by flowing water, which powers the machines

Source of water

WATER-POWERED LOOMS
The invention of new machines, meant there was no longer much need for skilled workers. Water-powered looms could be operated by anyone and carried out the process of weaving faster than any human, producing more cloth, more cheaply. For the factory workers, operating the looms was dull and repetitive.

Cast-iron power looms were in use from the 1820s.

THE DAWN OF A NEW ERA

The village of Coalbrookdale in Shropshire, UK, is often said to be the birthplace of the Industrial Revolution. The Coalbrookdale ironworkers realized how to use coal to cheaply and efficiently make large quantities of iron, which could easily be formed into larger and more complex items. The ironworks went on to experiment with and produce a wide range of industrial machines including early steam engines. Although at the time of this painting horses were still used to haul the iron, the age of industrialization and mechanization had begun.

▶ THE YEAR OF REVOLUTIONS

The revolutions of 1848 started with uprisings in France and Italy and spread across Europe. In some countries calls for reform were peaceful, but many of the revolutions were violent, with soldiers and protesters fighting in the streets. By the end of the year, many governments had regained control.

The king's throne was burned on the streets of Paris.

**FEBRUARY:
ANTI-MONARCHY RIOTS IN FRANCE**
In France, political meetings were banned to prevent people from criticizing King Louis-Philippe. Angry people poured into the streets of Paris, and riots began. Eventually, the king was overthrown, and the French monarchy was replaced by an elected government. All men were given the right to vote.

Austrian troops were forced to retreat through the Porta Tosa in Milan.

**MARCH:
UPRISING IN ITALY**
Large parts of northern Italy were ruled by the Austrian Empire. Rebellions sprang up in favor of uniting into one independent nation. After street fighting the Austrians were forced to retreat, but the revolutionaries failed to cooperate and the Austrians returned later in the year.

REVOLUTION GRIPS EUROPE

In the 19th century, many people in Europe were unhappy with how they were being ruled. They wanted more personal freedom, political change, and to have a part in ruling their own countries. In 1848, a wave of revolutions swept the continent. Although the protests were eventually suppressed, they awakened a new desire for national unity in divided countries such as Germany and Italy.

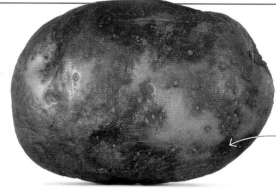

Black patches show the potato is rotten.

FAMINE IN EUROPE

Just before the revolutions, a disease called potato blight caused crops to fail all across Europe. In Ireland, around a million people died of starvation. The hunger and desperation were part of the reason so many people joined revolutions to demand change.

KARL MARX AND THE COMMUNIST MANIFESTO

German thinker Karl Marx wrote the *Communist Manifesto* in 1848, around the same time the wave of revolutions began. His book outlined a vision of a new system without private property in which all goods would be shared equally among the people.

The mythical warrior Germania represented the German nation.

RISE OF NATIONS

Many revolutionaries felt that people who shared the same language should be united in a single nation, not divided into small states or ruled by a different country. Despite revolutions failing, this new nationalist spirit survived and quickly began to gain popularity.

APRIL: REVOLUTION IN BERLIN

In the many small German-speaking states, people wanted the right to vote for their leaders, and to come together as a single, united country. Fighting broke out in the streets of Berlin, with calls for a new elected assembly.

OCTOBER: COUNTERREVOLUTION

An uprising of students, workers, and mutinous soldiers took place in Vienna, the capital of the Austrian Empire. The emperor fled the violence, and was forced to abdicate. However, before long, the army reoccupied the city, crushed the revolution, and placed the old emperor's nephew on the throne.

Imperial troops march back into Vienna after bombarding the city.

UNDERSTANDING DISEASE

Even with anesthetics, surgery was still very risky. In 1861, French scientist Louis Pasteur proved that some diseases were spread by "germs" entering the body. His germ theory showed that infections could be avoided by keeping wounds clean.

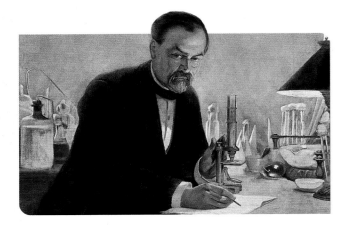

KEEPING GERMS AWAY

After germ theory was accepted, doctors began to introduce hygiene measures—wearing clean aprons and washing hands with soap. Wounds were sprayed with carbolic acid, and surgical instruments and dressings were sterilized with steam.

SURGERY TODAY

These breakthroughs opened the way for surgery today. With modern hygiene methods the risks are much reduced. Now, surgeons can replace failing organs, work on a minute scale with tiny cameras, and can even be assisted by robots.

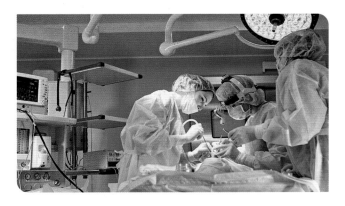

MODERN SURGERY IS BORN

Before the 19th century, surgery was a grisly business. There was little knowledge of cleanliness and no pain relief available, which meant any operation had to be basic and quick. Medicine was revolutionized by a series of breakthroughs, and pain-numbing anesthetics allowed surgeons to undertake more complicated operations than ever before. These developments paved the way for the cutting edge surgeries possible today.

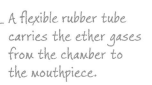

A flexible rubber tube carries the ether gases from the chamber to the mouthpiece.

▶ PAINLESS SURGERY

In the early days of medicine, surgery was very crude. The pain was intolerable and patients were unlikely to stay still. Anesthetics revolutionized surgery—they caused a temporary loss of sensation while the surgeon operated. Early anesthetics such as ether were inhaled, and left the patient completely unconscious. Surgery on quiet, still patients was safer, and more complex operations could be attempted.

EARLY ANESTHETIC
The first successful operation using an anesthetic was performed by a Japanese surgeon in 1804, years before anesthesia was attempted in the West. Hanaoka Seishū developed an herbal drink to put patients to sleep. He is pictured here performing an operation on an anesthetized patient with breast cancer.

Turning the control valve releases ether into the tube.

USING THE INHALER
In 1846, US surgeon William Morton was the first to publicly show the use of ether as an anesthetic. His patient inhaled the ether, making him unconscious. Morton was then able to operate, with his patient still and feeling no pain.

A mouthpiece fits over the patient's mouth and nose so they can inhale the fumes.

Ether gases collect in the glass chamber.

Ether-soaked sponges

ZULU WARRIORS
DEFEND THEIR KINGDOM

Large feather headdresses were intended to intimidate the enemy.

The province of Natal in southern Africa is the homeland of the Zulus. From 1816 to 1828, the Zulus were ruled by King Shaka, who led raids on neighboring groups to create a great Zulu kingdom. In the late 1870s, the Zulus were forced to defend their territory in a six-month war against the British. They were eventually defeated, and the Zulu kingdom became part of the British Empire. Today, there are roughly 11 million Zulus living in South Africa, making them the largest ethnic group in the country.

ZULU KING
King Shaka, also known as Shaka Zulu, was famed for his military skills. He revolutionized the Zulu army with new weapons and tactics. A ruthless fighter, he led attacks on neighboring villages and forced their people to become part of the Zulu state. In 1828, he was murdered by his half-brother Dingane.

BUFFALO HORN FORMATION
Shaka Zulu introduced a new battle formation known as the buffalo horn. The strongest fighters were placed at the chest, where they fought their enemies head on. The younger, faster fighters formed the horns, which encircled enemy troops, while the older, weaker soldiers fought from the loins at the rear.

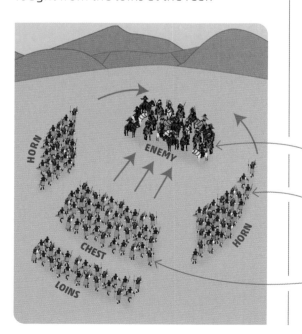

HORN

ENEMY

CHEST

HORN

LOINS

Enemy forces

The buffalo horn formation was used to attack and encircle enemy forces.

Zulu forces

FIERCE WARRIORS
Zulu warriors were highly trained and disciplined. They were divided into regiments, each with its own distinct uniform. In battle, soldiers carried shields made of ox skin and wore ornate headdresses decorated with feathers.

▼ WEAPONS OF WAR

Zulu soldiers were traditionally armed with shields, wooden clubs, and long throwing spears called *assegai*. Shaka Zulu introduced a shorter, stabbing spear, called an *ixwa*. During the Anglo-Zulu War, the Zulus also fought the British with firearms, such as muskets and rifles.

Strips were cut into the oval-shaped shield in order to attach a pole.

Long-bladed spear, or assegai, was thrown at enemy forces

Wooden club was used for both throwing and striking

BRITISH CONQUEST

During the Anglo-Zulu War in 1879, the Zulu army won several battles against the British. Their most decisive victory was at the Battle of Isandlwana, where more than 1,000 British soldiers were killed. The Zulus were eventually defeated at the Battle of Ulundi (pictured below) and their king, Cetshwayo, was sent into exile.

Food
storage

Metal
lantern

Frames to hold
canvas cover

Cooking
utensils

Driver's
seat

Bedroll

Pots and pans

CHUCK WAGON, 1800s

AMERICA EXPANDS
WEST

In 1776, when the US won independence from Britain, it consisted only of territory along the east coast. However, the new country quickly began to expand. From 1803, tens of thousands of people moved westward, believing it was the destiny of the new nation to control the land. In just 50 years, it had laid claim to a huge swathe of North America. In the process many Indigenous peoples were displaced from their ancestral lands and their cultures destroyed.

◀ **CHUCK WAGON**
Settlers moved west across the Great Plains in horse-drawn covered wagons, which were loaded with goods. They often traveled in convoy for safety, one wagon following another in a "wagon train." The wagon pictured here is a chuck wagon, which was used to carry food and cooking equipment.

OREGON TRAIL
Many settlers, miners, farmers, and ranchers made their way west along the Oregon Trail, a perilous route which stretched some 2,170 miles (3,490 km) east from Independence, Missouri, to Oregon City. Travelers included European migrants (eager to acquire farming land), Black Americans, and Latin Americans.

For safety, wagons formed a circle at night or when under attack.

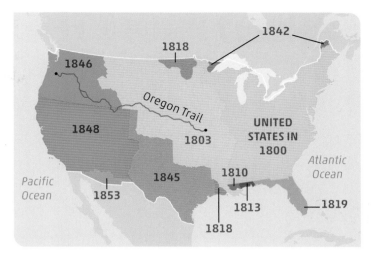

GAINING TERRITORIES
In 1800, large areas of North America were owned by other countries, including France, Britain, Spain, and Mexico. The US grew its territory by purchasing the land or claiming it through wars. This map shows the year when each area was acquired.

THE GOLD RUSH
The discovery of gold in California in 1848 brought nearly 300,000 people to the region. So many people panned for gold in the rivers that the first deposits were soon gone. The gold rush turned California into a major state.

TRAIL OF TEARS
The US's expansion forced some 60,000 Indigenous peoples to leave their ancestral homelands and travel thousands of miles along the Trail of Tears to reservations (see pages 214–215). Cherokee Elizabeth "Betsy" Brown was a survivor of the Trail of Tears.

FORCED FROM THEIR
HOMELANDS

As the US expanded, white settlers pushed Indigenous peoples out of ancestral homes they had lived in for thousands of years, breaking the bond between people and land. Many Indigenous peoples resisted, and even lost their lives fighting for their homes, but the US enforced the removals and people had no choice but to relocate.

LIFE ON THE RESERVATION
From the mid 1800s, all Indigenous peoples were forced onto reservations—land assigned to them by the US government. The US tried to eradicate traditional ways of life, and children on reservations were often forced to attend government-run schools such as the one in the background here.

FORCED RESETTLEMENT
The 326 Indigenous reservations in the US today make up just 2.3 percent of the country's total area, representing a huge loss of land. Due to forced relocations, many Indigenous nations have lost connection with their original homelands and some tribes have disappeared entirely.

Chinook
Yakima
Nez Perce
Crow
Lakota
CANADA
Abenaki
Massachusett
Iroquois
Pequot
Pomo
Cheyenne
Lenape
Shoshone
Arapaho
Pawnee
Miami
Powhatan
Paiute
Shawnee
Ute
Chumash
Navajo
Cherokee
Pueblo
Chickasaw
Apache
Comanche
Creek
Choctaw
Seminole
Gulf of Mexico

KEY
■ Current Indigenous land
■ Historic Indigenous land

Horses were extremely important to the Plains nations.

Guns were obtained through trade conducted at forts built by the US.

A US soldier rides with an Indigenous American. Some tribes fought alongside the US at times.

Plains people lived in tepees, portable dwellings made of buffalo hide. They are still used for ceremonial purposes today.

◄ PAINTED BUFFALO HIDE

This is a winter count—a way of recording history for future generations. It belongs to one of the Plains nations. Each pictograph (picture) represents a single significant event. This winter count covers the period in the 1800s when the US was forcing the Plains tribes to live on reservations. It shows that there were times of trade and cooperation, as well as conflict.

TELLING THE STORY

Indigenous peoples do not write their history. Instead, it has to be remembered and passed from generation to generation by a storyteller who uses tools such as winter counts to help recall events. This storyteller is from the Lakota nation.

Each feather in a headdress is sacred and has to be earned.

CLAN MOTHERS

After the forced relocation, family became more important than ever. Many Indigenous peoples trace their line of descent through the mother. A Clan Mother at the head of each family makes all the important decisions affecting its welfare.

THE BRITISH RULE
INDIA

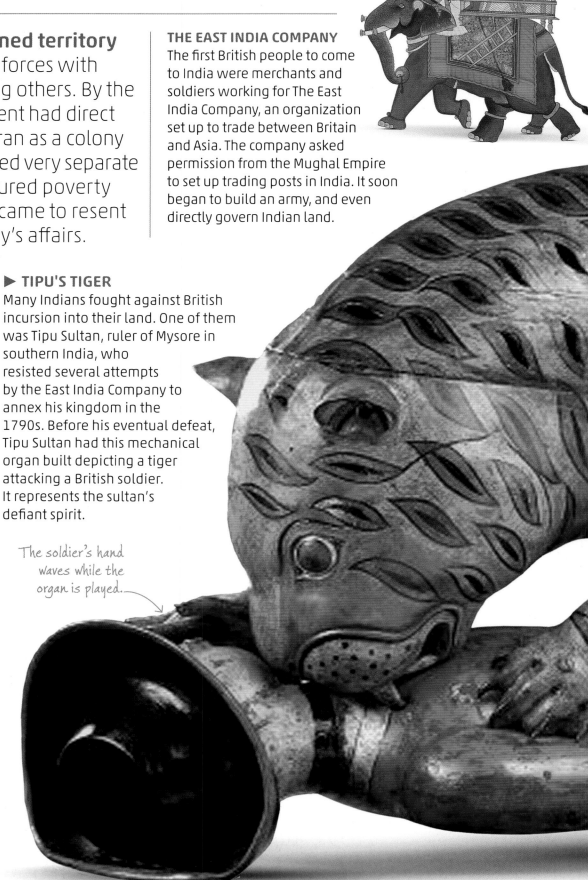

In the 18th century, Britain gained territory and influence in India by joining forces with some Indian rulers and conquering others. By the 19th century, the British government had direct control of much of India, which it ran as a colony to enrich Britain. British officials lived very separate lives from most Indians, who endured poverty and sometimes famine and who came to resent British domination of their country's affairs.

THE EAST INDIA COMPANY
The first British people to come to India were merchants and soldiers working for The East India Company, an organization set up to trade between Britain and Asia. The company asked permission from the Mughal Empire to set up trading posts in India. It soon began to build an army, and even directly govern Indian land.

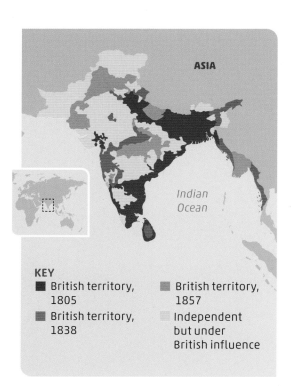

ASIA

Indian
Ocean

KEY
- ■ British territory, 1805
- ■ British territory, 1838
- ■ British territory, 1857
- ☐ Independent but under British influence

▶ TIPU'S TIGER
Many Indians fought against British incursion into their land. One of them was Tipu Sultan, ruler of Mysore in southern India, who resisted several attempts by the East India Company to annex his kingdom in the 1790s. Before his eventual defeat, Tipu Sultan had this mechanical organ built depicting a tiger attacking a British soldier. It represents the sultan's defiant spirit.

The soldier's hand waves while the organ is played.

GROWING BRITISH TERRITORY
The first British trading posts were set up by the East India Company with permission from the Mughal emperors in the 17th century. Later, the company took other areas from the empire by force. By the middle of the 19th century, Britain had direct control of much of India and even states that remained independent were subject to British influence.

THE REBELLION OF 1857
Throughout this period there were several military uprisings. The largest, in 1857, was sparked by the British insistence that Indian soldiers bite open gun cartridges that were rumored to be oiled with pig and cow fat, which was offensive to Hindus and Muslims. After the rebellion, the British government replaced the East India Company as rulers of India.

INDIAN NATIONAL CONGRESS
Resistance to the injustices of British rule grew, and in 1885, the Indian National Congress was established. This was a political movement made up of 72 delegates, one from each province. In its first few years, during a time of widespread poverty, it fought for Indians to have more rights under colonial rule. However, by the 20th century it was leading the struggle for independence from Britain.

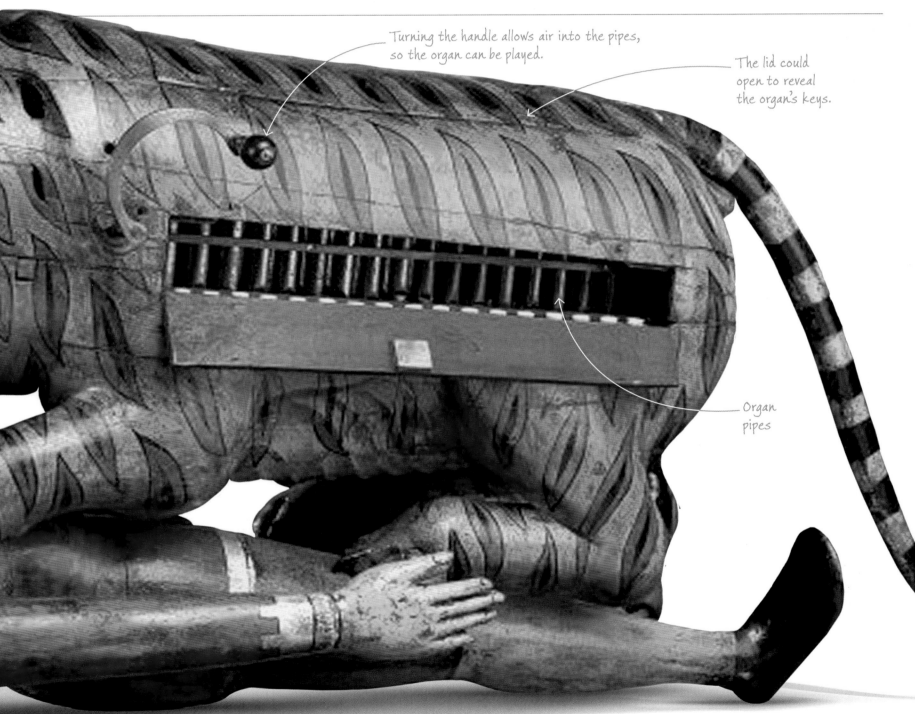

Turning the handle allows air into the pipes, so the organ can be played.

The lid could open to reveal the organ's keys.

Organ pipes

STEAM TRAINS OPEN UP THE WORLD

The coming of the railroads transformed the world.
For the first time, goods and people could travel long distances and at speeds no one had ever imagined. The first steam-engine passenger line opened in 1825 in Britain, and within 30 years railroad networks were spreading across the world, from Europe and the United States to parts of Asia and Africa. The railroads employed thousands of workers, boosted industry, and improved trade.

Chimney released steam and fumes

The boiler had to be well built to withstand the tremendous pressure that built up inside.

2. Steam pressure builds up inside the boiler.

1. Fire generated by burning coal heats the water in the boiler to make steam.

3. Pistons move, turning the wheels.

HOW A STEAM ENGINE WORKS
When coal is heated in a furnace it boils water, creating steam. The steam is forced into metal rods called pistons, which are connected to the train wheels. The force of the steam is so powerful it drives the pistons, which move the wheels.

EIR 22

The cowcatcher moved any obstacles off the track, so the train didn't have to stop.

▼ STEAM LOCOMOTIVE

The first steam locomotive was built in 1804, and by 1812 a commercially successful steam train for hauling coal ran in Britain. The US and Germany were not far behind. Locomotives, such as the 1855-built *Fairy Queen*, were made in Britain and taken to India. Britain and other European countries built railways to help them expand their empires in India and much of Africa.

Cabin protected the firebox underneath, where the coal was burned

STANDARD TIME

Before the railroads, time was slightly different from town to town. With the introduction of railroad networks, standard times were imposed in each country in order to create timetables, as well as publicize opening hours for stores and services.

BUILDING BRIDGES

The creation of great railroad networks, such as the Trans-Siberian Railway, created new job opportunities, from coal mining to iron and steel production. Skilled engineers designed great bridges to carry railroads over seemingly impassable regions.

TRANSCONTINENTAL RAILROAD

In North America, the first transcontinental railroad was completed in 1869, to much fanfare. Stretching 1,912 miles (3,077 km), it connected the eastern rail network with the Pacific Ocean in the west.

Japanese travel poster from 1935 promotes train journeys to Yamanashi Prefecture to see Mount Fuji

Wheels pushed this train to a maximum speed of 25 mph (40 km/h)

SEEING THE WORLD

Railroads revolutionized passenger travel, enabling people to travel for work and pleasure. A global tourism industry sprang up that ranged from cheap seaside trips to luxurious journeys on trains such as the Orient Express, which originally ran from Paris, France, to Istanbul, Turkey.

Abraham Lincoln, president of the United States, was morally opposed to slavery, but never called himself an abolitionist.

The eagle was a unifying symbol of the United States.

THE UNION
The 23 Union states had large, industrial cities, with plenty of opportunities and jobs available. As a result, they did not rely on enslaved labor, unlike the South. The North went to war in order to restore the Confederate States to the Union.

UNION $10 BANK NOTE

▶ ONE NATION, TWO GOVERNMENTS
During the Civil War, both the Union and Confederacy printed their own money. The imagery on these two bills reflects the two side's ideals. The North wanted to show that the country was stronger when it was united while the Southerners tried to present slavery in a positive light.

BATTLE OF GETTYSBURG
There were many battles in the Civil War, but the Confederate invasion of the North at Gettysburg, Pennsylvania, in 1863 was a turning point. The Union won after a three-day fight, and the Confederates never penetrated the North in force again.

In the early part of the war, the Southern capital was Montgomery, Alabama.

CIVIL WAR
DIVIDES THE UNITED STATES

Almost 100 years after independence, the US remained divided over slavery. Southern states allowed it, while Northern states generally did not. In 1861, the US elected President Abraham Lincoln, who was opposed to slavery. This led the Southern states to break away from the Union, forming their own government—the Confederacy. For four years the two sides fought a bitter civil war until the Confederacy surrendered in 1865.

NEW MILITARY TECHNOLOGY
The Civil War was one of the first conflicts to be fought using new technology and modern weaponry, including quick-firing rifles, early machine guns, and metal-covered steamships called ironclads.

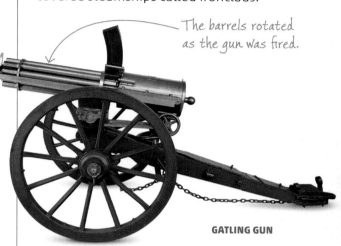

The barrels rotated as the gun was fired.

GATLING GUN

THE EMANCIPATION PROCLAMATION
In 1863, Lincoln issued the Emancipation Proclamation, freeing enslaved people in the Confederacy. He did not have the power to enforce the Proclamation, so this was mainly a symbolic gesture. Some enslaved people, such as these two men, escaped and joined the Union to fight for freedom.

CONFEDERATE $50 BANK NOTE

The bill paints a positive picture of enslaved labor that was far removed from the grim reality.

THE CONFEDERACY
In the 11 Confederate states, owners of huge farms called plantations used the labor of enslaved people to pick cotton and tobacco. These landowners were fighting to defend their right to own people as property.

BLACK AMERICAN REPRESENTATION
After the war, slavery across the US was abolished after three quarters of the states voted to end it. Black Americans were granted citizenship, and allowed to vote and buy land. In 1870, Hiram Rhodes Revels became the first Black American in the US Senate. However, in 1877 segregation laws were implemented, limiting Black American rights.

HIRAM RHODES REVELS

JAPAN
OPENS ITS BORDERS

In the second half of the 19th century, Japan transformed itself from a traditional society that was isolated from the rest of the world to a global power. For hundreds of years the island nation had kept its borders closed, but the arrival of US warships in the country's waters led people in Japan to push for social and governmental reforms that set the country on a path to modernization.

▶ THE ARRIVAL OF THE "BLACK SHIPS"

In 1853, steam-powered US warships sailed near Japan's coastline without permission, aiming to force unfair trade agreements on the country. Their arrival caused panic as the Japanese, with their wooden sailing vessels, were unable to stop the warships. People began to suggest Japan should reform itself to compete with the foreigners.

COMMODORE MATTHEW PERRY
Perry was commander of the four black ships. His expedition aimed to force Japanese ports to open to American vessels.

A Japanese print shows Perry in his naval uniform.

GOVERNMENTAL REFORM
After the arrival of the black ships, Japan was divided between those who wanted to modernize and those who didn't. The country's ruler, the Shogun, resisted change. In 1868, he was replaced as head of state by the Emperor Meiji (seen here). However, the emperor did not govern Japan. The real power was held by reformers acting in his name.

MAKING THE JAPANESE NATION

The new government quickly began to change Japan. The imperial capital was moved from Kyoto to the bustling port of Tokyo. The country began building factories, and education became compulsory.

THE END OF THE CLASS SYSTEM

Japan's ancient laws dividing people into classes were abolished, putting an end to the samurai, the warrior elite. Some samurai resisted but others, such as these men, were in favor of the reforms.

INDUSTRIALIZATION

The new government promoted industry by building factories, shipyards, railroads, and telegraph lines. The country's largest industry was silk making, and 80 percent of silk workers were female.

A JAPANESE RELIGION

Shintō is a Japanese religion revering natural sites such as these "wedded rocks." The government made Shintō the state religion to unite people under the new emperor, who was worshipped as a god.

PLANNING SAFER CITIES

From the late 18th century, huge industrial cities sprang up as people increasingly moved to urban areas in search of work. More and more people lived close together in cheap housing quickly built to accommodate the rising numbers of workers, and the existing sanitation could not cope. Raw sewage was emptied into the rivers and streets, causing deadly diseases. Flushing toilets and sewers transformed cities, making them safer and cleaner.

D-shaped handle is lifted to open the water supply and flush the pan

▶ FLUSHING TOILETS

By the late 1700s the flushing toilet had been invented, but they were uncommon. During the 19th century, cities were so overcrowded that many people had to use a communal toilet, shared by several families. These toilets often overflowed and sewage spilled out contaminating streets, rivers, and water supplies. In 1848, the British government insisted all new houses must be built with a flushing toilet.

Pump handle

DEATH PUMP

In 1854, cholera (a disease that causes severe diarrhea) broke out in Soho in London, killing more than 550 people. Many people thought the disease was airborne, but British doctor John Snow argued that sewage in the water was the cause. He traced the source to a water pump. Officials removed the handle of the pump, stopping access to the water and the epidemic ended.

S-bend traps water, stopping smells

THE GREAT STINK

During the 1800s, waste ran straight into London's Thames River, but in 1858, hot weather and raw sewage combined to make a horrendous smell. Cartoonists showed Death on the Thames and the situation prompted the modernization of London's sewers.

This flushing toilet dates from 1870.

Flushing mechanism drives waste along a drain

URBAN SLUMS
In the early 19th century, living standards for the poor were dreadful. Whole families lived in single rooms in inadequate slum housing. Open sewers ran with sewage and other filth, and disease was rife.

NEW SEWERS
After the "great stink," engineer Joseph Bazalgette designed an underground sewage system for London. By 1875 it carried 440 million gallons (2 billion liters) of waste daily. Paris, Chicago, and Tokyo built similar sewers.

GLOBAL SANITATION
Good sanitation is essential for public health. Despite today's vast sewage networks, sanitation worldwide is unequal. At least 2 billion people globally do not have basic sanitation such as toilets, and a similar number do not have access to clean drinking water.

A LIFE OF LABOR

As a result of the Industrial Revolution, it was common for children as young as four to have jobs. Children made popular employees because they were paid much less than adults. They swept chimneys and worked in factories and mines for up to 80 hours a week. Despite governments passing laws to improve labor conditions, the workplace was often dangerous—many children were killed or injured. These girls, working in a cotton mill in South Carolina, were photographed by Lewis Hine in 1908. Hine's images were used to campaign against child labor.

THE END OF IMPERIAL
CHINA

In the 19th century, after long decades of peace and stability, a series of crises plagued China's last imperial dynasty, the Qing. China's population had more than tripled, leading to famines and land shortages. At the same time, civil wars and foreign invasions weakened the authority of the emperors, paving the way for a republican revolution.

Europeans were often depicted on teapots made for export.

The pink glaze was first used in the 18th century.

The tea tin has text in both English and Chinese.

PACKED FOR EXPORT
Chinese tea was in demand and exported around the world in tins like this one from Hong Kong. The desire to control the tea trade prompted Britain to invade China in the Opium Wars.

▼ DESIRABLE COMMODITIES

From the 17th century, China sold luxury goods such as silk, tea, and porcelain products (like this teapot) to the West in exchange for silver. When Britain ran out of silver, British merchants began selling the Chinese an addictive drug called opium. China banned the drug, but the British Empire defeated China in the so-called Opium Wars, forcing the Qing to allow the drug trade to continue.

Teapots made of porcelain were in high demand in the West.

Long, looping handle

China was the world's largest producer of tea.

THE TAIPING REBELLION

From 1850 to 1864, China fought one of history's most devastating civil wars. Up to 50 million people died in the conflict between the Qing and an uprising called the Taiping Tianguo ("Kingdom of Heavenly Peace"). The Qing were victorious, but the upheaval left the dynasty severely weakened, contributing to its ultimate downfall.

EMPRESS DOWAGER CIXI

When, in 1861, the five-year-old Tongzhi Emperor came to the throne, his mother, Cixi, took an active role in state affairs. Cixi declared war on foreign powers in what is known as the Boxer Rebellion, resulting in another defeat for the Qing Empire and the capture of Beijing. She is often blamed for China's decline.

THE OPIUM WARS

In the 1840s and 1850s, China was defeated in two wars against Western powers. The victors forced China to cede territory in Hong Kong to Britain and allow foreign merchants to sell opium. The defeat humiliated China, weakening imperial authority.

A CHINESE REPUBLIC

After a successful uprising against the Qing called the Xinhai Revolution, China became a republic. This was the end of 4,000 years of imperial rule, and the beginning of modern China. Sun Yat-sen was elected provisional president. He was revered as the "Father of the Nation."

EUROPEANS COLONIZE
AFRICA

In the late 19th century, European countries began claiming territory across Africa. Europeans had been settling parts of West and Southern Africa—often pushing Africans off the most fertile land—since the 1600s, but the scale and intensity of colonization rapidly increased after about 1880. European companies wanted to extract the continent's resources and were willing to exploit African people to do so.

▶ THE BERLIN CONFERENCE

Between 1884 and 1885, German chancellor Otto von Bismark (pictured here on the far right) gathered leaders from 12 other European countries and the US to decide how to divide Africa between themselves. One outcome of the conference was the creation of the Congo Free State, a huge territory held by the Belgian King Leopold II. No Africans were present at the conference.

A COLONIZED CONTINENT

By the early 20th century, the majority of the African continent was in the control of European empires, with the French and British securing the largest territories. Only Liberia in the west and Ethiopia in the east remained independent.

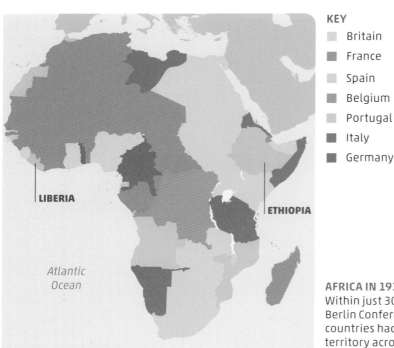

KEY
- Britain
- France
- Spain
- Belgium
- Portugal
- Italy
- Germany

LIBERIA

ETHIOPIA

Atlantic Ocean

AFRICA IN 1914
Within just 30 years of the Berlin Conference, European countries had claimed territory across the entirety of the African continent.

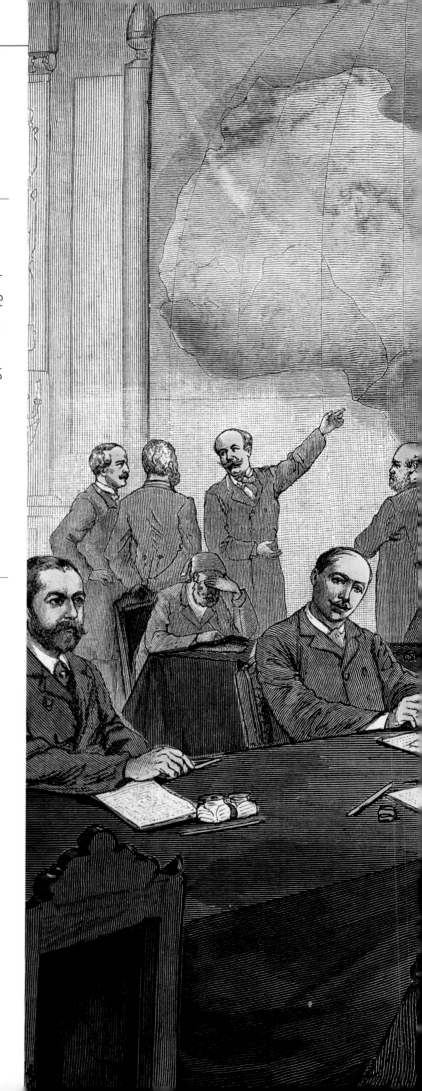

TECHNOLOGICAL ADVANTAGES

European empires took advantage of several technological innovations that made it easier to access and conquer the interior of Africa. Steamboats allowed the Belgians to expand into the Congo Basin, and the British to gain control over trade in the Niger River.

RESISTING THE COLONIZERS

From the moment Europeans began their attempts to colonize the continent, Africans fought back. This all-female military unit—"The Dahomey Amazons"—from Dahomey in modern-day Benin fought in two wars against French colonization in 1890 and 1892–1894.

"LEGITIMATE COMMERCE"

Europeans claimed they sought to trade with Africans for resources such as rubber and palm oil. In reality, Africans (above, with white overseers) were forced to work in brutal and violent conditions. In the Congo Free State, failure to meet quotas was punished by death.

COMMUNICATION
CONNECTS THE WORLD

In the 1830s, the invention of the telegraph allowed written messages to be passed through cables using electrical signals. Over the course of the 19th century, the development of other new technologies such as the telephone made it possible for people to speak to each other and share information over long distances.

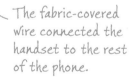

Mouthpiece

The user spoke into the mouthpiece of the handset.

▶ EARLY TELEPHONES
The first telephones were shaped like rectangular blocks and had separate ear and mouth pieces. In 1892 the Swedish company Ericsson released the model shown here, which combined these individual pieces into a single handset. It was immediately popular and became the standard design for corded telephones.

MAKING A CALL
Early phones were much more complicated than today's cell phones. To make a call, users had to lift the handset and speak to a switchboard operator, who connected them to the number they wanted.

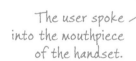

The wire would have connected to the rear of the phone.

The fabric-covered wire connected the handset to the rest of the phone.

The user spoke into the transmitter at this end.

THE INVENTION OF THE PHONE
The first telephone was invented by Alexander Graham Bell in 1876. It had two main parts. A transmitter (shown above) converted sound into an electrical signal. This was then sent along a wire to a receiver, where it was converted back into sound.

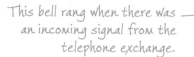

This bell rang when there was an incoming signal from the telephone exchange.

When not in use, the handset sat in a cradle on top of a heavy, cast-iron base.

NATIONAL TELEPHONE SERVICE

This part of the handset—the earpiece—was held up to the user's ear.

The user had to turn this crank handle to send a signal to the telephone exchange.

CROSSING THE ATLANTIC

HMS *Agamemnon* laid electrical cable on the seabed in 1858. After a few weeks, the cable failed and a second attempt was not made until 1866. When finally complete, the finished cable could send up to eight words every minute.

THE SWITCHBOARD

Early phones were connected to huge panels of plugs called switchboards. These were monitored by operators, who would take the caller's cable and physically connect it into the plug of the number they wanted to ring.

WIRELESS SOUNDS

As technology improved, it became possible for sound to travel without wires at all—by using radio signals. Early radios were big and expensive, but over time they got smaller and more affordable. Huge numbers of people tuned in to listen to the most popular radio shows.

RADIO IRIS

DIAGONAL. 460

The first radios were advertised in magazines as luxury goods.

MOTOR CARS
GET THE WORLD MOVING

In the late 19th century, a revolutionary new method of transportation was born—the first motorized cars. The invention of the internal combustion engine—a compact engine that burns fuel and air to drive a piston—opened up new possibilities for faster travel, and the car quickly became popular. Gasoline, diesel, and, later, electric cars soon dominated the globe, forever changing the way people traveled.

▶ A HORSELESS CARRIAGE

In 1885, German engineer Karl Benz produced the world's first gasoline-powered car. Modeled on the design of horse-drawn carriages, the Benz Patent-Motorwagen could only travel at speeds of up to 10 mph (16 km/h), but faster cars soon followed.

Instead of a wheel, the car was steered by a tiller—a lever commonly used to steer boats.

The front wheel mimicked that of a bicycle and could be moved to turn the car.

Each wheel was made out of steel covered in rubber.

PRODUCT TESTING

In 1888, Karl's wife, Bertha Benz, took the car for its first real test, driving her two sons 112 miles (180 km). Her journey—during which she fixed technical problems with a hat pin and garters— led to many improvements in the car's design.

A long lever acted as the car's brake.

The car's engine was powered by gasoline (petrol) and located at the back of the car, behind the seat.

A chain transferred power from the engine to the wheels.

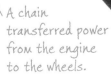

MASS-PRODUCED MACHINES

Early cars were hand crafted and very expensive, until American manufacturer Henry Ford launched the Model T-Ford—later the first mass-produced car—in 1908. His system of standardized parts and a moving assembly line made production much cheaper, and soon spread to other industries.

FREEDOM TO TRAVEL

As car prices fell and more people could afford them, increasing numbers of people used cars to drive to work, go on day trips and vacations, and quickly cover long distances. With so many new designs and types of cars becoming available, driving became for many a hobby and cars a luxury status symbol.

CITROËN
la voiture de montagne

SMOGGY SKIES

Today, there are approximately 1.4 billion cars on the road worldwide. However, cars emit carbon dioxide and other greenhouse gases, not only polluting the air but also contributing to global warming. With humans so reliant on cars for transportation, the race is on to find greener technologies to improve or replace them.

A NEW LIFE IN AMERICA

From the mid to late 19th century, hundreds of thousands of people from around the world made their way to the US. Many were fleeing poverty and oppression in their home countries. They traveled by ship, usually arriving at one of two islands that served as entry points: Angel Island, San Francisco, and Ellis Island, New York. In time, they helped shape a modern, multicultural American society.

▶ STARTING A NEW LIFE

From the 1850s, thousands of Chinese people fled to the US, escaping famine, civil war, and a struggling Chinese economy. They arrived in the US seeking well-paying jobs. Rich or poor, they carried with them objects of value that they owned. This suitcase shows some of the things that Chinese people might have brought with them, to remind them of home and to help in their new lives in the US.

ARRIVING AT ANGEL ISLAND

On arrival, immigrants had to undergo a series of interviews and medical tests (pictured). If they failed, they could be sent back home or detained in the US for months. Many Chinese people faced hostility and racism in the US. In 1882, the government passed the Chinese Exclusion Act, to halt immigration from China. The act was repealed in 1943.

As a child, Mabel Lee was held on Angel Island.

Silk was valuable, and merchants brought it to the US to show potential buyers.

Albert Wong and his brother were held on Angel Island.

Embroidered coin purse

Teapot, cups, and bowls were very useful everyday items.

Enamel box held medicine or snuff tobacco

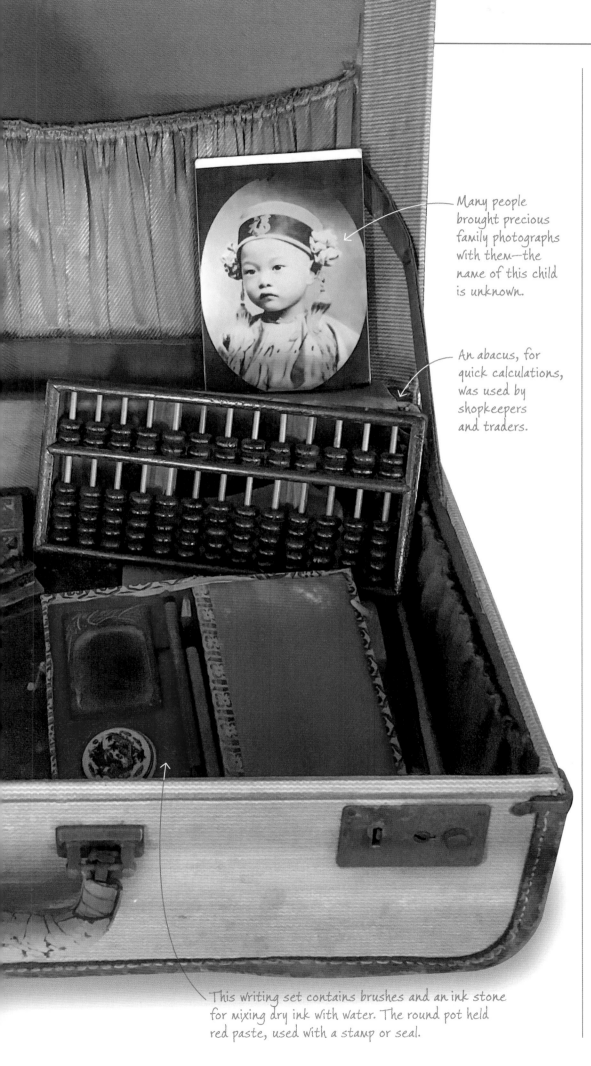

Many people brought precious family photographs with them—the name of this child is unknown.

An abacus, for quick calculations, was used by shopkeepers and traders.

This writing set contains brushes and an ink stone for mixing dry ink with water. The round pot held red paste, used with a stamp or seal.

ELLIS ISLAND

Immigrants from Europe arrived in the US at Ellis Island, in New York Harbor. Between 1892 and 1954, more than 12 million people passed through Ellis Island. These immigrants are thought to be the ancestors of around 40 percent of the current US population.

BUILDING THE NATION

Immigrants have made huge contributions to the US economy and infrastructure. The transcontinental railroad (pictured) was built by Chinese laborers, who were often mistreated. In New York, many European immigrants set up new businesses and worked in clothes factories.

THE US TODAY

People have moved to the US from all over the world, bringing their traditions, ideas, and labor with them, as seen in this image of Chinatown in New York. Around a million new immigrants continue to arrive in the US every year, creating a rich and diverse culture.

SHOPPING
TAKES OFF

Industrialization in the late 19th century made it possible to mass produce goods. As manufacturing increased, technology improved, and trade networks developed, the prices of goods became cheaper. People flocked to the cities to live and work, and their wages increased, which meant they had more money available to buy things other than food. Soon, shopping became a leisure activity—and not just for the rich.

▶ COME AND BUY!

As shopping became popular, companies began to change the way they advertised their products, with attractive posters aimed directly at potential shoppers. These advertisements were bright, colorful, and cheerful, and designed to tempt buyers to spend their money on things they wanted rather than needed, just as advertisements do today.

BUYING STATUS

Owning the newest, most expensive goods allowed people to display their wealth. Tea services popular with the aristocracy, such as those made by English pottery maker Josiah Wedgwood, became "must-have" items. Over time, prices fell and people had more money to spend, leading to a huge rise in consumer demand.

French poster from the early 20th century for tea and drinking chocolate

Children were often featured on early ads, such as this one from 1903.

Handbill from 1913 promoting a kimono shop in Japan

Advertisement promoting "toilet soap," to keep your skin soft, 1899

Many of the first products to be advertised are still familiar today— this poster dates from 1902.

SHOPPING EMPORIUMS
As cities grew and the demand for goods increased, department stores flourished. For the first time, a vast range of different items was available to buy all in one place. These huge new shops were often spread over several floors and their beautiful window displays were designed to entice shoppers inside.

CONSUMER SOCIETY
Today, at the heart of most towns and cities are shopping streets or malls—huge buildings full of stores. However, the advent of online shopping has made it possible to buy products from all over the world without even going into a store.

Poster advertising the toy section of a French department store, 1885

THE DOOMED *ENDURANCE*

In the early 20th century, European explorers turned their sights to icy polar regions. Norwegian Roald Amundsen was the first to reach the South Pole in 1911. In August 1914, Irish explorer Ernest Shackleton and his crew set sail for a new first—crossing Antarctica on foot. However, his ship, the *Endurance*, became trapped in coastal ice. The crew stayed with the doomed ship for months, until it was crushed by the weight of the ice. Shackleton and a small team sailed more than 620 miles (1,000 km) in a lifeboat to get help. Incredibly, the entire crew was rescued.

CROSSING THE ATLANTIC
In 1927, American aviator Charles Lindbergh became the first person to fly solo nonstop across the Atlantic Ocean. In a small plane, he flew more than 3,600 miles (5,800 km) from New York to Paris, France, in just under 34 hours. This feat paved the way for further international travel.

FLYING FOR FUN
The development of jet engines at the end of World War II led to more powerful planes, and commercial air travel soon boomed. Passengers in the 1950s and '60s traveled in style in roomy cabins. But flying was only for the well-off and did not become more accessible until decades later.

FLYING WITH WINGS
Before powered flight, many people experimented with lightweight gliders. In the 1890s, German engineer Otto Lilienthal used findings from his studies of bird flight to design a type of hang glider. Dangling below the wings, he steered the craft using a fixed bar.

▼ FLIGHT TAKES OFF
History was made in 1903 when American brothers Wilbur and Orville Wright achieved the world's first successful powered flight in a machine that was heavier than air. It had taken the brothers four years to develop the machine, which was called the Wright Flyer.

FLIGHT
SHRINKS THE WORLD

In the early years of the 20th century, travel took to the air. Airplanes meant people, freight, and mail could cross countries, continents, and even the entire span of the globe within hours and days rather than weeks or months. Soon, flying for both business and leisure became an affordable reality for many, and now more than 100,000 flights cross the skies every day.

The wings were made of wood covered with muslin cloth.

The pilot controlled the plane's pitch (up or down movement) with a lever, and pulled on wires to turn it left or right.

WRIGHT FLYER

Surfaces at the front of the plane, called elevators, tilted the plane's nose up or down.

Propellers pushed the plane through the air.

The wingspan of the plane was 40 ft (12 m) long.

THE FIRST FLIGHT
On the day of their first successful launch at Kitty Hawk, North Carolina, the Wright brothers carried out four flights. The first lasted only 12 seconds, flying just above the sand. The day's longest lasted almost a whole minute, covering 852 ft (259.6 m).

COAL MINING
FUELS INDUSTRY

From the mid-18th century, coal became a major energy source. Coal-powered steam engines drove machinery, while coal-fired furnaces produced iron and steel. As industrialization continued, the demand for coal soared, and coal mines were sunk ever deeper. But our dependence on coal has come at a heavy environmental cost.

Valve

Oxygen tank

When the valve is opened, oxygen flows through this pipe and into the box, reviving the canary.

The canary is visible through the window, so the miners could see if it was in distress.

▶ CANARY RESUSCITATOR

Miners faced hazards from explosions and gas poisoning. From the late 1800s, canaries were used to detect deadly gases, such as carbon monoxide. The canaries would show signs of gas poisoning before the miners, giving them time to escape. This resuscitator device held a canary to be used in this way. When the door was open, a grille stopped the bird from escaping. If it showed signs of distress, the door could be closed and the valve opened to allow oxygen in.

DEEP MINES

Coal exists in seams (layers) below the earth's surface. As coal production increased, mines got deeper and more dangerous for the workers who mined coal by hand. Deep, vertical shafts were sunk so miners could reach the seams. A network of tunnels enabled coal to be transported to a shaft and hoisted to the surface.

INCREASED DEMAND

From the 19th century, coal use accelerated to meet the demands of an increasingly industrialized world. Coal fueled huge furnaces hot enough to produce steel (seen below in a painting from 1885). It was also used to generate electricity and heat homes.

Door

FOSSIL FUELS

Coal is a fossil fuel found deep underground and is formed from fossilized plant and animal remains over hundreds of millions of years. Other fossil fuels include natural gas and crude oil, or petroleum. Much of the world's energy comes from these three fuels.

OIL

As well as producing fuels to power cars and planes, oil is also used in the manufacture of plastics and textiles. In 1859, American Edwin Drake drilled the world's first oil well, in Pennsylvania.

GAS

In the 19th century, gas was used for street lighting. Subsequently, gas has been used for cooking, heating, and to generate electricity.

A DESTRUCTIVE FORCE

Intensive coal mining has contaminated water, caused pollution, and destroyed landscapes, habitats, and ecosystems. Burning coal and other fossil fuels releases gases that contribute to the climate crisis. Today, people are increasingly looking for alternative ways to generate energy.

A LONG STRUGGLE

From the first ever women's rights convention, at Seneca Falls in 1848, it took American women more than 70 years to win the vote. Even when the right was won, not all were free to use it. US suffragists were inspired by the fight to abolish slavery. But while some women could vote from 1920, it was not until 1965 that voting rights were ensured for all, including Black women.

CAMPAIGNING WOMEN

Black women such as Nannie Helen Burroughs (holding the banner) campaigned for the vote, sometimes with white suffragists, but often separately as race became a dividing issue. White women put their own interests above those of Black people.

WOMEN
WIN THE VOTE

After centuries of inequality, in the late 18th century some women began demanding equal rights with men. They wanted equality before the law, in education, and at work. But they could not vote. Increasingly, from the mid-19th century, they turned their energies to fighting for the right to vote (suffrage) so that they could have a voice in government and law-making. It was a long, hard fight.

▶ TAKING ACTION

Most campaigners demanded the vote using peaceful methods. Known as suffragists, they petitioned, wrote letters, and held meetings. Other women adopted headline-grabbing methods, such as heckling or smashing windows. In the UK, they were known as suffragettes. They used leather belts and chains to attach themselves to public buildings as a means of protest.

Chains were used by suffragettes to attach themselves to railings.

FIGHTING TO BE HEARD

Suffragettes were met with police brutality and imprisonment. Police had difficulty removing women who chained themselves to buildings, which meant passers-by could hear women's speeches. This made front-page news. In prison, many went on hunger strike in protest.

Padlocks meant that police could not drag suffragettes away, giving the protestors time to attract attention.

FIRST IN THE WORLD
In 1893, women in New Zealand became the first in the world to gain the national vote, with both white and Maori women winning this right. The mural pictured left commemorates their victory. In 1902, some women in Australia won the right to stand for election too. Through the 1900s, women won the vote in other nations.

Bicycles were a recent invention that gave women new freedoms.

ANTI-SUFFRAGE
Some women and men opposed votes for women, saying politics was a man's world. While some said a woman's vote would be wasted, because women did not understand politics, others believed if women had the vote it would destroy family life.

This set of belt and chains was used by Australian suffragette Muriel Matters to chain herself to the UK Parliament buildings.

The sturdy leather belt fitted around the waist.

WOMEN IN POLITICS
Once women had the vote, they began running for parliament. In 1960, Sirimavo Bandaranaike was elected Prime Minister of Sri Lanka and so became the world's first woman prime minister. Today, women sit in parliaments around the world, but they are still outnumbered by men.

VOTING WORLDWIDE
Between 1893 and 2021, most of the world's women won the vote, but not always equally. In countries such as Canada and South Africa, white women could vote before Indigenous women or women of colour. In some countries, literacy is a bar to voting. Bolivia (above) has quotas that make sure women are represented.

Since the early 20th century, the pace of **technological change** has accelerated rapidly. New **innovations** and **inventions** have changed the way we communicate, put men on the **moon**, and **connected** far-flung parts of the globe as never before. But new **weapons** have also made conflict more **deadly**, and a reliance on fossil fuels to power this technological age has caused a **climate crisis**.

TIMELINE OF THE
MODERN WORLD

WWI FIELD GUN

1910

The beginning of this period is marked by two world wars, which killed millions of people. The map of the world changed again as European colonial empires collapsed and many countries gained their independence. The invention of computers and the Internet ushered in a new digital age.

1914–1918
World War I
War breaks out in Europe as two opposing blocs take up arms. The war soon spreads around the world.

SPUTNIK 1

1956
The Hungarian Uprising
Hungarians revolt against the Communist government in the first major threat to Soviet control of Eastern Europe. They are crushed by an invading Soviet force.

TOPPLED STATUE OF STALIN IN HUNGARY

1960
The Year of Africa
European colonial empires have begun to disintegrate. In Africa, 14 former French colonies are granted independence. By 1990, every African nation is independent.

1957
The space race begins
The Soviet Union sends *Sputnik I* into orbit. It is the first artificial satellite to orbit Earth in space and stays in orbit for three weeks until its batteries die.

1956
The Suez Crisis
Britain and France attack the Suez Canal, attempting to regain control from Egypt. They are humiliated and forced to withdraw.

1950–1953
The Korean War
War breaks out on the Korean peninsula as the Communist North attempts to take over the pro-Western South.

THE MARCH ON WASHINGTON, D.C.

1963
"I have a dream!"
US civil rights leader Martin Luther King leads a march on Washington, D.C., demanding civil and economic rights for Black Americans.

BUZZ ALDRIN

1969
The moon landing
Commander Neil Armstrong and Lunar Module pilot Buzz Aldrin become the first people to walk on the moon.

1989
Fall of the Wall
The Berlin Wall is pulled down as the Soviet Union withdraws troops and support from Communist governments in Eastern Europe, and the Cold War ends. The Soviet Union itself will collapse in 1991.

1965–1973
The Vietnam War
The United States sends half a million troops to support South Vietnam against Communist North Vietnam, before withdrawing them in 1973.

1967
The Six-Day War
Israel fears attacks by Egypt, Syria, and their Arab allies and so launches a series of pre-emptive strikes, occupying the Syrian Golan Heights, Jordanian West Bank, and Egyptian Sinai Peninsula.

1989
World Wide Web
British scientist Tim Berners-Lee invents the Web, an information system where documents and other resources are linked and accessible over the Internet, a global system of interconnected computers.

1991
The Gulf War
A coalition of 35 nations led by the US occupies oil-rich Kuwait and ends Iraqi occupation.

1917
Russian Revolutions
In February, a revolution overthrows the Russian czar and sets up a provisional government. A second revolution in October brings the world's first Communist state into existence.

1922
Fascist power
Benito Mussolini marches on Rome and takes power in Italy, becoming leader of the world's first fascist state.

1933
Hitler comes to power
Adolf Hitler, leader of the Nazi Party, is appointed German chancellor. He soon eliminates all political opposition, persecutes Jews, and begins to secretly rearm Germany.

REPUBLICAN SOLDIERS

1919
Treaty of Versailles
A peace treaty is signed in Paris, ending World War I. Germany is blamed for starting the war and made to pay reparations.

1929
Wall Street Crash
New York's stock exchange crashes. The Great Depression that follows will wreck the economies of many countries.

1936–1939
Spanish Civil War
Nationalist forces led by General Franco oppose the democratically elected Republican government of Spain, eventually seizing control.

THE FLAG OF ISRAEL

1948
The state of Israel
The independent Jewish state of Israel is declared in Palestine. Many Palestinians are forced to abandon their homes and go into exile.

1947
Indian independence
Britain hands over its vast empire in India to the newly independent states of India and Pakistan.

1945
The United Nations
An international organization is established to maintain international peace and security.

WWII GERMAN FIGHTER PLANE

1939–1945
World War II
The German invasion of Poland prompts Britain and France to declare war. The conflict widens in 1941 when Germany invades Soviet Russia and Japan attacks an American naval base at Pearl Harbor.

COMMUNIST TROOPS

1949
s China
The Communist Party of Mao Zedong defeats the Nationalist Chinese government and takes power, founding a new Communist state.

1945
Atomic bombs
American bombers drop two atomic bombs on the Japanese cities of Hiroshima and Nagasaki, bringing World War II to a devastating end.

1941
The Holocaust
Jewish people are murdered in mass shootings and the Nazis construct the first of six death camps. By 1945, six million Jews will have died.

COVID-19 VIRUS

2007–2008
Global economic crisis
Excessive risk-taking by banks, lax financial regulation, and the bursting of a housing bubble in the US cause an international financial and banking crisis.

2019
COVID-19
A global coronavirus pandemic begins in Wuhan, China, and spreads around the world. Economies grind to a halt and international travel is suspended.

2020

1994
Mandela is elected
After 27 years in prison, the South African anti-apartheid leader Nelson Mandela is freed in 1990. Four years later, apartheid ends and he is elected as the first Black president of South Africa.

2001
9/11
Islamist terrorists from a group called Al-Qaeda hijack aircraft. They attack the twin towers of the World Trade Center in New York and the Pentagon in Washington, D.C. Nearly 3,000 people are killed.

2011
World population
The total population of the world passes 7 billion people, of whom more than half live in cities. Forecasts suggest the population will continue to rise, reaching around 9–10 billion in 2050, but the pace of growth has slowed.

MACHINES
DRIVE WARFARE

World War 1 (1914–1918) was a war unlike any before. A global conflict, it was also the first mechanized war. Advances in technology had produced new weapons, which transformed how armies fought and resulted in massive casualties. The war between Allies (Britain, France, and Russia) and Central Powers (Germany and Austria-Hungary) was largely waged in Europe, but drew in troops from around the world.

British Mark IV tank

ALL TERRAIN
Tanks' maneuverability made them invaluable on uneven ground. They flattened barbed wire, plunged over shell craters, and provided cover for advancing infantry. Sometimes, though, the ground was so muddy even tanks became stuck.

▶ NEW WAYS OF FIGHTING
In previous wars, armies of foot soldiers and soldiers on horseback moved over large areas. They fought fast-moving battles in the open. During World War I, lethal bombs fired from new artillery made this impossible. Soldiers needed cover and started digging trenches. By the end of 1914, trenches stretched 400 miles (645 km) along the Western Front, from the Belgian coast to the Swiss border.

TRENCH WARFARE
On the Western Front opposing armies faced each other from trenches as little as 150 ft (50 m) apart, firing at anyone who stood up. Attacks took place at dawn or dusk. Following a signal, troops emerged from the trenches, often walking into murderous fire as they attempted to charge the troops opposite. Frequently, little or no ground was gained.

Iron caterpillar tracks meant tanks could cross any ground.

TANKS
As war became bogged down in the trenches, both sides desperately sought weapons that would break the stalemate. Developed by the British, tanks were a major innovation. Cumbersome but bulletproof, they could travel over churned-up ground and lumber into enemy trenches. The British Mark IV first saw action in 1917.

HEAVY GUNS
Artillery dominated the war. Heavy guns, such as howitzers, fired bombshells directly into enemy trenches in terrifying and relentless bombardments that destroyed men and the surrounding land. Some field guns were pulled by horses, many of which perished.

DEADLY FIRE, DEADLY GAS
Machine guns, firing up to 600 bullets a minute, mowed down advancing troops. In 1915, chlorine gas was used for the first time in war, choking anyone in its path. Gas hoods offered some protection.

An unditching beam could be lowered to enable the tank to travel over ditches.

One of two six-pounder guns

THE TANK MUSEUM
B46
BIG BRUTE

Bulletproof exterior

BATTLE DEVASTATION

Relentless bombardment during World War I (1914–1918) turned the landscape of the Western Front in Belgium into a nightmarish land of mud and shattered trees. In 1917, Britain launched a major offensive against German forces at Passchendaele. The attack was hampered by rain, which turned the ground into a swampy quagmire, and shell craters into treacherous pools. The army sent into battle was made up not only of British soldiers, but also of men from Australia, New Zealand, Canada, South Africa, India, the Caribbean, and other parts of the British Empire. These men suffered terrible casualties.

FIGHTING WOMEN

For the first time, women were enlisted into military forces. Mostly, they were not allowed to fight, instead taking on roles as, for example, telephone operators. There were exceptions: in Russia, Maria Bochkareva formed the Women's Battalion of Death.

NURSING ON THE FRONT LINE

By 1914, nursing was considered a suitable job for women. Many now went to the front line, driving ambulances and nursing the wounded in unsafe conditions. Some, such as the "Women of Pervyse," nursed under fire in Belgium.

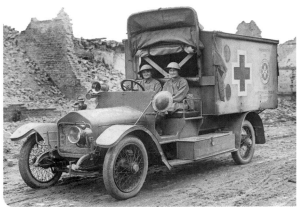

A net keeps long hair out of the way.

Women pack shells with TNT and tamp the explosive down.

DANGEROUS WORK

Work in munitions factories was hazardous and hard. Explosions were common. Women suffered from poisoning by the explosive TNT, which turned the skin yellow, causing them to be nicknamed "canaries."

WAR TRANSFORMS
SOCIETY

Women's lives were transformed during World War I (1914–1918). As men went to fight, women took over their jobs. Women's employment was not new. Working-class women had always been part of the labor force. But war brought women into a whole range of new work, from conducting trams to airplane engineering and policing. Some people were shocked at women doing what was traditionally seen as men's work, but most women embraced the chance to help the war effort, learn new skills, earn money, and gain independence.

◄ **MUNITIONS WORKERS**

In Britain, France, Germany, and Russia, thousands of women entered munitions factories to produce the huge numbers of shells that were needed for the war. Although governments promised that men would get their jobs back after the war, male trade unionists were opposed to women doing these jobs. Women were always paid less than men.

A HEAVY PRICE

Millions of young men died in the war. While women celebrated its end, they mourned, too. Most had lost at least one male relative—father, son, husband, brother, uncle—and friends. Welfare groups helped widowed mothers and children.

BEYOND THE DURATION

Post-war, women were expected to return to the home as wives and mothers. However, war work had given them independence. Those left single needed to earn. Slowly, new professions opened up, such as teaching and radio broadcasting.

REVOLUTION
ROCKS RUSSIA

A revolution took place in Russia in 1917 that changed the course of modern history. It ended centuries of imperial rule and created the world's first communist state. Out of it came the Soviet Union, a 20th-century superpower that rivaled the US, and communism as a powerful political force.

▶ **CELEBRATING REVOLUTION**
The 1917 Revolution was the first revolution to take power in the name of workers and peasants. It was inspired by communism, a belief that the people should own a country's resources, and that wealth should be shared according to need. Soviet propaganda art, such as this 1929 poster, glorified the Revolution.

IMPERIAL RULE ENDS
The Romanov dynasty had ruled Russia for 300 years. By 1900, the Russian people were fed up with inequality, poverty, and famine, and Czar Nicholas II was deeply unpopular. The 1917 Revolution ended imperial rule, and the whole family was later murdered.

REVOLUTION TRANSFORMS RUSSIA
In 1917, communist revolutionaries inspired by Vladimir Lenin (1870–1924) seized power. Under Lenin's leadership, the radical Bolshevik faction set up soviets (workers' committees), seized factories, and took ownership of land. Soon, however, the dream of a classless society was replaced by dictatorship.

THE SOVIET UNION BEGINS
In 1922, after a civil war, the Union of Soviet Socialist Republics (USSR) or Soviet Union, became the world's first communist state. Joseph Stalin (1878–1953) ruled from 1927, transforming the state into a major industrial power. A ruthless dictator, his policies brought famine and death to millions. He had opponents executed or sent to forced labor camps, known as gulags.

под Ленинским знаменем Коминтерна — вперед!

The flag of Lenin bears a slogan celebrating International Workers' Day. Soviet communists believed that revolution would sweep the world.

In this image, the heroic worker breaks free of his chains, which represent capitalist oppression, and stands on top of the world.

FARM WORKER
The Revolution promised equality to farm workers as well as industrial laborers. Many women supported it because of the hardship they endured. However, propaganda images such as this are far from the reality, in which peasants had their land taken away and millions died of famine.

THE GREAT DEPRESSION
SHAKES THE WORLD

In 1929, the world was plunged into the worst economic crisis in history—the Great Depression.
The US stock exchange (where shares in companies are traded) collapsed, causing businesses and banks to fail and unemployment to soar. The crisis spread to many countries around the world. Millions of people lost their jobs and faced hardship and hunger.

▶ FORCED TO FLEE
A few years into the Depression, another disaster hit parts of the central US. Severe droughts forced thousands of farmers and their families to pack up and leave their land. Many traveled west to California in search of work. However, they were not welcome when they arrived—jobs were in short supply and locals needed what work there was themselves.

HARD TIMES
Some people invested all their savings, or borrowed money to buy shares. When the US stock market crashed, the shares became worthless and they were left with nothing. Firms went bust and people were unable to repay loans, which meant many lost their homes. Shantytowns appeared across the US, and soup kitchens fed thousands of unemployed.

WORLD IN CRISIS
The Great Depression was triggered in the US, but its impact was global. All over the world fewer goods were produced, and unemployment and poverty grew. As the US economy failed, it canceled loans it had made to other countries. Paying this money back impacted economies across the globe. In Germany there were protest marches against the Depression (right). People began to lose hope in traditional politics, and groups appeared with new, extreme ideas, such as the Nazis.

ENDING THE DEPRESSION
In 1932, Franklin D. Roosevelt was elected president of the US. He championed a "New Deal," aiming to tackle the Depression by spending public money and creating millions of new jobs. The economy slowly began to recover, though unemployment was still high when World War II began in 1939.

THE DUST BOWL
In drought-stricken areas the soil dried out. The soil had been farmed heavily for years and plowed up repeatedly, making it light and loose, and turning it to dust. Strong winds blew the dust up into huge, choking clouds, killing crops, livestock, and people.

For those who had lost their homes in the Dust Bowl, cars provided shelter as well as a means of escape.

Farmers fleeing the Dust Bowl tied their belongings onto their cars.

FASCISM
RISES IN EUROPE

After World War I, a new political and social force emerged in Europe. Called fascism, it was a harsh, military-style movement. Its supporters were right-wing nationalists, who believed that the glory and strength of their nation was more important than individual rights and freedoms. In the 1920s and 1930s, fascist parties led by dictators gained hold in countries such as Italy and Germany, which had been devastated by the war.

RISE OF THE NAZIS
In Germany, fascism was known as National Socialism, or Nazism. Its leader was Adolf Hitler (1889–1945), who gained power in 1933 by promising to rebuild Germany. Nazism was extremely anti-Semitic, preaching hatred and prejudice against Jewish people.

▼ DISPLAYS OF POWER
Fascism relied on mass rallies; military-style uniforms; and strong, charismatic leaders to win popular support in the 1930s. The Nazis staged huge, popular rallies in Nuremberg, Germany, as propaganda—to spread their ideas and demonstrate their force to the world.

THE BIRTH OF FASCISM
In 1919, Benito Mussolini founded the Italian Fascist Party. He became dictator in 1922, making Italy the first fascist state in Europe. Italy later fought alongside Germany in World War II.

ECONOMIC PROBLEMS
Fascism grew after World War I. The war had left Italy shattered. By the 1930s, Germany also suffered economic hardship, with huge lines for homeless shelters. Fascist leaders won support by promising to restore wealth and national pride.

THE SPANISH CIVIL WAR
Between 1936 and 1939, civil war tore Spain apart as Republicans and Nationalists (fascists) fought for control of the country. Led by General Franco, the fascists gained power. Franco ruled Spain as a fascist dictator until his death in 1975.

The swastika became a key symbol of the Nazis and was used on their flag.

Black domed helmets were worn by the SS— a Nazi military organization that terrorized German citizens.

THE WAR IN EUROPE
On the orders of Nazi leader Adolf Hitler, German forces marched into Poland, annexed Denmark and Norway, and moved against France, occupying Belgium and taking Paris in June 1940.

DESERT WAR
To defend their colonial interests, Allied forces fought Italian and German troops in North Africa. In 1942, Germany's Afrika Korps was defeated at El Alamein, Egypt. In 1943, it surrendered.

WAR GOES GLOBAL

In 1939, war broke out when Germany invaded Poland. For the first two years, World War II was fought mainly in Europe and North Africa. This changed in 1941 when Japan attacked the US naval base in Pearl Harbor, drawing the US into the conflict, too. Almost the entire globe was now plunged into war—the most deadly war in history.

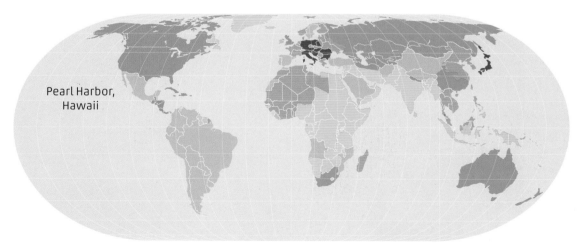

Pearl Harbor, Hawaii

THE WORLD AT WAR, 1941
Most of the world's countries were involved, in two opposing blocs: the Allies (led by Britain, the USSR, US, and China) and Axis (Germany, Italy, and Japan). Fighting took place on every continent but South America and Antarctica.

KEY
- Allied powers
- Allied colonies or occupied countries
- Axis powers
- Axis allies, colonies, or occupied countries
- Neutral countries

JAPANESE BOMBERS
The Japanese bombers were launched from aircraft carriers, which had sailed secretly to within 300 miles (480 km) of Pearl Harbor. Following the attack, fighting between Allies and Axis moved into Asia: on land in Hong Kong, Malaya (Malaysia), Singapore, and Burma (Myanmar), and at sea in the Pacific.

Attacking planes dropped torpedoes and bombs.

◀ ATTACK ON PEARL HARBOR
On December 7, 1941, Japanese planes launched a surprise attack on the US navy at Pearl Harbor in Hawaii. Within two hours, 19 of the US fleet's battleships had been destroyed and more than 2,400 American personnel had been killed. The US, which had remained neutral, joined the war. With the Soviet Union resisting German invasion in Europe, the course of the war began to change. By 1945, the Axis powers had been defeated.

THE UNITED NATIONS
Following the war, which ended in 1945, the United Nations (UN) was formed with a commitment to maintain international peace and security. Former First Lady Eleanor Roosevelt chaired the UN's Commission on Human Rights, which in 1948 issued a Universal Declaration of Human Rights. A response to the horrors of World War II, it declared all people free and equal.

DEADLY BOMBINGS

Aerial bombardment was a chilling feature of this war. Some bombing raids were strategic: aimed at dockyards or munitions factories. But cities, too, were bombed. In 1945, Allied bombing raids on Dresden, Germany, reduced the city center to rubble, killing some 25,000 civilians and making thousands homeless.

FOOD RATIONING

Food shortages affected most warring countries. Rationing was introduced, but in some places people starved from lack of food. Civilians in the USSR and Nazi-occupied territories suffered terrible hardship. There was no fresh fruit, eggs, or milk. Even in Germany, food substitutes, such as "ersatz coffee" made of acorns, were common.

WAR HITS HOME

World War II (1939–1945) is sometimes called a "total war" because the whole of society was involved, including ordinary people. Civilians had died in previous wars, but numbers were far greater during this war: as many as 45 million noncombatants lost their lives from bombing raids, hunger, and disease, as well as deliberate murder. War affected all aspects of life from food and housing to school and work.

▶ "MICKEY MOUSE" GAS MASK

When war began, governments worried about gas attacks on civilians. In some countries, everyone had to carry a gas mask. There were even novelty masks for children, which looked a bit like the Disney character. In the end, there were no gas attacks and masks were not needed.

Head strap

People in Leningrad, Russia, had only 4 oz (125 g) of bread daily during a 900-day siege of the city.

GAS MASK DRILL

Schoolchildren in the UK had to do a gas drill every day. They had to take the mask out of the box, put the mask on, check its fit, and then breathe normally. They became very skilled at making rude noises, such as blowing raspberries, when breathing out.

DISPLACED PEOPLE

Millions of people were displaced or driven from their homes during World War II—either forcibly removed or fleeing from invading armies. Many became refugees. An estimated 60 million Chinese people fled the Sino-Japanese War, which began in 1937. Even before war began in Europe, around half a million refugees fleeing the Spanish Civil War (1936–1939) had crossed into France.

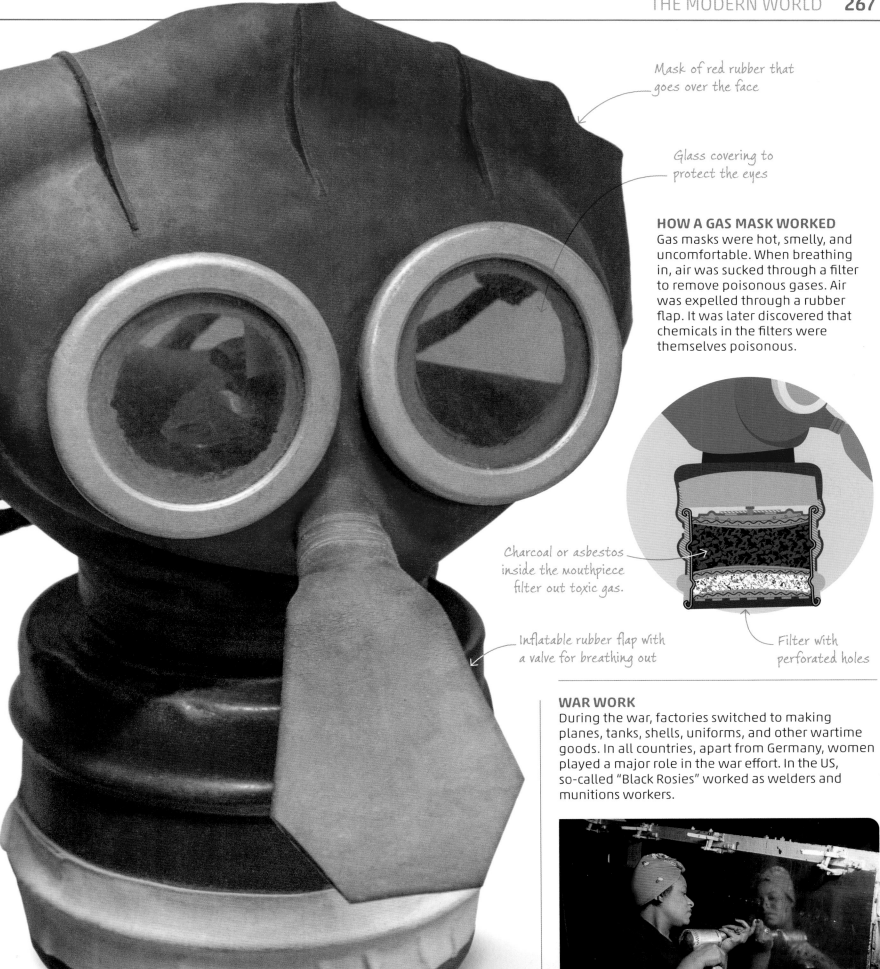

Mask of red rubber that goes over the face

Glass covering to protect the eyes

HOW A GAS MASK WORKED
Gas masks were hot, smelly, and uncomfortable. When breathing in, air was sucked through a filter to remove poisonous gases. Air was expelled through a rubber flap. It was later discovered that chemicals in the filters were themselves poisonous.

Charcoal or asbestos inside the mouthpiece filter out toxic gas.

Inflatable rubber flap with a valve for breathing out

Filter with perforated holes

Air filter

WAR WORK
During the war, factories switched to making planes, tanks, shells, uniforms, and other wartime goods. In all countries, apart from Germany, women played a major role in the war effort. In the US, so-called "Black Rosies" worked as welders and munitions workers.

THE HOLOCAUST

Six million Jewish people were murdered between 1941 and 1945, in what is now known as the Holocaust. Over the centuries, many Jews in Europe had experienced anti-Semitism (hatred of Jews) and persecution. In the 1930s, a new political group, the Nazis, took power in Germany. Its leader, Adolf Hitler, was anti-Semitic, and persecution intensified, giving way to murder. The Nazis also persecuted and murdered other groups, including Roma, disabled, and gay people.

▼ SHOES OF THE MURDERED
Jewish people began to be murdered in mass shootings in 1941. That winter, the Nazis constructed the first of six death camps. Over the following three years, Jews from across Europe were transported by train to these camps. On arrival, they were stripped of their clothes and then gassed. This pile of shoes is today displayed at Auschwitz as evidence of what took place there.

A WELL-TRAVELED BEAR
Many Jewish people who fled from Nazi forces became refugees. One was Stella Knobel. She and her family lived in Krakow, Poland. When the Nazis invaded, the family fled, first to the Soviet Union where they were in a labor camp, then to Iran. Finally, in 1943, Stella and her mother reached Israel. They had only a basket, five dollars, and Stella's teddy bear, Mishu.

AUSCHWITZ
Auschwitz was a complex that included a concentration camp and a death camp. It was the largest of its kind. More than 1.1 million people died there. These children were among the lucky few who survived.

PERSECUTION

In Germany, persecution of Jewish people began as soon as the Nazis came to power in 1933. Anti-Semitic laws forbade Jews from running businesses and banned them from public places. In 1939, Germany invaded Poland. Jews were herded into ghettos (separate areas) and forced to wear a yellow star, so they could be identified easily.

RESISTANCE

Jewish people resisted however they could. Some took up arms and fought; others worked hard to keep their Jewish culture and identity alive. Penalties were harsh but they observed religious festivals. This wedding was captured by Henryk Ross, who risked his life to photograph the lives of people in a ghetto.

IN HIDING

Courageous citizens risked their lives to hide Jews. One child who went into hiding was Anne Frank. For two years, her father's employees hid her and the family in a secret annex in Amsterdam. Throughout this time, she kept a diary, which her father, the only survivor, published in 1947. It is a powerful memoir of the Holocaust.

The shoes bear the imprint of the individuals who wore them.

THE DAWN OF THE
NUCLEAR AGE

The mid-20th century saw the invention of a terrible new weapon. By harnessing the power locked up inside the atom, scientists created a bomb with unprecedented destructive power—able to wipe out whole cities and kill tens of thousands of people. The knowledge that nuclear powers could now destroy each other at the touch of a button altered global conflict forever.

▶ NUCLEAR TESTING
Nuclear weapons were tested at remote locations, first above ground and then underground. From 1966 to 1996, 181 bombs were tested by the French at the Mururoa Atoll in French Polynesia. These tests, such as this 1971 detonation, caused long-lasting environmental damage and harm to the local population.

FROM BREAKTHROUGH TO BOMB
In December 1938, German scientist Otto Hahn and his assistant Fritz Strassmann made an incredible scientific breakthrough. They managed to split one of the tiniest bits of matter known to science—the center (nucleus) of an atom—releasing a large amount of energy. The discovery of this power led to the development of atomic weapons during World War II.

THE MANHATTAN PROJECT
At laboratories in the US, scientists from the US, UK, and Canada secretly produced the world's first atomic weapons in 1942. These huge bombs were tested in the New Mexico desert—the first in July 1945.

HIROSHIMA
On August 6, 1945, an American plane dropped a bomb on the Japanese city of Hiroshima. Up to 120,000 civilians were killed. When a second bomb was dropped on the city of Nagasaki, the devastation brought World War II to an end.

Anyone standing up to 85 km (53 miles) away from the blast would experience temporary blindness, due to the huge amount of heat and light emitted.

A distinctive mushroom-shaped cloud forms as energy from the explosion heats up the air and causes it to rise.

AN ARMS RACE

In 1945, the United States was the only country with nuclear weapons. When the USSR tested its own weapons in 1949, an arms race began as each superpower tried to stockpile the most weapons. Both developed even more powerful weapons able to destroy the other many times over.

NUCLEAR POWERS

After 1950, the number of nuclear weapons skyrocketed, reaching a peak in the mid-1980s. Numbers then fell as countries made efforts to disarm. Today, China, France, India, Israel, Pakistan, the UK, and North Korea as well as the US and Russia possess nuclear weapons.

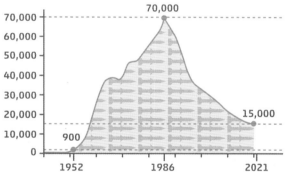

NUCLEAR ENERGY

The power unleashed by splitting the atom was also soon used to generate electricity. The first nuclear power station opened in Russia in 1954. Today, there are around 450 nuclear power plants in operation in 30 countries around the world.

THE PARTITION OF INDIA

At the stroke of midnight on August 15, 1947, India and the new state of Pakistan gained independence from British rule. The path to freedom had been painful and at times violent. Britain was reluctant to let go and leaders disagreed about the shape of a free India. The Congress party, led by Jawaharlal Nehru, wanted a united India, while Mohammad Ali Jinnah's Muslim League campaigned, successfully, for a separate nation for Muslims. The two men went on to lead the two new nations.

INDIA PARTITIONED
The final negotiations for independence took place in a rush. Britain agreed to divide the country in two. Sir Cyril Radcliffe, a British lawyer, was given five weeks to decide the border between India and Pakistan, which was divided into West and East. Kashmir was given the choice of which nation to join; both claimed it and went to war.

▼ MASS MIGRATION
Partition led to the greatest mass migration of people in history. About 14 million people were uprooted, Sikhs and Hindus leaving Pakistan for India, Muslims traveling the other way. A million lost their lives in riots, while others died of hunger and thirst.

Disputed territory of Kashmir
WEST PAKISTAN
Delhi
Karachi
Radcliffe Line, 1947
EAST PAKISTAN
Calcutta (Kolkata)
Arabian Sea
INDIA
Indian Ocean
SRI LANKA

GANDHI AND THE SALT MARCH
For many decades, the Indian National Congress party campaigned for Britain to leave India. In 1930, Mahatma Gandhi, its leader, led a march to protest a British salt tax. Thousands marched with him, among them poet Sarojini Naidu. Nonviolent civil disobedience promoted independence.

AN EQUAL INDIA
India's constitution laid the foundations for a liberal nation. Its architect was B. R. Ambedkar, who insisted that all people, including women, lower-caste Dalits, and the poor, were equal before the law. With more than 900 million voters, the country is the world's biggest democracy.

A NEW NATION
Pakistan was created as a nation for all, later declaring itself an Islamic Republic. The star and crescent on its flag represent Islam, and the white stripe other religions. It celebrates independence on August 14, a day before India. East Pakistan broke away to form Bangladesh in 1971.

Refugees crowded the trains, even sitting on their roofs.

People could only take what they could carry with them to their new lives.

THE CREATION OF ISRAEL

In 1948, a new nation called Israel was created in Palestine. It was established as a homeland for Jewish people. Demands for a Jewish state had begun in 1897 and intensified in the wake of the Holocaust. However, Palestinians objected to its creation. Many were driven from their homes and not able to return. Wars followed, and conflict in the region continues to this day.

KEY
- International Jerusalem
- Arab state
- Jewish state

LEBANON
SYRIA
Mediterranean Sea
Jerusalem
EGYPT
TRANSJORDAN

UN PARTITION PLAN
In 1947, Britain said that it intended to leave Palestine, which it ruled. The United Nations (UN) proposed to partition the territory into Jewish and Arab states, with Jerusalem under international control. While Jews accepted the plan, Arabs felt it took the rights to their homeland, and rejected it. When Britain left, Jewish leaders declared the creation of the state of Israel. It has since gained control of most of the land.

▲ JERUSALEM, DIVIDED CITY
The ancient city of Jerusalem is sacred to three major religions: Judaism, Christianity, and Islam. Israel has illegally occupied East Jerusalem since 1967, and in 1980 declared the reunited city its capital; this is not recognized by most nations. Jerusalem's status and access to its holy sites remain two of the most contentious issues dividing the Jewish Israeli and Muslim and Christian Palestinian communities.

THE DOME OF THE ROCK
On top of Temple Mount is the Dome of the Rock. Jews and Muslims believe that it is where God created the world. Muslims also believe that it was from here that the prophet Muhammad made his night journey to heaven.

A JEWISH HOMELAND
The Jewish people had left what they saw as their historic homeland in Palestine in Roman times. From the late 1880s, Jewish settlers immigrated to the "promised land" to avoid persecution in Europe. As anti-Semitism grew in the 1930s, a new wave of Jewish refugees started to arrive.

THE NAKBA
Israel's creation in 1948 forced more than 700,000 Palestinian Arabs—half the population—to flee their homes and go into exile. This is known as the Nakba (Arabic for "disaster"). Many Palestinians live as refugees, or under Israeli control in the occupied Palestinian territories.

THE ARAB-ISRAELI CONFLICT
When Israel proclaimed its existence, several Arab countries declared war on the state. Israel and its neighbors have since fought four major wars. Israeli-Palestinian tensions remain high. Israel has built a wall to limit Palestinian access from the occupied territories into Israel.

THE WESTERN WALL
Temple Mount was the site of the first Jewish temple, built by Solomon in 957 BCE. On one side is the Western Wall, part of a later temple completed in around 19 BCE. It is Judaism's most sacred site. Here, Jews come to pray.

THE HOLY SEPULCHRE
According to Christians, the Church of the Holy Sepulchre stands above the two holiest sites in Christianity: Calvary, where Jesus was crucified, and Christ's empty tomb. It has been a pilgrimage destination since it was built in 335 CE.

A DIVIDED WORLD

By the 1950s, the world was divided into two military superpowers. The capitalist United States faced the communist Soviet Union—both assisted by a host of allies who shared their economic ideas. Half the countries in the world, however, remained neutral.

The Soviet Union, or USSR, and its Warsaw Pact allies

The United States and its North Atlantic Treaty Organization (NATO) allies

THE COLD WAR DIVIDES THE WORLD

After the end of World War II, two rival superpowers emerged. The United States and the Soviet Union (USSR) began a "cold war," spying on each other and stockpiling nuclear weapons. Although no shots were fired, the war continued for decades, spreading hostility and distrust throughout the Western world and beyond.

SHOE TRANSMITTER

This apparent piece of poop was actually a homing beacon that could be used to send out a signal if a spy needed to be rescued.

TURD TRANSMITTER

A waterproof concealment chamber is hidden inside this tube, where information could be safely stashed.

TUBE CONCEALMENT

▶ SPY GADGETS

To gather intelligence (information) about each other, both sides used networks of spies. These were provided with a wide range of equipment that enabled them to gain access to secret information, copy it, and then get the information safely back to their spymasters at home. Many of these gadgets were miniaturized and cleverly disguised as ordinary objects.

THE IRON CURTAIN
After World War II, a barrier through the middle of Europe was erected, dividing communist countries from capitalist countries. Germany was split into two halves, as was the city of Berlin. Tough border controls made it hard for people to cross from one side to the other.

Both sides were testing nuclear weapons at the time of the crisis.

THE WAR HEATS UP
In 1962, the two powers almost went to war when the Soviet Union placed nuclear missiles in Cuba, pointing toward the United States. Tensions were high for 13 days, but an agreement was eventually reached and nuclear war prevented.

FIGHTING IN VIETNAM
Cold War rivalry also led to the two powers intervening in wars elsewhere. In Vietnam, conflict raged from 1955 to 1975, with the USSR sending troops to support the communists and the US sending hundreds of thousands to support the capitalist side.

American spies operating in Eastern Europe wore shoes fitted with a hidden microphone and transmitter.

f=4.45mm F2.8

LIGHTER CAMERA

This secret camera was made to look like a cigarette lighter.

Soviet operatives used lipstick pistols, capable of firing a single 4.5-mm bullet.

LIPSTICK SINGLE-SHOT PISTOL

Disguised as a tube of shaving cream, if squeezed the tube would squish and bend, just like normal.

The vast majority of badges feature an embossed image of Mao's head in profile, usually facing toward the left.

Some badges do not depict Mao, but show other Communist leaders or military commanders.

▲ DISPLAYING LOYALTY
Mao Zedong was the founding father of the People's Republic of China, and he ruled the country with an iron fist from 1949 until his death in 1976. Even before the Communist Party took power, badges with his image were produced, but during the Cultural Revolution, billions of Mao badges were made.

COMMUNISM
GRIPS CHINA

In the years after China's last dynasty was overthrown, rival factions fought for control of the country. After a long period of civil war, the Chinese Communist Party emerged victorious, and in 1949 established the People's Republic of China (PRC). The new Communist government reshaped China—taking industry and the economy under state control and forcing peasant farmers to work together on large collective farms. These policies enabled widespread social change, but also led to economic problems and millions of deaths.

Many badges carry Chinese characters meaning "The East is Red," in reference to a revolutionary anthem.

YOUNG MAOISTS
A cult of personality surrounded Chairman Mao during his time as leader. Even the youngest members of society wore Mao badges and carried the Little Red Book—a collection of Mao's revolutionary sayings—either by choice or to fit in.

THE LONG MARCH
China's Communist Party spent many years fighting the Kuomintang Nationalist Party before coming to power. In 1934–1935, around 100,000 Communist fighters fled, marching 5,600 miles (9,000 km) across China's harsh terrain. Mao's leadership on this Long March cemented his power.

THE GREAT LEAP FORWARD
After assuming power, Mao wanted to make China's farming and industry more productive. From 1958, he took land from peasants to set up rural communes, and urged people to produce steel in backyard furnaces. But these changes caused a great famine, in which at least 30 million died.

THE CULTURAL REVOLUTION
Seeking to revive Communist values and reassert his grip on power, from 1966 Mao began a purge of society. Groups such as intellectuals and landlords were forced to wear dunces' hats or placards listing their crimes against the revolution. Around one million people may have died.

FIGHTING FOR CIVIL RIGHTS

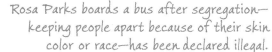

Rosa Parks boards a bus after segregation—keeping people apart because of their skin color or race—has been declared illegal.

Many Black Americans fought for equality during the 1950s and 1960s. Although slavery had been abolished in 1865, Black people in the US still faced discrimination and endured racism, especially in the South. The Civil Rights Movement won equal rights under the law in areas including education and voting. Black people could now work in the same jobs as white people and sit wherever they wanted on buses and in restaurants. However, the fight for full civil rights is still not over.

A SHARED EDUCATION

Before the 1950s, many schools in the US were segregated: some taught only white pupils and others only Black pupils. In 1954, the Supreme Court ruled that all should be treated equally after seven-year-old Linda Brown (in the front row on the right, below) was rejected from the all-white schools in Topeka, Kansas.

▲ MONTGOMERY BUS BOYCOTT

In 1955, activist Rosa Parks was arrested for refusing to give up her seat on a bus to a white man. Her protest, and that of others including teenager Claudette Colvin, led to a bus boycott in Montgomery, Alabama, that lasted for 381 days. In 1956, the Supreme Court said bus segregation was illegal.

THE MARCH ON WASHINGTON
In August 1963, more than 200,000 people marched on Washington, D.C., to demand rights for Black Americans. At the march, civil rights leader Martin Luther King, Jr., gave his famous "I Have A Dream" speech calling for an end to racism in the US.

BLACK POWER POLITICS
Some believed that Black people should take action to gain power. These included Black nationalist Malcolm X, revolutionary socialist Fred Hampton, and the Black Panther Party, which said Black people should carry weapons for self-defense.

The autobiography of Malcolm X was published after his death.

BLACK LIVES MATTER
Black Americans had gained many rights by the end of the 1960s, but inequalities remained. Black Lives Matter is a movement calling for the human rights of Black people to be respected. It was founded after 17-year-old Trayvon Martin was killed by a white vigilante in 2012.

SEPARATE SEATING
Before the boycott, many buses across the US were racially segregated. In Montgomery, Alabama, the law required that Black people rode in the back and white people rode in front.

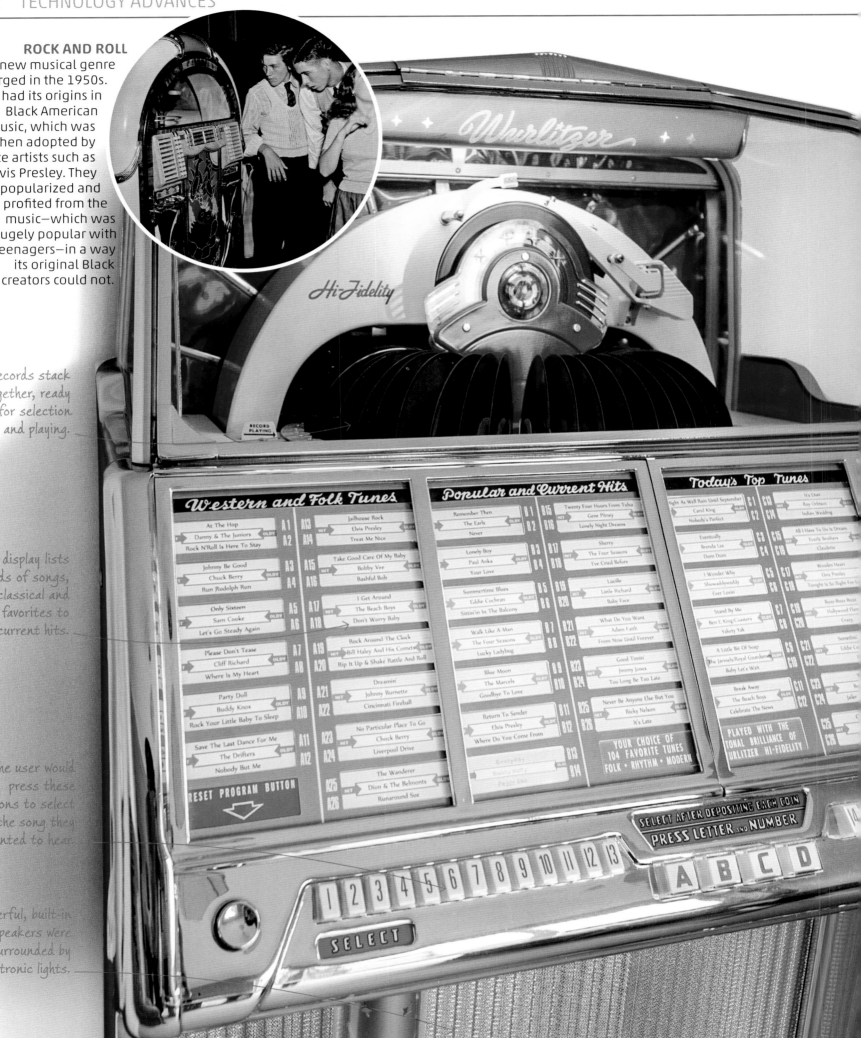

ROCK AND ROLL
This new musical genre emerged in the 1950s. It had its origins in Black American music, which was then adopted by white artists such as Elvis Presley. They popularized and profited from the music—which was hugely popular with teenagers—in a way its original Black creators could not.

Records stack together, ready for selection and playing.

The display lists hundreds of songs, from classical and old favorites to current hits.

The user would press these buttons to select the song they wanted to hear.

Powerful, built-in speakers were surrounded by electronic lights.

TEENAGERS REBEL

In the 1950s, many countries in the West began to recover from the hardship of World War II. At this time, a new phenomenon emerged: the teenager. Before, young people were seen as adults in waiting. But now they had more independence and free time, and a distinctive "youth culture" emerged. Teenagers began to rebel against authority, and looked to movie stars and musicians for inspiration. Today, the tastes of young people are a driving force of modern culture.

◀ **MUSICAL MACHINE**
Jukeboxes are machines that hold records to play music on demand. They were invented in 1889, but became very popular in the mid-20th century when young people gathered around jukeboxes in diners and video arcades to listen to music, especially the newly popular rock-and-roll songs.

Coins go in a slot to operate the jukebox.

TEENAGE TRENDS
The transition between childhood and adulthood is called adolescence. There have always been adolescents, but after World War II, advertisers started treating them as a distinct group, and marketed products to them, including cars, music, and movies.

MUSIC FOR ALL
In the US in the 1950s there were laws designed to keep Black and white people separate. But rock-and-roll concerts broke down racial barriers. Regardless of race, many teenagers enjoyed this music, dancing together to musicians such as Little Richard (above).

TEEN IDOLS
Many young people started rebelling against their parents and other authority figures' way of life. Lots of teenagers admired actors that their parents didn't like, such as Marlon Brando and his outlaw character in the 1953 movie *The Wild One*.

STUDENT PROTESTS
As young people started to develop their own cultural identity, they began to speak their minds on political issues. In 1968, student protests like this one in Berlin, Germany, took place around the world, speaking against wars and authoritarian rule, and in favor of civil rights.

LIBERATION
IN AFRICA

Through the mid-20th century, African nations won independence from their European colonizers. Before 1910, when white settler–controlled South Africa broke free from Britain, all but Liberia and Ethiopia were colonies. Many Africans had fought colonialism since it began, but the world wars boosted liberation struggles as African troops returned from abroad with new ideas of freedom.

▶ AFRICAN NATIONS GAIN INDEPENDENCE

The struggle for liberation in Africa picked up pace slowly, but between the mid-1950s and 1975 most of the continent cast off colonial rule. Egypt became free from Britain in 1922, although British influence was strong until 1956. Other countries in northern Africa, such as Tunisia and Morocco, followed. Ghana's independence in 1957 is often seen as a tipping point, inspiring many nations to declare their freedom.

PAN-AFRICANISM
Many Black people globally were Pan-Africans who believed Black people should fight together against racism and colonialism. A black star symbolizing Pan-Africanism was incorporated in Ghana's new flag.

GHANA
Ghana was the first Black African country to gain freedom from colonial rule, becoming independent from Britain on March 6, 1957. Kwame Nkrumah, who became president of the new nation, was a powerful speaker who wrote several books about the evils of colonialism.

FREEDOM-FIGHTING WOMEN
Many women played vital roles in Africa's liberation, from Huda Sha'arawi, who was a leading light in Egypt's independence struggle, to Bibi Titi Mohammed (above), who mobilized women's opposition to colonial rule in what became Tanzania.

ALGERIA
Algerians engaged in a war of independence with France between 1954 and 1962. Algeria gained independence on July 5, 1962, but as many as 1.5 million Algerians may have died during the war. A memorial to those who lost their lives was set up in the capital, Algiers.

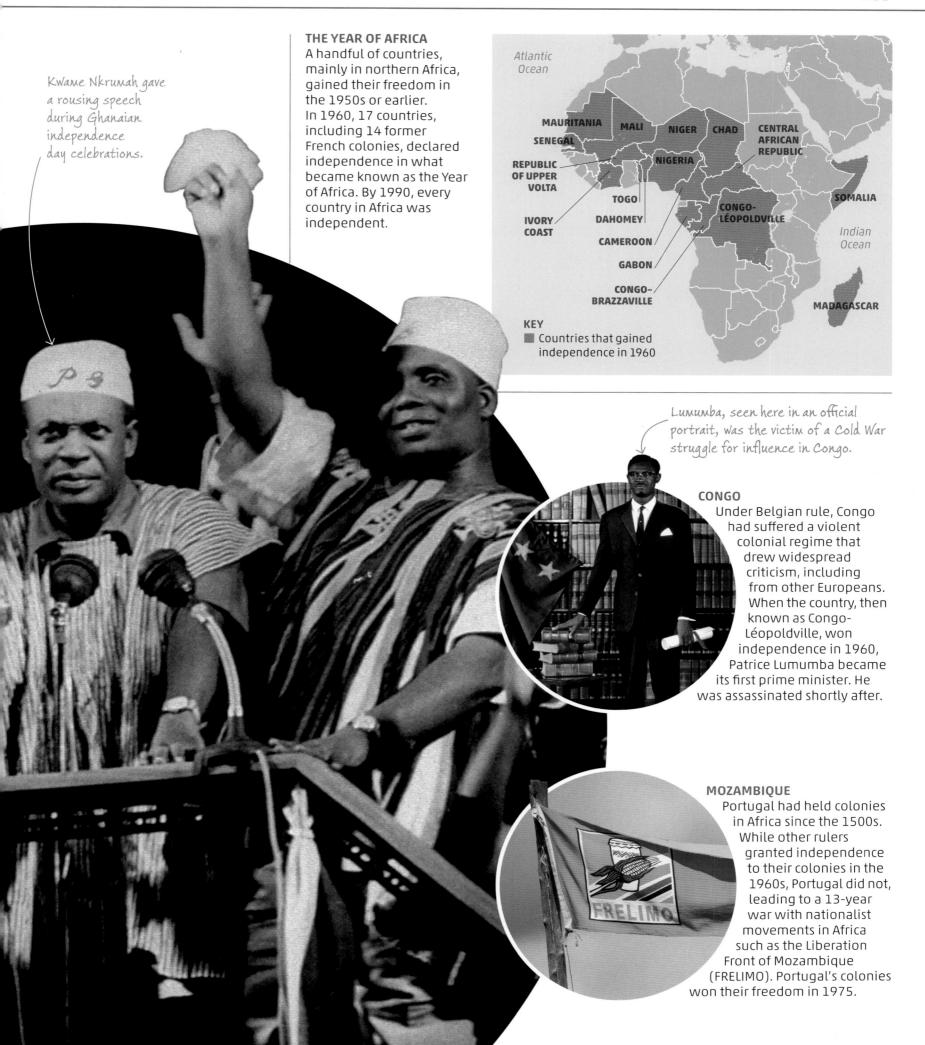

Kwame Nkrumah gave a rousing speech during Ghanaian independence day celebrations.

THE YEAR OF AFRICA
A handful of countries, mainly in northern Africa, gained their freedom in the 1950s or earlier. In 1960, 17 countries, including 14 former French colonies, declared independence in what became known as the Year of Africa. By 1990, every country in Africa was independent.

Atlantic Ocean

MAURITANIA
SENEGAL
MALI
NIGER
CHAD
CENTRAL AFRICAN REPUBLIC
REPUBLIC OF UPPER VOLTA
NIGERIA
TOGO
IVORY COAST
DAHOMEY
CAMEROON
CONGO-LÉOPOLDVILLE
SOMALIA
GABON
CONGO-BRAZZAVILLE
Indian Ocean
MADAGASCAR

KEY
■ Countries that gained independence in 1960

Lumumba, seen here in an official portrait, was the victim of a Cold War struggle for influence in Congo.

CONGO
Under Belgian rule, Congo had suffered a violent colonial regime that drew widespread criticism, including from other Europeans. When the country, then known as Congo-Léopoldville, won independence in 1960, Patrice Lumumba became its first prime minister. He was assassinated shortly after.

MOZAMBIQUE
Portugal had held colonies in Africa since the 1500s. While other rulers granted independence to their colonies in the 1960s, Portugal did not, leading to a 13-year war with nationalist movements in Africa such as the Liberation Front of Mozambique (FRELIMO). Portugal's colonies won their freedom in 1975.

RACE TO THE MOON

Starting in the mid-1950s, two global superpowers competed to dominate space exploration. This space race between the Soviet Union and the United States grew out of Cold War rivalry between the two states. Each wanted to be the first to achieve space flight. Initially, the Russians took the lead, sending the Sputnik satellite, a dog called Laika, and then the first man into space. However, the Americans triumphed when they landed men on the moon. Today, many nations cooperate in space research and exploration, while private ventures have launched a new race for space travel.

The Command Module was the spacecraft's control center.

The Service Module took the spacecraft into lunar orbit and back to Earth.

The Lunar Module was used to land on the moon's surface.

The third stage took it on toward the moon.

The second stage carried it until almost in Earth's orbit.

The first stage lifted the rocket off the ground.

FIRST PERSON IN SPACE

Flying in the Vostok 1 spacecraft, Russian fighter pilot Yuri Gagarin made a complete orbit of Earth on April 12, 1961. He was the first person to travel into space, claiming a major victory for the Soviet Union in the space race.

THE SATURN V ROCKET

The Apollo 11 mission was propelled into space by a powerful rocket. The Saturn V was made up of three "stages." As the fuel in each stage was used up, that part was jettisoned. It remains the largest and most powerful rocket ever made.

A layer of aluminum foil protected the craft from extreme temperatures.

▶ REACHING THE MOON

In 1969, the US became the first nation to land people on the moon. TeChe Apollo 11 mission carried three astronauts into space. Neil Armstrong and Buzz Aldrin explored the moon's surface, while Michael Collins flew the Command Module in orbit around the moon. The US is still the only country to have sent its citizens to the moon.

Only the top part of the Lunar Module returned to space, leaving the bottom section behind on the moon.

KATHERINE JOHNSON
Years before the advanced computer technology that we have today, planning Apollo 11's path required people to make precise, complex mathematical calculations. A team of female mathematicians, including Katherine Johnson, undertook these. Along with her colleagues, she made a huge contribution to space travel.

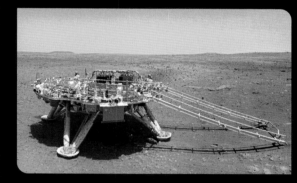

MARS ROVER
Since the US moon landing, many other countries, including China, have ventured into space. In 2021, China landed a space rover on Mars. The remote-controlled robot studied the planet's surface rocks and atmosphere. It also looked for signs of life, including water or ice below the surface, sending data back to Earth to be researched.

Wide footpads stopped the Lunar Module from sinking into the moon's surface.

Astronauts explored the moon's surface for more than two hours.

ENIAC MACHINE

The earliest computers had big panels of wires, switches, and tubes. This made them unwieldy and large. One of the earliest computers, the Electronic Numerical Integrator and Computer (ENIAC), took up a whole room. ENIAC was first developed to calculate weapons data for the military in the 1940s.

▶ THE RISE OF PERSONAL COMPUTERS

Early computers were huge and expensive, and used only by the military and big business. With the invention of new technologies such as the microprocessor, computers became smaller and affordable for personal use in the home. Smartphones today fit increasing computing power into a pocket-size device.

A TV screen could be plugged into the Apple I's circuit board to display results.

1 KIT COMPUTERS
The first personal computers available were sold as simple circuit boards, such as the Apple I. The user had to add or build elements, such as keyboards, screens, and even the computer's casing. They were expensive and only for experts.

COMPUTERS FOR ALL 2
Over time, personal computers became more affordable. Some families were able to buy ready-made computers to use at home. The Commodore 64, released in 1982, sold over 17 million units and is still considered the best-selling computer of all time.

COMPUTERS
REVOLUTIONIZE SOCIETY

First invented in the 1940s for doing military calculations, computers today are powerful machines able to store huge amounts of data and process it at incredible speeds. They have transformed how we work, learn, and communicate and impact every area of our world, from buying and selling goods to controlling a space mission.

3 A CONNECTED WORLD
The World Wide Web, a global collection of linked documents, was launched in 1991 (see pages 296–297). Cybercafés (pictured above) became popular in the mid-1990s and gave travelers or those without a computer access to the Web.

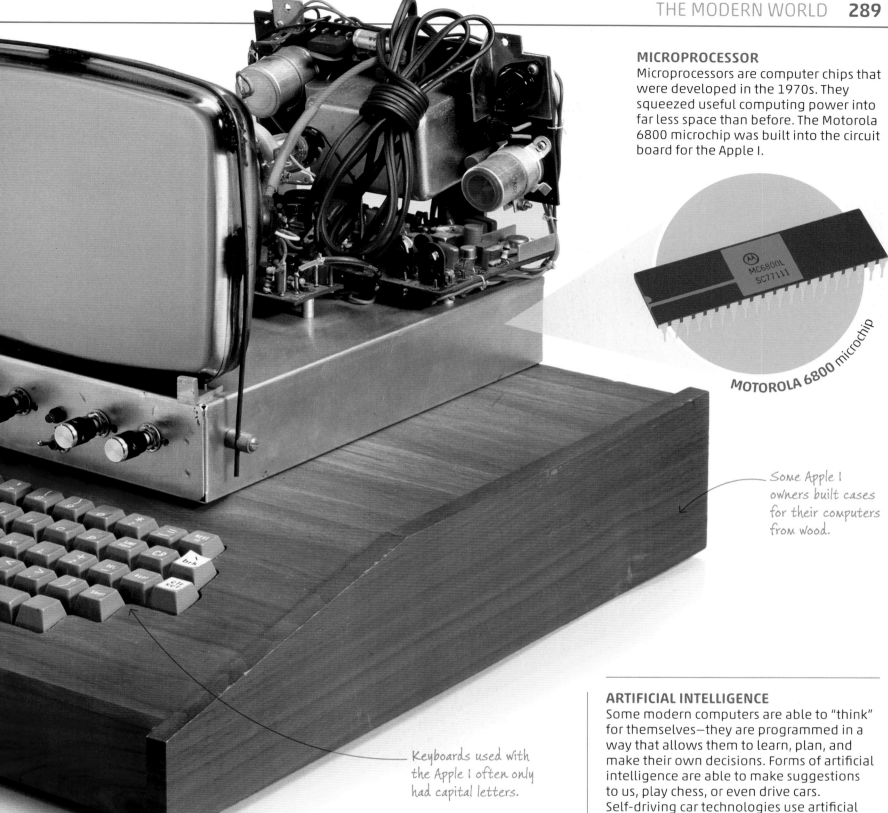

MICROPROCESSOR

Microprocessors are computer chips that were developed in the 1970s. They squeezed useful computing power into far less space than before. The Motorola 6800 microchip was built into the circuit board for the Apple I.

MOTOROLA 6800 microchip

Some Apple I owners built cases for their computers from wood.

Keyboards used with the Apple I often only had capital letters.

ARTIFICIAL INTELLIGENCE

Some modern computers are able to "think" for themselves—they are programmed in a way that allows them to learn, plan, and make their own decisions. Forms of artificial intelligence are able to make suggestions to us, play chess, or even drive cars. Self-driving car technologies use artificial intelligence to identify hazards on the road.

4 **PORTABLE DEVICES**
Modern computers such as smartphones and tablets are small and light—we are able to carry them with us wherever we go. Most can connect to the Web, giving us easy access to information on a regular basis. It is estimated that half the world's population own a smartphone.

A tiny canister replaced the fuel tank.

HIDDEN INSIDE
The BMW Isetta or "bubble car" was a tiny car with a single bench seat. The fuel tank was replaced with a tiny canister containing just enough gasoline to get the car across the border to freedom, allowing space for a person to hide. When Jacobi approached the military checkpoint at the border, the East German guard checked his papers and waved him through, unaware of the stowaway inside.

The upholstery has been removed to show where the stowaway would have been concealed.

All unnecessary parts were removed to make just enough room to fit one person inside.

THE END OF THE
COLD WAR

In 1991, the Cold War that had divided the world came to an end. In November 1989, the East German government had opened up the Berlin Wall, the symbol of a divided Europe, and within a year the country was reunited with West Germany. Two years later, following worsening economic conditions and protests in communist countries, the Soviet Union (USSR) that enforced communism in the East fell apart. After 45 years of confrontation, the conflict was at an end.

▼ **MAKING AN ESCAPE**

For 28 years, the German city of Berlin was divided by a wall splitting the communist East from the capitalist West. Many people in East Berlin resented economic hardship and being separated from friends and being separated from friends and family, and tried to cross the wall. Some even died attempting to do so. In 1963, West German Klaus-Günter Jacobi used a modified BMW Isetta to smuggle a friend from East Berlin to the West.

The door was at the front—it opened forward and had the steering wheel attached.

This replica of the original car is in a museum in Berlin.

PROTESTS AGAINST COMMUNISM

Poland was one of the countries where protests against communism broke out—beginning with demonstrations against price rises in 1970. Strikes followed, in 1980, and opposition grew against other communist governments over the next few years.

REFORMING THE USSR

In 1985, Mikhail Gorbachev (above, left) became leader of the Soviet Union. He began to reform the country economically and politically. He also sought better relations with the US, signing treaties to get rid of nuclear weapons with US president Ronald Reagan (above, right).

THE FALL OF THE WALL

In 1987, Gorbachev began to withdraw Soviet troops from communist countries. In East Germany protests were raging and many people had already fled to Hungary. In 1989, East Germany opened its borders and people flooded through the Berlin Wall, tearing it down.

APARTHEID
DIVIDES SOUTH AFRICA

The Union of South Africa was created in 1910 by white settlers, and gained full independence from the United Kingdom in 1934. In 1948, the South African government introduced apartheid, a policy that favored the white minority and discriminated against non-white people, particularly the indigenous Black population. Under apartheid, different racial groups were forced to live in separate neighborhoods and were not allowed to visit the same venues, from schools to places of work.

THE DIVISIONAL COUNCIL OF THE CAPE
WHITE AREA
BY ORDER SECRETARY
DIE AFDELINGSRAAD VAN DIE KAAP
BLANKE GEBIED
OP LAS SEKRETARIS

LIVING UNDER APARTHEID
Most white South Africans spoke Afrikaans. In this language apartheid means "apartness." During this time, Black people were forcibly moved to poor areas, and could only enter "white areas" to work menial jobs. This sign marked a beach as only for white people.

Many South Africans waited for hours in long lines so they could cast their vote.

PROTESTS GAIN ATTENTION
Throughout apartheid rule, many white and non-white South Africans protested against this hateful policy. In the Soweto protests of 1976, Black schoolchildren marched on the streets. Hundreds of these children were shot at and killed by police, sparking international outrage and increasing global solidarity in the fight against apartheid.

TRUTH AND RECONCILIATION
Apartheid ended in 1994. Following this, a Truth and Reconciliation Commission was set up to help all South Africans come to terms with its legacy and find a way to move forward. The commission's chairman was archbishop Desmond Tutu (above, right). The deputy chairman was white anti-apartheid activist Alex Boraine (above, left).

MODERN SOUTH AFRICA
Following the end of apartheid, a new constitution guaranteeing equal rights and dignity was created. Yet, there is still widespread inequality in South Africa today. Many Black South Africans continue to live in low-income townships (above), while white South Africans tend to live in rich and prosperous areas.

▲ THE FIRST FREE ELECTIONS
In 1994, South Africa held its first elections in which everyone had a right to vote, including Black South Africans. Millions lined up to exercise their democratic right to vote, and more than 19 million votes were counted. Of all of the political parties in the running, the African National Congress gained the most seats. This party, founded in 1912, had played a key role in the fight to end apartheid.

MANDELA WINS
Prominent anti-apartheid activist, and head of the African National Congress, Nelson Mandela became South Africa's first Black president in 1994. Mandela had spent 27 years in prison, and was freed in 1990 after pressure on the apartheid government from home and abroad.

ORBITING EARTH

The International Space Station (ISS) is a huge research station that is in constant orbit 250 miles (400 km) above Earth. The first modules (parts) of the ISS were launched into space in 1998 in a groundbreaking collaboration between the US and the USSR. Since then, a series of modules have been added—to date, 15 different organizations and countries have been involved in building the ISS. Today, it has 16 modules, measures 356 ft (109 m) across, and can house up to six people at a time. It is visited by astronauts and cosmonauts from all over the world.

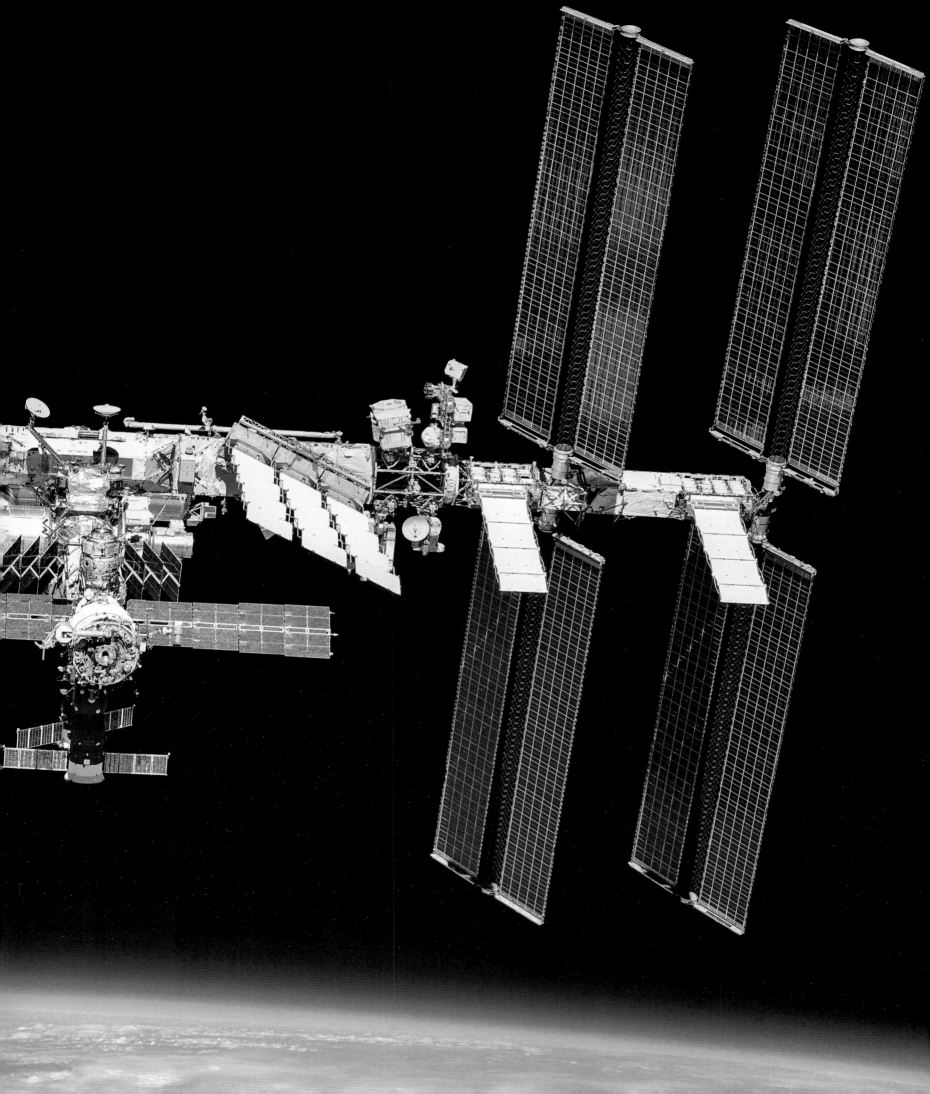

THE WORLD GOES ONLINE

The rapid rise of the Internet and the World Wide Web has changed how people interact with each other. Information can be accessed and shared much more easily. The Internet allows us to explore the world as never before and social media can bring us closer together. Billions of people are now connected online.

▼ LIVING ONLINE

The increased use of smartphones means that, for many, life has moved online as part of a vast international community. Everything we do, say, and watch can be recorded and broadcast to family and friends through numerous apps. Online communities, however, have dangers—they can also spread hate speech, incorrect information, and conspiracy theories.

RISE OF SOCIAL MEDIA

Social media websites and apps allow users to create their own content, such as broadcasting ideas and news, and writing their own stories or poems. Apps on smartphones allow users to post photos, text, and multimedia content to friends. Users can communicate directly with each other in a way never possible before.

Smartphone cameras record videos that can be shared quickly around the world.

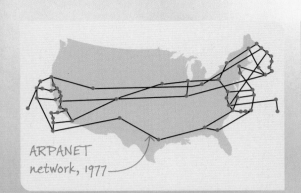

ARPANET
network, 1977

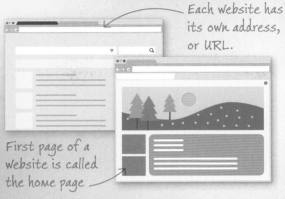

Each website has
its own address,
or URL.

First page of a
website is called
the home page

BIRTH OF THE INTERNET

The Internet began in 1969 when the Advanced Research Projects Agency Network (ARPANET) connected four west-coast US colleges using phone lines. By 1977, this network stretched across the US. Today, more than half of the world's population is estimated to be online.

WORLD WIDE WEB

Invented in 1989 by British scientist Tim Berners-Lee, the World Wide Web is a global information system that operates over the Internet. Each entry in this system is a website, often containing many pages. Hyperlinks connect entries and enable people to navigate the Web quickly.

REACHING THE MASSES

Social media can be used as a marketing tool by businesses, but it can also be used by social and political movements for communication and organization. Demonstrators used a messaging app to organize a large protest against President Alexander Lukashenko in Belarus in 2020.

Live music can be
recorded and
replayed later.

MORE THAN A PHONE

The first handheld cell phone was developed by Motorola in 1973, but early cell phones only made and received phone calls. Later versions supported text messaging and Internet access. Smartphones, invented in 2007, are phones, computers, cameras, and music players all rolled into one.

CHINA
BECOMES A SUPERPOWER

In 2010, China became the world's second-biggest economy, after the US. Economic reforms since the 1980s have allowed the country to dominate world trade, generating huge wealth. At the same time, its influence around the globe has grown. But while China has embraced global money, it has maintained a strong control over its people.

SHANGHAI IN THE 1980S
The district of Lujiazui sits on a peninsula formed by a bend in the Huangpu River. Before China's economic reforms, this district mainly held small factories, warehouses, and storage yards.

GLOBAL TRADER
China's economic growth has been driven by the volume of goods it exports. Three of the world's five busiest ports are in China, including Shanghai. These ship a wide variety of goods around the globe. Due to the demand for Chinese products, foreign money has poured into China, creating billionaires and lifting millions out of poverty.

MADE IN CHINA
A huge manufacturer, China produces electronic goods, clothes, toys, and many other products. It is the world's largest maker of both gasoline and electric cars, produces more than half the world's steel, and is second only to the US in financial services. Its success depends on a vast work force of cheap labor and college graduates.

▼ SOARING SHANGHAI

Shanghai's growing skyline is a symbol of China's soaring economic success. The city has long been an important port, but since the 1980s, when China opened up to foreign markets and private businesses, the city has boomed. Today, it is the world's busiest container port, and its Lujiazui district has become a global center for trade and finance. It is one of around 10 Chinese megacities with of more than 10 million people.

At 2,073 ft (632 M), the Shanghai Tower is the second-tallest building in the world.

CONTEMPORARY SHANGHAI
Today, Lujiazui is Shanghai's financial center, dominated by towering skyscrapers. Ten of the world's 20 tallest buildings are in China, with more under construction.

A NEW APPROACH
In 1978, Deng Xiaoping came to power. He made market reforms while maintaining strong state control. After decades of economic problems caused by Mao's policies (see page 279), Deng opened China up to trade and enterprise. Not all have benefited equally.

Deng's image is paraded at the 60th anniversary of the People's Republic of China in 2009.

POPULATION CONTROL
The country's large population helped its global rise, but it soon grew so rapidly that, in 1980, the Chinese government limited urban families to one child only. This controversial decision prevented up to 400 million births and resulted in more boys than girls being born. In 2021, China changed this policy to three children as it faces an aging population.

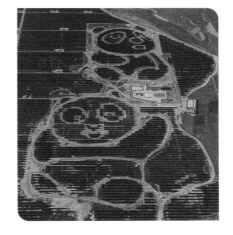

A GREEN FUTURE?
Economic growth has come at a cost to the environment. China today emits more carbon dioxide than any other country, making it a major contributor to climate change. However, it is also the world's largest producer of green technology—such as wind turbines and this array of solar panels—and of clean energy.

GOING GLOBAL

The world has become an increasingly connected place. People travel for business and leisure, and billions of tons of goods are shipped around the world every year. Multinational companies (companies that operate in more than one country) increasingly control trade. This has led to growth in international trade and a mass exchange of ideas and cultures. This process is called globalization.

▼ MOVEMENT OF GOODS
Multinational companies make their products wherever labor or materials are cheapest, and then ship them around the world. When we shop online, goods arrive quickly and efficiently. These goods are carried on container ships and processed through massive fulfillment centers.

TRANSPORTATION ❶
Manufactured goods are shipped around the world in identical metal containers on massive cargo ships. Once the loaded containers arrive in port, they are taken by rail or road to distribution warehouses.

Some ships can carry more than 21,000 containers at a time.

FULFILLMENT CENTER ❷
Goods leave the warehouse packed on large pallets and are brought to fulfillment centers—large facilities where the goods are unpacked, sorted, and stored.

Each item has its own place in the fulfillment center's storage facilities.

ONLINE ORDERING ❸
When a customer orders a product online, it is processed through the fulfillment center. With the help of robots and using a network of conveyor belts, the goods are boxed up, ready for delivery.

GLOBAL MANUFACTURING
Many multinational companies assemble their products in different factories around the world. The product is built in stages, with one part being assembled in one country and a second part in another country. The assembly line pictured left is building smartphones in India, using parts made in many different countries.

A SHRINKING WORLD
Air travel has increased hugely in the 21st century. As people fly around the world for both business and pleasure, those with different cultures and world views are able to interact and share ideas with each other.

Orders are packaged, ready to be sent out for delivery.

Orders are gradually processed and assembled stage by stage throughout the fulfillment center.

GLOBAL BRANDS
The spread of brands and businesses that operate around the world, such as McDonald's, means that the same goods and services are found almost everywhere. Some people worry this could lead to less cultural diversity and overwhelm local cultures and traditions.

ENVIRONMENTAL COSTS
It is easier and cheaper than ever before to buy consumer goods. But this has come at a cost to the environment, from the pollution caused by shipping to the exploitation of raw materials. The disposal of used and unwanted goods is leading to overflowing landfills.

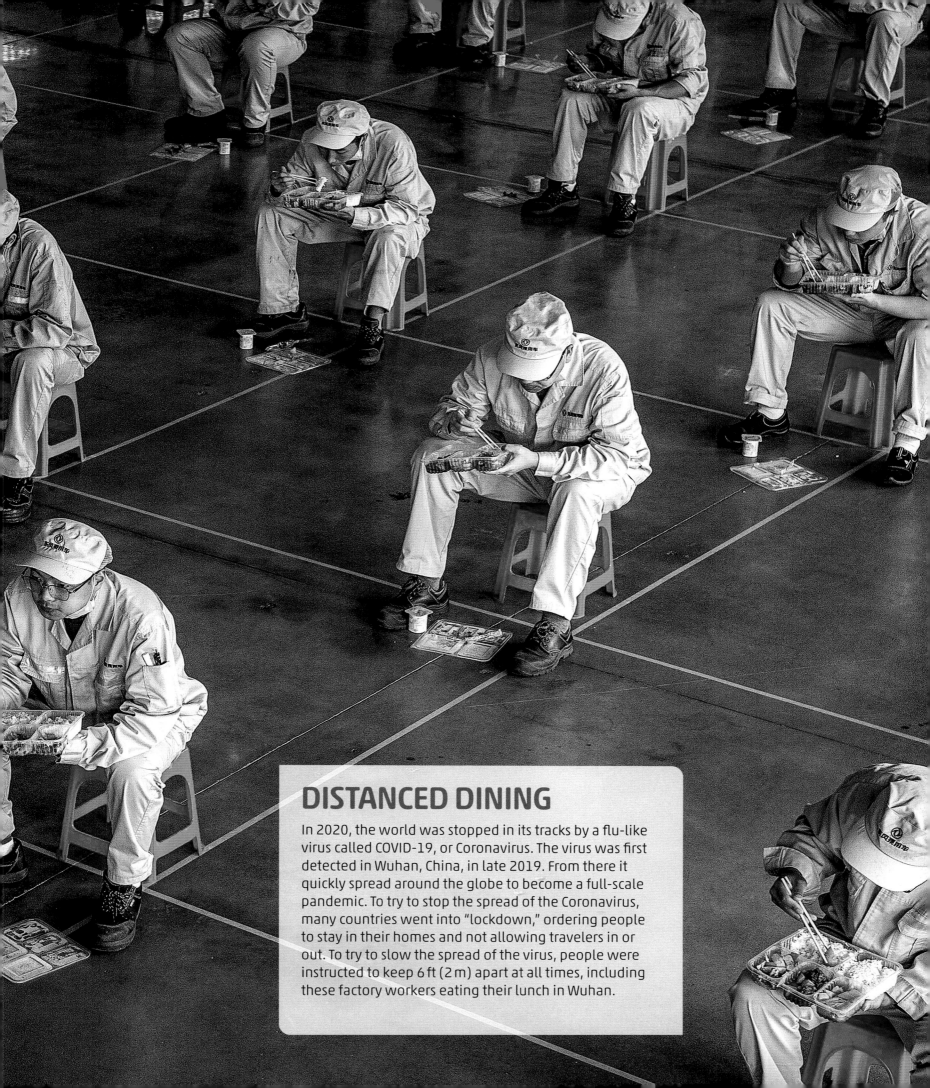

DISTANCED DINING

In 2020, the world was stopped in its tracks by a flu-like virus called COVID-19, or Coronavirus. The virus was first detected in Wuhan, China, in late 2019. From there it quickly spread around the globe to become a full-scale pandemic. To try to stop the spread of the Coronavirus, many countries went into "lockdown," ordering people to stay in their homes and not allowing travelers in or out. To try to slow the spread of the virus, people were instructed to keep 6 ft (2 m) apart at all times, including these factory workers eating their lunch in Wuhan.

THE CLIMATE CRISIS

For the past two centuries, people have used the energy generated by burning fossil fuels to heat and power homes, factories, and transportation systems. As a result, Earth's temperature has started to rise. The effects of this global warming will impact every living thing on the planet. Many countries have agreed to limit their reliance on fossil fuels, but drastic action is needed from governments and individuals to slow the effects of climate change.

▶ **STUDENT PROTESTS**

Growing awareness of climate change has inspired many young people to take action. In 2018, 15-year-old Greta Thunberg skipped school to protest outside the Swedish parliament. Inspired by her example, students around the world—like this group in Lisbon, Portugal—have also come together to call for climate action.

FOSSIL FUELS

Humans burn fossil fuels such as oil, coal, and gas to produce heat, light, and energy. The use of these fuels releases carbon dioxide and other greenhouse gases that trap heat in the atmosphere, warming the surface of the Earth. Fossil fuel use has accelerated in the last 50 years as the global population and demand for energy have grown.

RISING SEA LEVELS
Higher temperatures have melted glaciers, increasing the amount of water in the oceans and causing sea levels to rise. This leads to severe floods (as seen here in West Bengal, India) that threaten low-lying coastal areas.

INTENSIFYING WILDFIRES
Hotter, drier environments have created the ideal conditions to make wildfires more frequent and intense. Fires, such as those that raged for six months beginning in September 2019 in Australia, can destroy homes and animal habitats.

GREEN ENERGY
In order to combat climate change, people must reduce their reliance on fossil fuels. One alternative is to make use of renewable energy. Wind farms such as this one use the strength of the wind to generate energy without producing greenhouse gases.

GLOSSARY

ABOLITIONIST
A person who was opposed to the transatlantic slave trade and slavery.

ALLIES
People or countries working together. In World War I and World War II, the Allies were the countries fighting Germany and other forces.

ANCESTOR
A person who lived in the past, and who is a distant relative of people who are alive today.

ANESTHETIC
A drug or gas given to a patient to make them unconscious before and during surgery.

ANTI-SEMITISM
Hatred of or prejudice against Jewish people.

APARTHEID
In South Africa, a government policy of racial segregation that lasted from 1948 to 1994.

AQUEDUCT
A special channel (either raised up or buried underground) that carries water.

ARTILLERY
Large guns used in warfare.

AXIS POWERS
Nations that were allied with Germany in World War II.

BACTERIA
Tiny microscopic life forms that live all around us and can cause disease and infections in humans.

BARBARIANS
The name given by Romans to Germanic and other peoples outside the Roman Empire.

CALIPHATE
An Islamic empire, ruled by a leader called a caliph.

CAPITALISM
An economic system based on the private ownership of property, industry, and profit, with few regulations for business.

CARAVAN
A train of animals, usually camels, used to transport goods across long distances. Camel caravans were often used on the Silk Roads.

CAVALRY
A part of an army made up of troops mounted on horseback.

CHANCELLOR
An official position in the government of a country. In Germany, the chancellor is the head of government.

CITIZEN
A person who belongs to a city or a bigger community, such a state or country, and has certain rights.

CITY-STATE
A city, and its surrounding territory, that has its own independent government.

CIVILIZATION
The culture and way of life of people living together in a complex society.

CIVIL RIGHTS
The rights of citizens to be socially and politically equal. Often used to refer to campaigns by Black people and other ethnic groups to gain the same equal rights and treatment as their white counterparts.

CIVIL WAR
A war fought by opposing inhabitants of the same country.

CLASSICAL
Relating to the ancient Greeks or Romans and their civilizations. Most commonly used to describe their art and architectural styles.

CLIMATE CHANGE
Long-term changes to Earth's weather patterns, due to natural causes or human activity.

COLD WAR, THE
The period of hostility between Western capitalist countries, such as the US, and the communist countries dominated by the Soviet Union. It lasted from shortly after World War II until 1991.

COLONIZATION
The act of sending settlers to establish a colony in another country, often involving taking political control over the people already living there and exploiting the natural resources. Colonization of many parts of the world still leaves a legacy today.

COLONY
An area under the political control of another state, usually in a foreign country.

COMMERCIAL
To do with commerce and selling goods and services for profit.

COMMUNISM
An economic system under which ownership of property and wealth is shared.

CONFUCIANISM
A Chinese religion based on the teachings of Confucius. Followers are taught to respect people of a higher rank than themselves.

CONGRESS
A formal group of representatives from countries or areas who discuss ideas and information. In the US government, Congress is the legislative (law-making) body.

CONQUISTADORS
Spanish soldiers and explorers who colonized parts of America occupied by Indigenous peoples.

CONSTITUTION
A set of laws that determines the political principles of a nation or state and its government.

CRUSADES, THE
Military expeditions of the 11th to 13th centuries, in which Christian knights from Europe tried to seize Jerusalem and other places from Muslim control.

CULTURE
The customs, beliefs, and behavior shared by a society.

DECOLONIZATION
The process of giving back political control to a former colony, resulting in its independence.

DEMOCRACY
A political system in which people have power to control their government, usually by electing politicians to represent their views.

DESCENDANT
The offspring of a person or family.

DICTATOR
A leader who rules a country alone with no restrictions on the extent of their power.

DIPLOMAT
A person appointed by a country or other political body to carry out negotiations and maintain relationships with other countries.

DOMESTICATION
The taming of wild animals and plants to make them more useful to humans.

DYNASTY
A family ruling a country for successive generations.

ECONOMIC DEPRESSION
A severe, long-term decline in economic activity, in which unemployment rises and people may face hardship.

ECONOMY
The organization of money and resources in a region or country.

EDICT
An official command or instruction issued by a government or person in authority.

ELECTRUM
A mixture of gold and silver sometimes used to make coins.

EMBALMER
A person who treats a dead body to stop it from decaying.

EMIGRATION
The act of people leaving their home country to settle permanently in another.

EMPEROR/EMPRESS
The absolute ruler of an empire.

EMPIRE
A group of lands or peoples under the rule of a government or person from another country.

ENLIGHTENMENT
In Hinduism and Buddhism, enlightenment means insight gained through meditation and other spiritual practices. Also an 18th-century movement in Europe that placed great value on reason.

EPIDEMIC
An outbreak of an infectious disease.

EVOLUTION
The process of gradual change in living things over many generations.

EXPORT
The sale of goods and services to another country. The opposite of imports.

EXTINCT
Describes a species that has no living members.

FAMINE
A severe shortage of food, causing widespread hunger.

FASCISM
A political movement characterized by nationalism, which places the strength of the state above individual citizens' interests.

FEUDALISM
A social system in which knights pledged allegiance and military service to nobles in exchange for land, and people of the serving classes (such as laborers and peasants) pledged their labor in exchange for a portion of that land.

RT
A strong building or set of buildings, designed to protect its defenders.

FRONTIER
A border separating two countries.

GHETTO
An area of a city in which a particular group of people are required to live separately from other inhabitants of the city. The name originated in 16th-century Venice, to describe the part of the city to which Jewish people were confined.

GLACIER
A slow-moving mass of ice.

GLOBAL WARMING
The rise in global average temperature, caused by human activities that release greenhouse gases into the atmosphere.

GREENHOUSE GAS
A gas, such as carbon dioxide, in Earth's atmosphere that traps heat from the sun and causes Earth to warm faster.

GUILD
A company or association connected with a particular craft or skill, such as shoemaking or weaving.

HABITAT
A place where animals and plants live naturally.

HELLENISTIC
An adjective used to describe the period following the death of Alexander the Great, when the Greek way of life spread throughout the lands he had conquered. It can also be used to describe the art and culture produced as a result of his influence.

HIEROGLYPHICS
An ancient Egyptian system of writing in which pictures (hieroglyphs) represented sounds, objects, and ideas.

HOLOCAUST
The mass murder of the Jews by Nazi Germany in World War II.

HOMININ
A member of the biological group that includes humans and their relatives. Humans are the only species in the group to survive in the present day.

HOMO ERECTUS
A prehistoric member of the human family that lived around 1.9 million years ago. *Homo erectus* evolved in Africa but spread to Asia.

HOMO HABILIS
A prehistoric member of the human family that lived around 2.5 million years ago and which developed some of the earliest stone tools.

HOMO HEIDELBERGENSIS
A prehistoric member of the human family that lived around 700,000 years ago.

HOMO NEANDERTHALENSIS
A prehistoric member of the human family that lived between 400,000 and 40,000 years ago. Known as Neanderthals, they are the closest relatives to *Homo sapiens*.

HOMO SAPIENS
The scientific name for modern humans (our own species). *Homo sapiens* evolved around 300,000 years ago.

IMMIGRATION
The process by which people move to a new country to settle there.

IMMUNITY
The quality or state of being immune (protected from) a particular disease.

IMPERIAL
Of or relating to an empire.

IMPORT
The purchase of goods and services from other countries.

INDEPENDENCE
The freedom of a country, state, or society to be self-governing.

INDIGENOUS PEOPLES
The first people to live in a particular place.

INDUSTRIAL REVOLUTION
The changes that took place in Britain and other countries during the 18th and 19th centuries as a result of industrialization.

INDUSTRIALIZATION
The development of industries, such as steelmaking and weaving, which used mills and other factories with power-driven machinery on an extensive scale.

INFANTRY
A part of an army made up of soldiers fighting on foot.

KINGDOM
A state or area ruled over by a king or queen.

LIBERTY
The state of being free.

MANUSCRIPT
A document written by hand.

MARTYR
An individual who dies for his or her religious or other principles.

MEDITATION
A practice found in several religions that involves emptying the mind of thoughts.

MEGALITH
A large stone that is part of a prehistoric monument.

MERCHANT
A person who buys or sells goods.

MESOAMERICA
An ancient region of present-day Mexico and Central America. Before the 16th-century Spanish conquest, Mesoamerica was home to civilizations such as the Aztecs (Mexica) and the Maya.

MESOPOTAMIA
The region of modern-day Iraq lying between the Tigris and Euphrates rivers, where the earliest civilizations began.

METAL
A material, usually hard and shiny, that can be shaped to make a variety of objects, including tools and weapons.

MIGRATION
The mass movement of humans (or animals) from one place to another. Early human species migrated out of Africa and later moved all around the world.

MONARCH
A king or queen who rules a country or state and generally passes their title to their children.

MOSAIC
A decoration made from small pieces of glass, stone, or tile cemented into position to make a picture or pattern.

MUMMIFICATION
The process of preserving a dead body to prevent it from decaying. Mummification can also occur naturally when bodies are exposed to certain conditions.

MUNITIONS
Weapons and other military equipment.

NATION
An independent country, or a group of people who share historical and cultural ties.

NATIONALISM
Loyalty and devotion to a nation, and the political belief that its interests should be pursued as the primary goal of a political party.

NATURALIST
A scientist, such as a biologist, who studies the natural world.

NEOLITHIC
The later Stone Age, during which improved stone weapons were made and the first farming began.

NOMAD
A member of a tribe or people which has no permanent home, but moves around constantly.

PAPYRUS
A material for writing on, used by the ancient Egyptians. Strips of reed were laid together and beaten to form long rolls like paper.

PARLIAMENT
The law-making branch, or legislature, of a country's government, often made up of elected politicians.

PATENT
A legal document that grants sole rights to an individual or company to make, use, and sell an invention.

PEASANT
A worker on the land, usually an agricultural laborer.

PHARAOH
A title given to a king in ancient Egypt. People believed that Pharaohs had sacred powers and were descended from the sun god, Ra.

PHILOSOPHER
Derived from the ancient Greek for "lover of wisdom," someone who thinks about deep questions of human existence.

PICTOGRAPH
A picture representing a word, sound, or idea. Some of the earliest languages used pictographs.

PILGRIM
A religious person who makes a journey to a holy place.

PILGRIMAGE
A religious journey to a holy place.

PLANTATION
A farm or estate on which cotton, tobacco, coffee, rice, hops, and other crops are grown and where the workforce lives on site. Plantations were common in the Americas during the period of slavery, when enslaved people worked on them.

PREHISTORY
The time before the invention of writing and therefore before written records.

PRESIDENT
A term for a country's head of state, usually elected by the people.

PRIMITIVE
A early form of something in human history.

PRINCIPALITY
A state ruled by a prince or a princess.

PROPAGANDA
A method used to influence how people think and behave. It may take the form of posters, broadcasts, air-dropped leaflets, or digital media, for example.

RATIONING
The controlled distribution of scarce resources, often put into place during wartime.

REINCARNATION
The belief that humans live many different lives on Earth, and that each soul will be reborn into another body after death.

REFORM
A change made to a way of doing things in order to improve it.

RELIC
An ancient object, which often has religious significance.

RELIEF
A carved or molded image that stands out from its background.

RENAISSANCE, THE
A period of European history, beginning in the 14th century, when art and literature were influenced by the rediscovery of ideas from the ancient world.

REPUBLIC
A form of government in which supreme power lies with the people and their elected representatives.

RESERVATIONS
Areas of land in the US managed by Indigenous peoples. These were allocated by the government to specific peoples after they were forced off their ancestral homelands by the western expansion of the US.

REVOLT
An organized uprising intended to overthrow whoever is in authority.

REVOLUTION
A sudden and fundamental change in society brought about by an organized group of protesters.

Can also be used to mean a major change in the way people do or think about things.

ROUNDHOUSE
A circular house with a conical thatched roof built in western Europe before the Roman occupation.

SACRED
Considered holy and with religious significance, possibly related to a god or goddess.

SANITATION
The safe disposal of sewage and refuse and the supply of clean, running water to people's houses.

SATELLITE
An object orbiting Earth. Artificial satellites can be used to help people communicate, navigate, and predict the weather.

SATIRICAL
Poking fun at society, often using literary devices such as sarcasm.

SARCOPHAGUS
A stone coffin, often elaborately carved and decorated.

SCRIPT
The written characters that make up a writing system, such as an alphabet.

SEGREGATION
A system of separation, particularly of one race from another within a racist society.

SETTLERS
People who settle in a new region. Settlers often move into an area to colonize it, seeking to replace the indigenous peoples with a new society of their own in a process called settler colonialism.

SHANTYTOWN
An area in or around a city where people live in temporary shacks, often without basic services such as running water.

SHOGUN
A title given to military leaders who ruled Japan in the name of the emperor from the 1100s to the 1800s.

SHRINE
A building or place considered sacred and usually dedicated to a god, spirit, or holy object.

SIEGE
The surrounding and blockading (blocking its entrances and exits) of a castle, town, or other fortified structure in order to capture it.

SILK ROADS
Several trade routes from China to West Asia and Europe, named after the most valuable product traded, silk.

SLAVERY
The system of owning people as property. Enslaved people have no rights and work with no pay.

SMELTING
A process used to extract metals from rocks, known as ore, containing them.

SOCIALISM
A political system that aims to establish social and economic equality through collective ownership.

SOCIETY
A group of people who live together or who are involved together in a community.

SOVIET UNION
After the Russian Revolution of 1917, the Russian Empire was renamed the Union of Soviet Socialist Republics (USSR), or Soviet Union for short. The Soviet Union broke apart in 1991.

SPECIES
A group of organisms that are similar to, and can breed with, each other.

STAPLE
A basic product that is important to people's lives. For example, a staple food is a food that makes up a large part of a person's, or community's, diet.

STATE
A country, or region within a country, which has its own government.

STELE
An upright stone monument, often carved with an inscription. Stelae have been set up by rulers to honor the gods, list laws, or mark a tomb.

STEPPE
A large area of grassland or semi-desert without any trees.

STERILIZATION
The process of killing off harmful germs from something, in particular on medical equipment.

STUPA
A mound-shaped structure typically containing the remains of the Buddha or a Buddhist monk or nun.

SUBCONTINENT
A large landmass that is a part of a continent, such as the Indian subcontinent in the continent of Asia.

SUFFRAGE
The right to vote in an election. Universal suffrage refers to the right of citizens to vote regardless of their gender, race, social status, wealth, or other factors. Women's suffrage describes the right of women to vote on the same basis as men.

SUFFRAGETTE
Activists who fought for women's right to vote through organized, sometimes, violent protests.

SUFFRAGIST
Activists who fought for women's right to vote through peaceful means, such as petitions.

SUPERPOWER
A country with great political and military power, capable of influencing international politics.

TERRITORY
A geographic area that has come under control of another government.

TRANSCONTINENTAL
Extending or going across a continent.

TREATY
An official written agreement between states.

TRIBE
A group of people who share a common language as well as customs and religious beliefs.

TUNDRA
Treeless areas of low-growing plants tolerant of the cold.

TURBINE
A machine that turns one type of energy into another, which can be used to power equipment.

UNITED NATIONS (UN)
A global organization set up after World War II to help maintain international peace, security, and cooperation.

USSR
See Soviet Union

VACCINE
A substance used to stimulate the body's defenses against an infectious disease.

WEST, THE
Usually used to refer to Europe and North America, or their ideals and culture when seen in contrast to other civilizations.

INDEX

ACKNOWLEDGMENTS

DK would like to thank:
Elizabeth Wise for the index; Hazel Beynon for proofreading; Simon Mumford for help with the maps; Bharti Bedi, Hazel Beynon, Carron Brown, Priyanka Kharbanda, Ashwin Khurana, Annie Moss, and Lizzie Munsey for additional editing; Chrissy Barnard for additional design; Eve Anderson for advice and support; Zhui Ning Chang for additional reading; Yoko Machida for advice about Heian Japan.

The publisher would also like to thank the following people for their help sourcing and advice about images: Professor Ryan Shosted and Stephanie Chen, University of Illinois, School of Literatures, Cultures and Linguistics, for the cuneiform tablet; Casey Dexter-Lee, Angel Island State Park, for the suitcase; Dr James Dilley, University of Southampton for the Bronze Age axe-casting sequence; Louise Evanni, Arkaeologerna, Sweden, for the Sundveda Hoard; Professor Steven Hooper, Director, Sainsbury Research Unit, University of East Anglia, for the Polynesian drua; Bita Pourvash, Assistant Curator, Aga Khan Museum, Toronto, Canada, for the astrolabe.

Glasshouse Images (cra). **Bridgeman Images:** (b). **92-93 Bridgeman Images:** (c). **93 Bridgeman Images:** (cr); Photo Josse (br). **Getty Images:** DEA / A. Vergani (tr). **94-95 Alamy Stock Photo:** Sorin Colac. **96-97 Andy Crouch, Sainsbury Centre, University of East Anglia:** (c). **97 Alamy Stock Photo:** Scott Anderson (cr). **98 Alamy Stock Photo:** Cannon Photography LLC. **99 123RF. com:** Boris Philchev (tr). **Alamy Stock Photo:** Artokoloro (br); Lanmas (c). **100 Alamy Stock Photo:** The History Collection (bl). **Dorling Kindersley:** Angela Coppola / University of Pennsylvania Museum of Archaeology and Anthropology (r). **101 Alamy Stock Photo:** Imaginechina Limited (br). **Dorling Kindersley:** Angela Coppola / University of Pennsylvania Museum of Archaeology and Anthropology (cla, cra, cr). **Science & Society Picture Library:** © Science Museum (bc). **102 Getty Images:** Ian Forsyth (bl). **102-103 Powerhouse Museum / Museum of Applied Arts & Sciences. 103 Alamy Stock Photo:** North Wind Picture Archives (br). **Bridgeman Images:** Iberfoto (cr). **Getty Images:** Michal Fludra / NurPhoto (tl). **104 Alamy Stock Photo:** OJPHOTOS (bl). **Bridgeman Images:** National Museums Scotland (tr). **National Historical Museums Of Sweden:** Bengt A Lundberg (cl). **104-105 Getty Images:** Thos Robinson / Draken Harald Harfagre (b). **106 Alamy Stock Photo:** agefotostock (br). **Bridgeman Images:** Luisa Ricciarini (bl). **107 Bridgeman Images:** Fitzwilliam Museum (br). **108 Alamy Stock Photo:** Artokoloro. **109 Depositphotos Inc:** pugalenthi28 (cr). **Shutterstock.com:** photo-world (crb). **110-111 Alamy Stock Photo:** Science History Images. **112 akg-images:** De Agostini Picture Lib. / G. Nimatallah (r). **Getty Images:** Sepia Times / Universal Images Group (cl). **113 Alamy Stock Photo:** Lebrecht Music & Arts (tr); Uber Bilder (tr). **Bridgeman Images:** Michel Guillemot (cr). **Getty Images:** The Print Collector (br). **114 Bridgeman Images:** Royal Albert Memorial Museum (br). **© The Trustees of the British Museum. All rights reserved:** (l, ca). **115 Alamy Stock Photo:** Ivan Batinic (bl). **Bridgeman Images:** Heini Schneebeli (r). **116 Alamy Stock Photo:** Album (tr). **116-117 Swiss National Museum:** (c). **117 Alamy Stock Photo:** funkyfood London - Paul Williams (br). **Getty Images:** Heritage Art / Heritage Images (cr). **119 Bridgeman Images:** (tc); Tallandier (tr). **120-121 Getty Images:** Vyacheslav Argenberg (b). **121 Bridgeman Images:** (tc). **122 Alamy Stock Photo:** Kairi Aun (tr). **122-123 Getty Images:** Cyrus McCrimmon / The Denver Post (c). **123 akg-images:** Pictures From History (br). **124 Alamy Stock Photo:** agefotostock (cl); Heritage Image Partnership Ltd (bl). **Bridgeman Images:** Dirk Bakker (br). **125 Bridgeman Images:** Dirk Bakker (cl, r); Lebrecht History (tl). **126 Alamy Stock Photo:** Mauricio Abreu (bl);

incamerastock (cl). **Gabriel Moss:** (tl). **126-127 Getty Images:** Brent Stirton. **128-129 Alamy Stock Photo:** Jan Wlodarczyk. **130 Alamy Stock Photo:** The History Collection (br). **Bridgeman Images:** National Museums Liverpool (cl). **Getty Images:** Jean-Pierre Courau / Gamma-Rapho (bc). **131 © The Trustees of the British Museum. All rights reserved. 132 Alamy Stock Photo:** Aleksandra Kossowska (tl); David Wall (bl). **132-133 Alamy Stock Photo:** Kult Heaton. **134 Alamy Stock Photo:** ART Collection (bl). **Getty Images:** Leemage / Universal Images Group (c). **134-135 Dorling Kindersley:** Peter Anderson / Saxon Village Crafts East Sussex (c). **135 Alamy Stock Photo:** imageBROKER (cr); mauritius images GmbH (tr); World History Archive (bl). **136 Alamy Stock Photo:** petographer (bl). **136-137 Alamy Stock Photo:** adam eastland (c). **137 Bridgeman Images:** Art Museum of Estonia (tr). **Getty Images:** Science & Society Picture Library (br). **138 Alamy Stock Photo:** China Images (t). **138-139 Alamy Stock Photo:** J.Ellis Photography. **139 Alamy Stock Photo:** Chris Hellier (tc); travellinglight (tl). **© The Metropolitan Museum of Art:** Gift of Robert E. Tod, 1937 (tr). **140 Alamy Stock Photo:** Aytug Askin (c). **© The Trustees of the British Museum. All rights reserved:** (r). **TopFoto.co.uk:** Granger, NYC (bl). **141 Alamy Stock Photo:** Album (br). **Bridgeman Images:** Johnny Van Haeften Ltd., London (tr). **© The Trustees of the British Museum. All rights reserved:** (l). **143 Courtesy of The Washington Map Society www. washmapsociety.org. 144 Alamy Stock Photo:** The Picture Art Collection (br); Uber Bilder (tl). **Dorling Kindersley:** Gary Ombler / University of Aberdeen (tr). **Getty Images:** MPI (bl). **145 Alamy Stock Photo:** musk (cr). **Dorling Kindersley:** Angela Coppola / University of Pennsylvania Museum of Archaeology and Anthropology (cl). **Dreamstime. com:** Christianm (br). **Getty Images:** Sepia Times / Universal Images Group (t). **146 Alamy Stock Photo:** Bailey-Cooper Photography (tl); The Picture Art Collection (cl); Ted Horowitz (bl). **147 Alamy Stock Photo:** incamerastock (br). **Getty Images:** Thomas Samson / AFP (c). **148 Bridgeman Images:** Look and Learn (l). **Courtesy of The Washington Map Society www.washmapsociety.org:** (tr). **149 Alamy Stock Photo:** Lalith Herath (cra). **Science Photo Library:** Eye of Science (tr). **Courtesy of The Washington Map Society www. washmapsociety.org:** (c). **150 akg-images:** Roland and Sabrina Michaud (tl). **150-151 Alamy Stock Photo:** Stephen Bay (c). **151 akg-images:** Roland and Sabrina Michaud (tr). **Alamy Stock Photo:** Pavel Dudek (br); Jonathan ORourke (cr). **152 Alamy Stock Photo:** Peter Righteous (bl). **153 Alamy Stock Photo:** World History Archive (tr). **Bridgeman Images:** (br); Deutsches Historisches Museum / © DHM (tr). **154 Alamy Stock Photo:** H.

Mark Weidman Photography (r). **155 Alamy Stock Photo:** FL Historical 1A (cr); Prisma Archivo (tr). **Kėdainiai Tourism and Business Information Centre:** (l). **156-157 Alamy Stock Photo:** Azoor Photo (c). **156 akg-images:** Album / Oronoz (br). **Bridgeman Images:** (bl). **157 Alamy Stock Photo:** Witold Skrypczak (br). **Bridgeman Images:** Archives Charmet (tr). **Shutterstock. com:** Everett Collection (bl). **158 Alamy Stock Photo:** CPA Media Pte Ltd (bl). **158-159 Photo Scala, Florence:** The Metropolitan Museum of Art / Art Resource (c). **159 Alamy Stock Photo:** CPA Media Pte Ltd (br). **© The Trustees of the British Museum. All rights reserved:** (bc). **160-161 Bridgeman Images:** (c). **161 Alamy Stock Photo:** Allison Bailey (tr); david pearson (cr); The Picture Art Collection (br). **162 Alamy Stock Photo:** GL Archive (tl). **162-163 Alamy Stock Photo:** Reuters. **163 Alamy Stock Photo:** Gina Rodgers (cr). **Bridgeman Images:** Ashmolean Museum (tr); Don Troiani (br). **164-165 Alamy Stock Photo:** Michel & Gabrielle Therin-Weise. **166 Bridgeman Images:** Pictures From History (bl). **166-167 Dreamstime.com:** Jasonjung (c). **167 akg-images:** Pictures From History (tr). **Bridgeman Images:** Pictures From History (bl, bc, br). **Getty Images:** Michael Nicholson / Corbis (cr). **168 akg-images:** van Ham / Saša Fuis, Köln (t). **Alamy Stock Photo:** CPA Media Pte Ltd (l). **Photo Scala, Florence:** (bc). **169 akg-images:** (tr); van Ham / Saša Fuis, Köln (l, tc, bc). **Bridgeman Images:** Pictures from History (cr). **170 Åland Maritime Museum Trust:** (cl). **Bridgeman Images:** (tl); Granger (tr). **171 Alamy Stock Photo:** Stuart Abraham (tr); Randy Duchaine (l). **Bridgeman Images:** New York Historical Society (cr); Prismatic Pictures (br). **172 Alamy Stock Photo:** Royal Armouries Museum (r). **Bridgeman Images:** The Stapleton Collection (l). **173 Alamy Stock Photo:** mauritius images GmbH (l). **Dreamstime.com:** Elenatur (br). **Getty Images:** Sepia Times / Universal Images Group (tr). **174 Alamy Stock Photo:** GL Archive (tr); World History Archive (cl, bl); The Granger Collection (cr). **175 Getty Images:** Science & Society Picture Library. **176-177 Bridgeman Images:** GraphicaArtis. **178 Alamy Stock Photo:** GL Archive (br). **Bridgeman Images:** Museumslandschaft Hessen Kassel (bl). **178-179 Royal Danish Collection:** Iben Kaufmann (c). **179 Alamy Stock Photo:** Granger Historical Picture Archive (br). **Getty Images:** Fine Art Images / Heritage Images (tr). **180 Alamy Stock Photo:** Niday Picture Library (l). **180-181 Alamy Stock Photo:** Granger Historical Picture Archive (c). **181 Alamy Stock Photo:** Album (br). **Shutterstock.com:** WindVector (cra). **182 Alamy Stock Photo:** Georgios Kollidas (t). **182-183 Alamy Stock Photo:** Chronicle of World History (c). **183 Alamy Stock Photo:** Artokoloro (tr/Fanmaking); Niday Picture Library (tl); Classic Image (tc);

Florilegius (tc/Lion, tr/Fencing). **184 Alamy Stock Photo:** Pictorial Press Ltd (bl). **184-185 akg-images:** (c). **185 Alamy Stock Photo:** Nicolas De Corte (tr). **Bridgeman Images:** Leonard de Selva (br). **186 Alamy Stock Photo:** Album (cr). **Getty Images:** Joe Raedle (t). **187 Alamy Stock Photo:** B Christopher (bc); morten larsen (t); Ian Dagnall (br). **Getty Images:** Universal History Archive / Universal Images Group (bl). **188 Alamy Stock Photo:** agefotostock (bl); Science History Images (tl); Niday Picture Library (c); Chronicle (cr). **189 Getty Images:** Damien Meyer / AFP. **192 Alamy Stock Photo:** Chronicle (cla); Niday Picture Library (clb). **Dorling Kindersley:** Clive Streeter / The Science Museum, London (b). **Getty Images:** Science & Society Picture Library (cra). **193 Alamy Stock Photo:** Pictures Now (cla). **Dorling Kindersley:** Geoff Dann / Powell-Cotton Museum, Kent (tr); Martin Cameron / Shuttleworth Collection, Bedfordshire (crb). **Dreamstime.com:** Magnus Binnerstam (clb). **194 Alamy Stock Photo:** incamerastock (bl). **194-195 Alamy Stock Photo:** Jaubert Images (c). **195 Alamy Stock Photo:** GL Archive (tl). **Bridgeman Images:** (br); Giancarlo Costa (cr). **196 © The Trustees of the British Museum. All rights reserved:** (t). **196-197 © The Trustees of the British Museum. All rights reserved:** (c). **197 Alamy Stock Photo:** Christian B. (tr); incamerastock (cr); KGPA Ltd (bl); Doug Steley A (br). **198 Alamy Stock Photo:** Randy Duchaine (cl); Granger Historical Picture Archive (br). **Bridgeman Images:** Gerald Bloncourt (tl). **Getty Images:** Photo12 / Universal Images Group (tr). **199 Alamy Stock Photo:** Granger Historical Picture Archive (t); Universal Images Group North America LLC (cr); Science History Images (br). **200-201 Getty Images:** DEA / M. Seemuller (c). **201 Alamy Stock Photo:** Zoonar GmbH (tc). **Bridgeman Images:** (br); Look and Learn (cr). **202 Alamy Stock Photo:** Classic Image (cl); Granger Historical Picture Archive (bl, br). **202-203 Science & Society Picture Library:** © Science Museum (t). **203 Alamy Stock Photo:** Granger Historical Picture Archive (br). **204-205 Alamy Stock Photo:** World History Archive. **206 akg-images:** MPortfolio / Electa (cb). **Bridgeman Images:** Archives Charmet (tl). **206-207 Alamy Stock Photo:** Niday Picture Library (tc). **207 Alamy Stock Photo:** Nigel Cattlin (tr); GL Archive (cr); INTERFOTO (br). **Getty Images:** DEA / G. Dagli Orti (bl). **208 Alamy Stock Photo:** Georgiy Datsenko (tr); Science History Images (br). **Getty Images:** Universal History Archive / Universal Images Group (cl). **208-209 Science & Society Picture Library:** © Science Museum (c). **209 Alamy Stock Photo:** North Wind Picture Archives (c); Science History Images (tr). **210 Alamy Stock Photo:** Album (l); Niday Picture Library (cr). **Bridgeman Images:** Heini Schneebeli (tr). **211 Alamy Stock Photo:** Universal Images Group North America LLC (br). **Dorling

Kindersley: Gary Ombler / Board of Trustees of the Royal Armouries (c, cr); Geoff Dann / Powell-Cotton Museum, Kent (l). **213 Alamy Stock Photo:** ClassicStock (bl); FLHC11 (br). **Getty Images:** Bettmann (cr). **214-215 Courtesy of Smithsonian. ©2020 Smithsonian:** Department of Anthropology, Smithsonian Institution. **214 Alamy Stock Photo:** Granger Historical Picture Archive (cl). **215 Getty Images:** Fine Art Images / Heritage Images (br). **216 Bridgeman Images:** (tr). **216-217 Alamy Stock Photo:** CPA Media Pte Ltd (b). **217 Alamy Stock Photo:** CPA Media Pte Ltd (tr). **Bridgeman Images:** Look and Learn (tl). **218-219 Dorling Kindersley:** Gary Ombler / National Railway Museum, New Dehli (c). **219 Alamy Stock Photo:** Benjamin John (tr); Niday Picture Library (br); Apic (cr); Buyenlarge (bc). **220-221 Bridgeman Images:** Don Troiani (c). **220 Alamy Stock Photo:** Artokoloro (bl). **Bridgeman Images:** Don Troiani (t). **221 akg-images:** Science Source (cr). **Alamy Stock Photo:** Science History Images (br). **222 Alamy Stock Photo:** Chronicle (c). **Bridgeman Images:** Pictures from History (l). **222-223 © The Metropolitan Museum of Art:** Bequest of William S. Lieberman, 2005 (c). **223 akg-images:** Pictures From History (tr). **Alamy Stock Photo:** CPA Media Pte Ltd (cr); Sean Pavone (br). **224 Alamy Stock Photo:** Maurice Savage (l); Science History Images (br). **224-225 Science & Society Picture Library:** © Science Museum (c). **225 akg-images:** WHA / World History Archive (tr). **Alamy Stock Photo:** Heritage Image Partnership Ltd (cr); Zoonar GmbH (br). **226-227 Alamy Stock Photo:** David Massey. **228-229 Alamy Stock Photo:** Ian Shaw (c). **228 Alamy Stock Photo:** Pictures From History (bl). **229 Alamy Stock Photo:** colaimages (br); Alexander Tarassov (bc); Niday Picture Library (tr). **Bridgeman Images:** Pictures From History (bl, cr). **230-231 Alamy Stock Photo:** Photo 12 (c). **231 Alamy Stock Photo:** Sueddeutsche Zeitung Photo (br). **Getty Images:** Chris Hellier / Corbis (cr); Royal Geographical Society (tr). **232 Alamy Stock Photo:** Vintage Images (cra). **Getty Images:** Science & Society Picture Library (bl). **232-233 Bridgeman Images:** (c). **233 Alamy Stock Photo:** Retro AdArchives (br). **Bridgeman Images:** The Stapleton Collection (tr). **Getty Images:** Hulton Archive (cr). **234 Getty Images:** National Motor Museum / Heritage Images. **235 Alamy Stock Photo:** Imaginechina Limited (tr). **Bridgeman Images:** Christie's Images (cr). **Getty Images:** National Motor Museum / Heritage Images (tr). **236-237 Angel Island State Park Immigration Center. 236 U.S. National Library of Medicine, History of Medicine Division:** Western Photo Company, (bl). **237 akg-images:** Science Source (cr). **Getty Images:** Maremagnum (br); Photo12 / Universal Images Group (tr). **238-239 Getty Images:** Fine Art Images /

Heritage Images (c). **238 Alamy Stock Photo:** CPA Media Pte Ltd (br); History and Art Collection (bl); Marcus Harrison - adverts (cr); Lordprice Collection (tl). **Getty Images:** Popperfoto (tr). **239 Alamy Stock Photo:** Contraband Collection (cl); INTERFOTO (bc); Lordprice Collection (br); Danita Delimont (cr). **Getty Images:** Popperfoto (bl). **TopFoto.co.uk:** Granger, NYC (tr). **240-241 Alamy Stock Photo:** IanDagnall Computing. **242 Alamy Stock Photo:** Granger Historical Picture Archive (tl). **Getty Images:** William Gottlieb / Corbis (cl). **243 Alamy Stock Photo:** Pep Roig (t). **244 Alamy Stock Photo:** IanDagnall Computing (br). **National Coal Mining Museum:** Illustrator : Jane Peryer (bl). **244-245 Science & Society Picture Library:** © Museum of Science & Industry (c). **245 Alamy Stock Photo:** Avalon / Construction Photography (cr); Glasshouse Images (tr). **Getty Images:** Bettmann (br). **246 Alamy Stock Photo:** Everett Collection Inc (tl). **246-247 © Museum of London:** (c). **247 Alamy Stock Photo:** Chronicle (tr); robertharding (tl); Everett Collection Historical (cr). **Shutterstock.com:** Jorge Saenz / AP (br). **249 Alamy Stock Photo:** Andy Gibson. **250 Alamy Stock Photo:** colaimages (cr). **Dorling Kindersley:** NASA (br); The Tank Museum, Bovington (tr). **Getty Images:** AFP (bl). **251 Alamy Stock Photo:** Granger Historical Picture Archive (tr, bl). **Dreamstime.com:** Sdecoret (br). **252 Alamy Stock Photo:** Universal Art Archive (tr). **Bridgeman Images:** Tarker (bl). **253 Alamy Stock Photo:** Christopher Jones (b). **Bridgeman Images:** Peter Newark Military Pictures (tr). **Getty Images:** Lt. J W Brooke / Imperial War Museums (tl). **254-255 Alamy Stock Photo:** Granger Historical Picture Archive. **256 Alamy Stock Photo:** Chronicle (tl). **Getty Images:** Lt. Ernest Brooks / Imperial War Museums (cl). **Imperial War Museum:** (bc). **256-257 www.mediadrumworld.com:** Royston Leonard (c). **257 Getty Images:** Hulton-Deutsch Collection / Corbis (bc). **Science Photo Library:** Science Source (br). **258 Alamy Stock Photo:** Zoonar GmbH (bl). **Colourised by Olga Shirnina:** (cl, c). **258-259 Alamy Stock Photo:** Shawshots (c). **259 Alamy Stock Photo:** Glasshouse Images (br). **260 Alamy Stock Photo:** IanDagnall Computing (cl); Universal Images Group North America LLC (cr). **Getty Images:** General Photographic Agency / Hulton Archive (bc). **261 Alamy Stock Photo:** RBM Vintage Images (tl); Jim West (b). **262 Getty Images:** Hulton Archive (tr). **262-263 Alamy Stock Photo:** Shawshots (b). **263 Alamy Stock Photo:** IanDagnall Computing (tr); Shawshots (tl); Sueddeutsche Zeitung Photo (tc). **264 Alamy Stock Photo:** Shawshots (tl). **Shutterstock.com:** Eliot Elisofon / The LIFE Picture Collection (tc). **264-265 Getty Images:** Universal History Archive / Universal Images Group (c). **265 Alamy Stock Photo:** Granger Historical Picture Archive (br). **266 akg-images:** ullstein

bild (bl). **Alamy Stock Photo:** ITAR-TASS News Agency (clb). **Getty Images:** Bettmann (br); Fred Ramage / Keystone Features (tl). **267 Alamy Stock Photo:** Maurice Savage (l). **Getty Images:** Photo12 / Universal Images Group (br). **268 Alamy Stock Photo:** Pictorial Press Ltd (cr). **268-269 Alamy Stock Photo:** David Harding (b). **269 Alamy Stock Photo:** Vintage_Space (tc). **Getty Images:** Anne Frank Fonds Basel (tr); Fine Art Images / Heritage Images (tl). **270 Alamy Stock Photo:** MeijiShowa (bl). **Science Photo Library:** Los Alamos National Laboratory (clb). **270-271 Getty Images:** Galerie Bilderwelt / Contributor / Hulton Archive (c). **271 Alamy Stock Photo:** aerial-photos.com (br). **Getty Images:** Rolls Press / Popperfoto (tr). **272-273 Getty Images:** Bettmann (b). **272 Alamy Stock Photo:** Stuart Forster India (tc). **273 Alamy Stock Photo:** Dinodia Photos (tl); Reuters (tr). **274 Getty Images:** AWAD AWAD / AFP (br). **274-275 Shutterstock.com:** JekLi (b). **275 Alamy Stock Photo:** CPA Media Pte Ltd (tc). **Getty Images:** Nick Brundle Photography (br); Dan Porges (tr); Artur Widak / NurPhoto (bl). **Shutterstock.com:** Dmitri Kessel / The LIFE Picture Collection (bl). **276-277 Getty Images:** Saul Loeb / AFP (tc). **276 Dorling Kindersley:** Gary Ombler / H Keith Melton Collection (br). **277 Alamy Stock Photo:** 2ebill (tr); Andrew Twort (cl); INTERFOTO (br). **Dorling Kindersley:** Andy Crawford / H Keith Melton Collection (bc). **Getty Images:** STR / AFP (cr). **278-279 Alamy Stock Photo:** VisualHongKong (t). **279 Alamy Stock Photo:** Everett Collection Historical (br); Sally and Richard Greenhill (cr); MARKA (bl). **The International Institute of Social History (Amsterdam):** Private Collection (bc). **280 Getty Images:** Carl Iwasaki (bl). **280-281 Getty Images:** Don Cravens (c). **281 Alamy Stock Photo:** Richard B. Levine / Sipa US (cr). **Getty Images:** Tony Savino / Corbis (br). **Shutterstock.com:** Francis Miller / The LIFE Picture Collection (tr); Hank Walker / The LIFE Picture Collection (bl). **282 Alamy Stock Photo:** Andy Gibson (c). **Getty Images:** Photo12 / Universal Images Group (tl). **283 Alamy Stock Photo:** Sueddeutsche Zeitung Photo (br). **Getty Images:** FPG (bc); GAB Archive / Redferns (tr); Michael Ochs Archives (cr). **284 Alamy Stock Photo:** Leonid Andronov (bc). **Dreamstime.com:** Aliaksei Kruhlenia (tr/blue sky background). **Getty Images:** Gianluigi Guercial / AFP (tr); Keystone / Hulton Archive (l). **285 Alamy Stock Photo:** Africa Media Online (br). **Shutterstock.com:** SIPA (cr). **286 Alamy Stock Photo:** Heritage Image Partnership Ltd (cb); Science Photo Library (tr). **286-287 Alamy Stock Photo:** AF archive (c). **287 Alamy Stock Photo:** Xinhua (cr). **Getty Images:** Smith Collection / Gado (tr). **288 Alamy Stock Photo:** Kim Karpeles (br); Science History Images (tl); Reuters (c). **288-289 Getty Images:** Science & Society Picture Library (c). **289 Alamy

Stock Photo:** Ekkasit Keatsirikul (br); Kumar Sriskandan (bl). **290-291 Alamy Stock Photo:** David Cooper (c). **290 BMW AG:** Illustrator: Jan Stein (tl). **291 Alamy Stock Photo:** agencja FORUM (tr). **Getty Images:** Dirck Halstead (cr); Gerard Malie / AFP (br). **292 Getty Images:** Keystone (tr). **292-293 Getty Images:** Peter Turnley / Corbis / VCG (b). **293 Getty Images:** AFP (tl); Peter Turnley / Corbis / VCG (br); Oryx Media Archive / Gallo Images (tc). **Getty Images / iStock:** JohnnyGreig (tr). **294-295 Alamy Stock Photo:** Geopix. **296 Alamy Stock Photo:** Geoff Smith (t). **296-297 Alamy Stock Photo:** Aliaksei Skreidzeleu (b). **297 Alamy Stock Photo:** ifeelstock (br). **Getty Images:** Artur Widak / NurPhoto (tr). **298 Getty Images / iStock:** (bl). **Getty Images:** Chen Xingyu / VCG (br). **Reuters. 299 Alamy Stock Photo:** Barry Lewis (bl); WENN Rights Ltd (br). **Getty Images:** guowei ying (c); Visual China Group (br). **300 Alamy Stock Photo:** Gary Blake (ca); Geoffrey Robinson (bl). **300-301 Alamy Stock Photo:** Geoffrey Robinson (c). **301 Alamy Stock Photo:** Friedrich Stark (br). **Dreamstime.com:** Antartis (tr). **Getty Images:** Miguel Candela / SOPA Images / LightRocket (tl); Mandy Hong (cr). **302-303 Getty Images:** STR / AFP. **304 Alamy Stock Photo:** Anton Lebedev (l). **304-305 Reuters. 305 Alamy Stock Photo:** Cavan Images (cr); ZUMA Press, Inc. (tl). **Getty Images:** Steve Ramplin / EyeEm (br).

Cover images: *Front and Back:* **123RF.com:** Cobalt c/ (Inner circle), Nick8889 (Outer circle); **Dreamstime.com:** Christos Georghiou (Screws), Mario Lopes / Malopes (Metal texture); *Front:* **123RF.com:** Trezvuy (Text texture), (Rim rust texture); **Dreamstime.com:** Ilkin Guliyev cr, cl, Nejron c; *Back:* **123RF.com:** Trezvuy (Text texture); **NASA:** c; *Spine:* **123RF.com:** Trezvuy (Text texture), (Rim rust texture); **Dreamstime.com:** Ilkin Guliyev cl, cr, Nejron cb.

Endpaper images: *Front:* **123RF.com:** Nick8889 (Outer circle); **Alamy Stock Photo:** J.Ellis Photography (Right), Jon Arnold Images Ltd (Left); **Dreamstime.com:** Christos Georghiou (Screws), Mario Lopes / Malopes (Metal texture); *Back:* **123RF.com:** Nick8889 (Outer circle); **Alamy Stock Photo:** Science History Images / Photo Researchers (Left); **Dreamstime.com:** Christos Georghiou (Screws), Mario Lopes / Malopes (Metal texture), Zoom-zoom (Left- sky); **Getty Images:** Galerie Bilderwelt / Contributor / Hulton Archive (Right).

All other images © Dorling Kindersley

For further information see: **www.dkimages.com**